W9-BVV-068

WHERE WE WANT TO LIVE

WHERE
WE WANT
TO LIVE

RECLAIMING INFRASTRUCTURE FOR
A NEW GENERATION OF CITIES

RYAN GRAVEL

St. Martin's Press
New York

www.stmartins.com

Library of Congress Cataloging-in-Publication Data

Gravel, Ryan, 1972– author.
  Where we want to live : reclaiming infrastructure for a new generation of cities / Ryan Gravel.
      pages   cm
  Includes bibliographical references and index.
  ISBN 978-1-250-07825-4 (hardback)   978-1-4668-9053-4 (e-book)
  1. City planning—Social aspects—United States. 2. Land use, Urban—United States. 3. City and town life—United States. I. Title.
  HT167.G73   2016
  307.1'2160973—dc23

2015026371

Our books may be purchased in bulk for promotional, educational or business use. Please contact your local bookseller or the Macmillan Corporate and Premium Sales Department at 1-800-221-7945, extension 5442, or by email at MacmillanSpecialMarkets@macmillan.com.

First Edition: March 2016

10 9 8 7 6 5 4 3 2 1

For the people of Atlanta . . .

especially Karen, Lucia, and Jonas.

CONTENTS

Acknowledgments   ix

Preface   xi

1   As Many Gains as Losses   1

2   "Infra-Culture"   13

3   Cycles of Change   23

4   There's Nothing Wrong with Sprawl   41

5   Tough Love   55

6   An Idea with Ambition   77

7   A Wide-Open Place   89

8   An Expandable Vision   109

9   Breaking Ground on Hope   127

10   Catalyst Infrastructure   137

11   An Infrastructure for Health and Well-Being   179

12   An Infrastructure for Economic Prosperity   187

13   An Infrastructure for Equity   195

14   An Infrastructure for Civic Identity   207

15   Up Ahead   217

Notes   225

Index   231

ACKNOWLEDGMENTS

I NEVER WOULD HAVE SURVIVED THE ATLANTA BELT-line, including the writing of this book, without the determined and loving support of Karen Mahoney Gravel, who has been with me on this wild journey from the beginning. Thanks to her and also to our children, Lucia and Jonas, who showed up along the way and patiently awaited the completion of this work. Thanks to my family and friends who not only have supported me but have themselves become a part of this amazing story; special thanks to my parents, Alan and Sheri Gravel.

This book would not have been possible without support and encouragement from Annik La Farge, Hannah Palmer, Howard Lalli, and Justin Heckert—thanks also to them and to Kirby Kim and Elisabeth Dyssegaard.

Special thanks to Perkins+Will, especially CEO Phil Harrison for the firm's commitment to this work and its generosity.

Thanks also for the contributions and support of Cathy Woolard, Helen Robinson, Matt Hicks, Mark Arnold, Sarah Edgens, Ed McBrayer, Mtamanika Youngblood, Ethan Davidson, Aaron Fortner, Danielle Roney, David Green, Leigh Christy, Filo Castore, Clara Axam, Anna Foote, Panke Miller, Bill Seay, Greg Levine, Jim Langford, Rob Brawner, Andy Schneggenberger, Randy Roark, Richard Dagenhart, Arthur C. Nelson, Catherine Ross, Alex Garvin, Bart Everson, Tim Springer, and Mark Pendergrast; the late Doug Allen and Paul vanMeter.

Many thanks to the city of Atlanta, and all of its departments, especially mayors Kasim Reed and Shirley Franklin; to the Atlanta BeltLine Inc. staff and board; and to the Atlanta BeltLine Partnership staff and board.

Of course this book would not exist without the Atlanta Beltline, and in the category of people, agencies, businesses, and organizations who made our vision come to life, there are far too many to name. Special thanks to them and also to all the other catalyst infrastructure projects out there, along with the people who inspire and support them. Thanks most of all to the people of Atlanta—for your active participation and love, and for your ownership and authorship of this vision. Please continue to be vigilant throughout its implementation.

PREFACE

THE STORY OF PEOPLE CAN BE TOLD THROUGH OUR infrastructure. In the rise and fall of cities throughout history, the places best positioned for a thriving future have always been those that offer systems and structures to support the timely needs of people. Relevant variables including politics, culture, technology, and business help us leverage those systems to create the lives that we want. And we can see that as the innovations of canals, aqueducts, railroads, and highways did in their time, the kind of infrastructure that we build today matters to our success. If we do it right, it will forever transform our way of life.

Our lives are already changing, and today we find ourselves participants in an organic and unplanned, but also irresistible, response to the advances and limitations of these changes. The culmination of millions of individual decisions is generating a new prevailing cultural momentum that is appreciably different from our experience over the last half century. People everywhere are responding to this new cycle of change by harnessing its energy to create new opportunities for their lives. As their efforts organize instinctively around physical infrastructure—the underlying construction of cities that also happens to form the foundation of our economy, culture, and social life—these active participants are doing more than making their lives more interesting. They are charting a brighter path forward for cities.

As we stare ahead in both wonder and disgust at the metropolis sprawled before us, these kinds of actions are important. They are the first breaths of a beautiful, tangible, and growing new cultural life that is just beginning to be constructed in physical form. Though still small, their collective legacy will be comparable to the revolution that came with the automobile, and they will help resolve the most daunting challenges of our time. By taking action through businesses, governments, nonprofits, and even unorganized citizen campaigns, grassroots leaders are testifying to our ability, opportunity, and desire to grab hold of this amazing cycle of change and create places where we actually want to live. In the process, they are demonstrating how ordinary people can leverage their pragmatic instincts for self-preservation and prosperity to support a more sustainable, healthy, and equitable way of life for everyone.

My confidence in this cycle comes from daily validation of the vision we created for the Atlanta Beltline, a 22-mile circle of repositioned infrastructure that is changing both the physical form of my city and the decisions people make about living here. It began with a kernel of vision as my graduate school thesis in 1999 and has evolved into an astonishing journey of transformation that is now in the early stages of construction. As the project slowly reclaims a set of mostly abandoned railroads and fallow industrial land as a continuous loop for transit, trails, parks, and redevelopment, it is turning what was once a barrier into a linear common meeting ground for over 40 neighborhoods surrounding downtown. While my version of our story is not an official or comprehensive account for the hundreds of people and dozens of agencies and organizations required to make the project come to life, it sets the tone for a much larger unifying narrative about the strategic role of infrastructure in catalyzing a more desirable future for ourselves.

That role for infrastructure was first revealed to me during a college year in Paris and then continuously throughout my journey. It is an invaluable and intimate lesson that also, perhaps subconsciously, captivated the imagination of the people of Atlanta and made the project possible. And in my travels to share our story, I have found it reinforced in the work of people from Memphis to Singapore who are also reinventing their infrastructure to support new ways of living. Whether they are finding new life for old railroads, degraded waterways, or obsolete roadways, the concurrent emergence of these efforts, outside any common ideology, suggests that they are part of a larger movement brewing—the zeitgeist of our time. Their efforts range in scope and scale from the small but powerful High Line in New York City to sublime proposals for the revitalization of the Los Angeles River. They vary widely in the breadth of their programs, their progress to date, their politics, and their partnerships, but together, these inventive, popular, community-driven public works projects illustrate how people everywhere are reclaiming infrastructure as renewed conduits of urban life.

The technical metrics of this new generation of infrastructure are worth noting, but my primary interest is what they mean and why they matter. My lens for this investigation is our extraordinary and unexpected success in Atlanta, which has developed into one of the most wide-ranging urban regeneration projects in the country. It is reinforced by people working the ground game on these other efforts and by my observation that the decisions fueling them are not coming from Congress or City Hall. They're made by ordinary people like you and me, and the force of their shared momentum is growing more powerful by the day. Common lessons from a broad range of projects across a vast geography are uniting into a powerful, messy, organic, and grassroots transformation that touches nearly every aspect of our lives.

By claiming a more conscious role for infrastructure, we can help shape and advance this cycle of change and use its energy to establish the foundation for a better life. This will allow us to finally forget tired old arguments about traffic, pollution, blight, and sprawl and instead leverage those conditions as assets in the creation of something far more interesting than anything we've seen so far. If we are thoughtful, if we work hard, and if we care, this new claim will allow us to leverage change to work for us, not against us, and in the process, catalyze the creation of places where we want to live.

WHERE WE WANT TO LIVE

AS MANY GAINS
AS LOSSES

THE TREE-LINED STREETS OF THE 16TH ARRONDISSE-
ment immediately behind the Trocadéro had suddenly and somehow un-
expectedly broken through the long, beige, bleak Paris winter. It seemed
that, exactly at the moment that I emerged from the Métro, they exploded in the sunlight with impossibly green young leaves at the end of
every branch. They led me behind an imposing wall into the Cimetière
de Passy, which had also burst to life with bright flowers and singing
birds. A spirit of lightness shone through the stained-glass windows of the
cemetery's many mausoleums, lifting the gloom of winter, and the smiles
on every passerby confirmed that I wasn't the only one who had noticed.

I discovered the joy of springtime in Paris on that April day in 1995.
It was the satisfactory result of a homework assignment from my professor, a scholar of the Situationist International, to conduct a *dérive,* or
unplanned journey. In mid-twentieth-century Paris, the situationists
deliberately created situations that would build critical awareness of the
spaces and actions in people's everyday lives. They used the concept of the
dérive (literally, drift) to help break the monotony of life's routine. Rather
than slogging through each day, retracing the exact same steps with the
same low gaze upon the sidewalk, conducting a *dérive* requires you to pay
attention to the world around you, to allow your feelings, intuition, and

experiences to guide you through an exploration of the urban landscape. Such wanderings "express not subordination to randomness but complete insubordination to habitual influences."[1] The larger goal of the exercise was to gain an appreciation for the city in hopes of stopping its destruction at the hands of what the situationists saw as the greed of capitalism, highway building, and other midcentury assaults. My assignment had been to conduct a *dérive* in a part of the city I had not yet seen. I enjoyed it so much that I immediately made it a habit wherever I went.

With each discovery, the city came alive to me. Of particular interest were its inner workings—the physical systems that support its mechanical functions but also breathe life into the streets and public spaces and give each district or place its identity. The origin of my *dérive,* the Place du Trocadéro, radiates typical Parisian boulevards to the north and west and frames a dramatic vantage point to the southeast of the Eiffel Tower across the River Seine on the majestic Champ de Mars. Classic Parisian plane trees surround the square, performing their technical duties of making oxygen, shading the sidewalk, cooling and cleaning the air, and simultaneously providing intangible benefits like beauty, artistic inspiration, and smiles at the onset of spring. The surrounding streets carry a nonstop parade of pedestrians and other people on tour buses, city buses, cars, mopeds, bicycles, and subways. They provide conduits for utilities, emergency response, signage, and deliveries. But more than these utilitarian functions, the streets of Paris furnish the city's people with a stage for their lives. They become places for daily exchanges with strangers, friends, and neighbors, for sitting in cafés to read the news or observe the bustle of urban life. They are venues for innocent flirtations, arguments, or marriage proposals. For my part, an American student wandering around rather aimlessly, I discovered who I am one night walking down one of those dark streets in the "City of Light."

In Paris or in any place where people live in relatively close quarters, layers of shared infrastructure networks, including communication systems, storm-water drainage, transportation, and power, are developed to support them. These systems interact with local conditions including history, geography, topography, and climate. The resulting assembly is occupied and used by people in both expected and unexpected ways, both successfully and unsuccessfully over time, and those activities build economies, culture, and social life. The position of this assemblage, the strength of each part, and the skill with which people utilize the assets made available to them, result in a unique, complex living organism called a city. It is not fully comprehensible, and its complexity defies both the rationality of planners and the passion of designers. Yet there I was in Paris to study both. My immediate interest was to figure out how I could work within this complexity to improve cities like my own hometown. Long before my springtime *dérive,* I had come to the perhaps not-so-insightful observation that the best way to learn how to make cities great is to leave the classroom and walk the streets of great cities.

Fortunately, I didn't have to walk far. I found relevant instruction every morning when I left for school. I lived half a block off the Rue de Lyon in the 12th arrondissement. Every day I walked its most eastern block on the way to the Métro, where it terminates at the Gare de Lyon. Like the Place du Trocadéro, this short five-block link between the train station and the Place de la Bastille was lined with Paris's distinctive plane trees. The Rue de Lyon was part of the transformative vision that Louis-Napoléon Bonaparte, known as Napoleon III, implemented in the mid-1800s. The plan's overarching premise was to open up the city's tangle of dim and narrow streets to improve both military access and public-health conditions. He gave his prefect of the Seine, Baron Georges-Eugène Haussmann, the financial resources and political backing to plow the now-famous grand boulevards through the heart of medieval Paris. And Haussmann, for his part, had the steely will to implement such an audacious vision. His dramatic alterations resulted in iconic new streets like the Avenue de l'Opéra, Boulevard Haussmann, and Boulevard Saint-Germain, as well as the lesser-known Rue de Lyon and the Place du Trocadéro. Haussmann oversaw dozens of projects like these from the 1850s through the 1870s, although some work continued to the end of the century.

The construction of the grand boulevards completely destroyed entire city blocks, along with homes, businesses, and livelihoods. The scale of

Boulevard Haussmann, Paris. (Ryan Gravel, 2010)

change was enormous, and reconstruction continued for decades. Public opposition eventually got Haussmann fired, but while the personal and social costs to the people of Paris and the loss of its medieval character were real and significant, Napoleon III's vision also transformed Paris for the better. It implemented a physical plan for a more robust infrastructure network that still serves the city well today.

The grand boulevards were designed to accomplish many goals—not the least of which was the deterrence of social uprisings. The streets drained low-lying land and brought sunlight into formerly dark spaces in order to create healthier conditions. They strengthened commerce by providing pavement to improve the movement of wheeled carts and wagons. Underground pipes conveyed water and sewage. The boulevards also included a generous new public realm with plazas, monuments, fountains, and trees. Eventually, they brought street lighting, electricity, and other utilities. Starting at the turn of the century, they evolved to also accommodate an amazingly intricate and expansive network of underground subways. With all of these changes, the grand boulevards laid the literal foundation for the life of Paris, enabling its rise to global prominence as an economic, political, and military powerhouse.

But what really set the grand boulevards apart from an ordinary capital investment program is that they bestowed on Paris a distinct and profound physical identity that stimulated a cultural life in the city that has in turn become the engine of its economy and that remains recognizable around the world. In addition to the boulevards, Napoleon III's vision included new landmark structures like the Opéra Garnier, renovated public spaces like the Place de la République, and new parks like the Bois de Vincennes and the Parc des Buttes-Chaumont. The newly sundrenched districts and lighted streets evoked the city's spirit—a "City of Light"—and that lightness was captured by painters like Gustave Caillebotte and Camille Pissarro in a radical new style called Impressionism. Over time, these places created a fertile environment for change, stimulating the city's legendary café culture of artists, musicians, and writers who by the first half of the twentieth century mingled there with cultural luminaries like Simone de Beauvoir, Ernest Hemingway, and Pablo Picasso.

Of course, Napoleon III's vision is only one part of the story that propelled Paris into a region of over 12 million people with one of the largest city GDPs in the world. The grand boulevards, parks, and public spaces support other investments in business, housing, and the arts to create a city that is both highly functional and culturally desirable. One example is the region's enviable rail transit network that itself works in multiple layers. Bullet trains carry passengers to major European capitals in a matter of hours. Other high-speed trains connect Paris to cities throughout France. The commuter train network links the far-flung suburbs within the urbanized parts of Île de France. And the iconic Métro, with its warren of tunnels and trains crowded with college students, suits, and tourists, performs almost effortlessly the demanding task of transporting 4.5 million people a day. Back above ground, several other modes of transportation support the network, including buses, trams, taxis, water taxis, and one of the world's first and most expansive bikeshare programs.

Rue Traversière, Paris. (Ryan Gravel, 2010)

The signature element of this transportation network, however, is found at the beginning and end of every trip. Whether along one of Haussmann's straight, broad boulevards or one of the remaining narrow medieval lanes like Rue Traversière where I lived my year abroad, the sidewalks of Paris are not relegated to a subordinate, utilitarian role as they are in many cities. They are the system's signature element.

Everything comes to life in the city's streets, squares, parks, and gardens. In the decades during and following the construction of the grand boulevards, the new promenades became the territory of the flâneur. Unlike a wanderer on a *dérive,* a flâneur was a conscious actor in the theater of the city—a "passionate spectator," as described by Charles Baudelaire. The flâneur strolled confidently along the city streets, offering observations and commentary about the built environment and, by doing so, played a valuable role in defining the new lifestyle offered by Paris's transformation. Toward the end of the nineteenth century, the flâneur embodied a bourgeois aspiration of leisure and a cultural life for

Rue de Lyon, Paris. (Ryan Gravel, 2010)

the city that remains the foundation for Paris's defining global identity today.

The situationists despised that lifestyle as much as they railed against the city's destruction in their own century. "From any standpoint other than that of police control, Haussmann's Paris is a city built by an idiot, full of sound and fury, signifying nothing."[2] To them, the bourgeois environment of the flâneur was only the beginning of a capitalist appropriation of Paris. Their focus, therefore, became the present, and their predictions about the impact cars would have on the city were prescient. They accused contemporary planners of being interested only in "ensuring the smooth circulation of a rapidly increasing quantity of motor vehicles."[3]

As the situationists grew more concerned about these motives, the targets of their frustration became clear. They "regarded all the social sciences, including urbanism, with a suspicion proportional to the field's pretense of neutrality and expertise."[4] They challenged the status quo in modern city building efforts and in the very legitimacy of city planning practice, much like Jane Jacobs and other contemporaries who were fighting the similar transformation of New York under Robert Moses.

Like that of Jacobs, and unlike most criticism of urban development patterns today, the situationists did not emphasize environmental matters such as climate change, air or water quality, land consumption, or the destruction of wildlife habitat. Their attention was less on economics or any concern for public health. Their focus was social and cultural—"the stifling functionalism of postwar urbanism, as seen especially in the autocratic housing schemes built around Paris and other cities, which they felt curbed the individual's creative capacities."[5] In addition to the *dérive*, they engaged in dozens of other spectacles and activities that called attention to changes needed to reform contemporary society.

The situationists were unable to force change from the top, so they attempted to deliberately change individual cultural expectations through a kind of grassroots movement. It had radical, artistic overtones, but it was essentially community organizing. They challenged the individual to do something—to take responsibility for making change. The founder of the Situationist International, Guy Debord, wrote, "It is not a question of knowing whether this interests you but rather of whether you yourself could become interesting under new conditions of cultural creation."[6] He saw full participation in the life of the city as not only an opportunity but also our responsibility.

Of course by the time I lived there in the mid-1990s, Paris, like most any city in the West, had been significantly altered by its long flirtation with the automobile. The flâneur's demise, presumably due to habitat loss, reflected a cultural shift toward driving cars and the physical space needed to accommodate them. The River Seine was lined with highways, divorcing its banks from urban life. The city had narrowed its sidewalks, compromised its public spaces to make room for automobile traffic and parking, and developed large, detached social housing districts around its periphery. While the situationists had been responding in real time to these "atrocities" as they happened in the 1950s and 1960s, they were far too marginal a group to stop them. They made contributions in writing and actions, like the *dérive*, and they also played a role in the protests in

France in 1968. But for the most part, they represented only a small fringe of the intellectual, political, and artistic avant-garde. Like Jacobs, however, they did portend with crisp accuracy the kinds of challenges people would face as a result of the city's transformation.

The irony of my satisfaction with that *dérive* at the Place du Trocadéro, a part of Paris that had been radically altered at the hands of Haussmann, is not lost on me. But by acknowledging the viewpoint of both the situationist and the flâneur, a more enlightened picture is painted that illustrates what was—and still is—happening in the world. Alongside Jane Jacobs, parallel environmental arguments, and even more contemporary campaigns like Tactical Urbanism that are emerging at a grassroots level, the overwhelming sentiment seems to be that there is something very wrong with the way we have been building cities for well over the last half century.

The durability and diversity of this movement and the increased clarity of that larger picture also suggest that those of us who care should push more aggressively against the status quo of most city building practices. Even if we're not yet sure exactly what constitutes our collective success, we need to act, quickly and with confidence and urgency, as we move along any or all of these paths—social, cultural, environmental, economic, health related, or otherwise. We don't need everyone to agree on any one ideology before we start doing something. And in our data-heavy culture, we need to get more comfortable navigating through the sea of information rather than being paralyzed by its expanse. We need to be smart about data, of course, but we can't afford to pretend that a clear understanding is even possible—as if the city, in contrast to any other time in human history, is somehow now more knowable or less complex because of our ability to measure it with new technology. What has become clear is that whichever path each of us takes, and for whatever reason we take it, we need to actually start doing something.

AT THE TIME THAT BARON HAUSSMANN took up the job of implementing Napoleon III's vision, the little railroad junction that would become Atlanta had only been around for about 20 years. Up to and following the American Civil War, which ended in 1865, the city enjoyed significant growth as a result of the expansion of rail service throughout the state. Later, hundreds of miles of streetcar routes opened up new land for development to support a growing population well into the twentieth century. The region's truly explosive growth, however, came after mid-century, when the same car culture that lined the Seine with highways was creating an entirely new way of life in the United States.

I returned home to Atlanta from my time abroad in Paris and took a year to readjust to a life dependent on my car. I then went back to graduate school in city planning, deciding after another year to stick around for my architecture degree as well. I imagined that somewhere in between the stifling comprehensiveness in much of professional planning practice, and the commodification of design as just a collection of cheap boxes, there might be some ideas about the future of the city. There might be some space to uncover that would challenge the way people see the places in which they live, much the way that Paris had dramatically changed my worldview.

The dominant dialog between these disciplines, however, became frustrating. It sounded so much like the same arguments we had heard a generation ago. For example, we shouldn't be discussing whether sprawl is a good idea or not, I thought. It's done. Surely we are creative enough to look forward, take what we have, and invent ways to make it work for our future and for future generations. I wondered why we weren't talking more directly about that.

At home in Atlanta I somehow merged the practices of urban examination that I had learned in Europe with my native car culture. I was wandering the city with a little more intent than a *dérive* and a little less show than a flâneur. Maybe it was more like a field investigation. I explored the infrastructure of the city by foot, bike, and car. I followed the main-line railroads that gave the city its reason for being, as well as the belt line railroads that supported its economic expansion in the form of an industrial ring around the city. I found neighborhoods on the rebound and some stuck in decline; people everywhere trying to make a difference. In the process, I realized that there's more to this town than conventions and traffic, and if we paid more attention, we might find the city to be a much more satisfying place than we thought. We also might make a few changes.

In graduate school I became increasingly interested in the relationship between the design of public infrastructure and the way it influences private-market development—the way a new bridge, transit station, or exit ramp influences what kind of development takes place there. I think I was drawn to the topic of infrastructure because, while incredibly influential in the development and life of a city, it seemed relatively under the radar as a tool for social and cultural change. For my thesis in the fall of 1999, I developed an idea that might generate a future Atlanta that I wanted to live in. I was inspired by a quote from Rem Koolhaas, a Dutch architect who had quite a lot of not-so-nice things to say about metropolitan Atlanta, but who, unlike any other critic I was reading, at least offered what seemed like a sincere hope for our future. I interpreted what he said to mean that as we develop solutions to the problems we have created, we have the opportunity to make Atlanta into an amazing and new kind of place. The very first page of my thesis begins with two paragraphs split by that influential quote.

> In *Toward the Contemporary City,* Rem Koolhaas observes that the project of the modern city was built only in fragments and the challenge now is to remodel and augment the different parts of the city without destroying them, much the way Milan or Paris did in the nineteenth century. By working in between the different fragments, both the idealism of modern urbanism and the imagery and scale of the traditional city are compromised, but valuable new themes to work with are opened up that allow us to deal with the complexities of contemporary life.[7]

>> The contemporary city . . . ought to yield a sort of manifesto, a premature homage to a form of modernity, which when compared to cities of the past might seem devoid of qualities, but in which we will one day recognize as many gains as losses. Leave Paris and Amsterdam—go look at Atlanta, quickly and without preconceptions.[8]

> If Atlanta may be considered the poster child of the new American city, then we need look no further for the challenges and complexities

of contemporary urban life. This metropolitan area, with both un-controllable suburban growth and extensive inner city gentrification, suffers most of all from traffic congestion and the ecological conse-quences of unmitigated sprawl. . . . Real change in the way we build our city will require a significant shift in the attitude of a region that has for too long prioritized the automobile as the primary tool for ur-ban expansion.[9]

TAKING KOOLHAAS'S CHALLENGE quite seriously, the Atlanta Beltline was conceived as my graduate thesis. Based on the idea that the creative design of infrastructure systems can direct private investment to accomplish public goals, it was born as a way to reinvigorate Atlanta's in-town communities with appropriate new development and improved transit mobility. In an amazing story that has followed that inception, the idea has been nurtured by people who believe in its vision; an engaged public that has expanded it into a remarkably ambitious proposal for ur-ban regeneration.

Even more important than the project's physical implementation, however, is the fact that its progress is proving exactly the proposal's origi-nal promise and intent. It is not only changing the physical form of the city. It is changing the way we think about Atlanta. In the process, it is reflecting a much larger story of change in cities everywhere that is calling all of us to discover a new kind of infrastructure for our lives.

"INFRA-CULTURE"

GENERAL JAMES OGLETHORPE FOUNDED GEORGIA BY charter in 1732 as the thirteenth British colony in the New World and established Savannah as its capital the following year. Far away, working in earnest from his home near London, Oglethorpe fashioned the town as a critical prototype for an ambitious but ultimately unsuccessful regional utopia.[1] For Savannah, resting high on a bluff at the edge of the coastal plain, Oglethorpe laid out an extraordinary plan to provide each citizen with access to a town lot, a garden plot, and a farm on the edge of town.[2] He made what is now one of the most famous city street plans in the world, and for me, he also created the perfect venue to challenge my understanding of cities. Just over a year after my experience in Paris, an innocent question about his plan had me rethinking again the relationship between our lives and the places we live, even those as lovely as Savannah.

We might imagine that, in drafting the new city's subtle hierarchy of blocks and parcels and its elegant network of streets, avenues, and squares, Oglethorpe foresaw how his plan would be built out over time. He might have predicted that the city's modest houses would one day make way for the townhouses, theaters, and commercial buildings that now offer a pleasing architectural expression of his plan, and even that one of them might become a Banana Republic. He might have projected that there would be dramatic technological innovations related to travel along the city's streets, from horse-drawn carts in his time to trolleys, buses, and automobiles, and that one day we might stack those individual driving machines ten stories high in buildings called "garages" that would be as easily accommodated within the town plan as its magnificent churches and public buildings. But it is hard to imagine that Oglethorpe would ever have envisioned a day when our cultural perspective was warped to such a point that my cousin could challenge the very essence of the place he had created.

I had stopped by Savannah with Leanne on the way to a wedding on the coast. We were both in our mid-twenties and had both grown up in sprawl, although her version was from north Alabama and her cultural perspective was far less tainted than mine. It had not been misshapen by "The History of Urban Form," a course taught by the late legendary Georgia Tech professor Doug Allen, who, referring to constant attempts by students to reinvent the way cities fit together, once told us, "It is easier to bake a cake with sugar and flour than with raw chemical elements." Those fresh ingredients—the kind you get at the grocery store, not in the science lab—were all around us that day in Savannah: sidewalks, porches, fountains, and all the rest in a magnificent display of urbanity. We were standing there in the street near one of Oglethorpe's famous squares, embedded fully and three-dimensionally in what is arguably the most delightful and sophisticated urban plan in America, when she turned to me and asked, "Does Savannah have a real city?"

The question caught me off guard. After all, regardless of Oglethorpe's failure to realize his utopian vision, the inherent beauty and utility of Savannah's street plan, combined with the city's southern hospitality, enchanting colonial history, and graceful architecture, embody the perfect marriage of the Old and New Worlds and makes it one of the most profound and "real" cities that either of us had ever stepped foot in. I had spent the last several years of my life studying cities and was sufficiently confident about that fact. Yet with the dappled sunlight of summer's midday dancing through the Spanish moss, and with the gentle ebb and flow of people and cars behind us in their daily ballet around Johnson Square, she clarified, "I mean, does Savannah have a mall?"

IT IS CLEAR THAT THE sprawling kind of urban development pattern that is so conventional today—strip malls fronted by parking lots and lined with chain restaurants and gas stations in a dizzying array of traffic lights and turn lanes—has altered our perspective of the city itself. These consumer-oriented landscapes have dissolved the clarity of relationships that once gave coherence and identity to older places like Savannah's famous squares. Still, I stood there, speechless. All I could think about was how the streets and public spaces there in that place were so clearly designed for people like us; not only for cars, like the places where we had been raised. They provide a coherent sense of order for finding our way through the city, for a productive economy, and for the enthusiastic living of life itself. That's what makes a city "real," isn't it?

The problem with the way we have been building cities over the last sixty years is not just the lack of venues for such celebration, however. It's not only the physical separation of people by income, race, and age. It's not just the separation of places where we spend our time, like home, work, stores, and parks. It's not only the inefficient use of public resources like water, sewers, schools, and emergency services, or the wasteful use of our private resources, including our time, wealth, and health. We'll discuss all of those things later. The real problem is much less part of our public discourse, but is perhaps even more important, and my cousin's question in Savannah zeroes in exactly on this point. There have been generations of people, she and myself included, who grew up with the shopping mall as the highest standard of how we build our cities. Not only did we never go shopping downtown during the formative years of our youth, but we didn't live in neighborhoods with people who were significantly different from ourselves, or in places where we didn't have to get in our car to go practically everywhere. To many of us, the mall, or its more recent form, the open-air "lifestyle center" and all of its accoutrements like highways, outparcels, and drive-throughs, is the physical manifestation of our preferred lifestyle. This is what we want.

For this reason, I have come to realize that "Does Savannah have a real city?" is actually the perfect question for our time. We shouldn't be afraid to ask it. It's honest. It eventually challenged me to consider how my individual perspective on the world helps to shape the decisions I make about living. We all develop ideas and expectations about the way the world works over the course of our lives and sometimes, in order to move forward, we need to deliberately break those expectations.

That's basically what Oglethorpe was doing with the Georgia colony. He wanted to make political reforms, and they were reflected in challenges to conventional practices in town planning.[3] He drew a thoughtful physical frame for shaping the public's view of the world, one unlike the relatively disordered urban blocks that had evolved in other North American colonial cities like New York (before the 1811 Manhattan grid), Boston (before Back Bay), or Charleston. The town plan took a more rhythmic, rectilinear form that embodied both its social and functional purposes. While he may have been unsuccessful in his social goals, Oglethorpe did create a clear, efficient framework for infrastructure to support a high quality of life and a reasonably successful economy.

More pertinent to this story, perhaps, is that Oglethorpe's plan did for Savannah what Napoleon III's grand boulevards, parks, and public spaces did for Paris. It produced a unique physical expression that captured and defined an enduring character and identity found nowhere else on Earth. His deliberation also formed a valuable social, cultural, and physical model for shaping the places where we live with intention. This attention to purpose and the public interest made Savannah not only quite lovely as a physical place, but also a very "real" city for living—at least in my opinion.

Savannah's exquisitely deliberate expression of interlocking avenues and squares and its sophisticated composition of public and private buildings has left an indelible impression not only on me, but also on the lives and perspectives of its people over time. The physical place, along with its infrastructure networks and functional qualities, has combined with the region's history and climate and the people who live there to produce a unique economy, culture, and social life. The allure created by such a

Savannah's historic district as seen from a parking garage. (Ryan Gravel, 2006)

distinctive physical place inspired many people to fight for the plan's protection all these years—through the dark days of car dependency when
Ellis Square was sacrificed for a parking garage and two other squares
were erased to improve the flow of automobiles; when the mall was built
on the edge of town and the population sprawled into the coastal plain
with much less care or vision.

Thanks to those efforts, the city's original plan and the buildings and
squares that give it form all remain remarkably intact. They have proved
to be more highly valued culturally and more resilient physically than almost anything we build today. And it is important to remember in our assessment that compared to those car-dependent communities, the historic
core of Savannah is designed primarily for people. Its utility as a place to
live, therefore, remains exceptionally well positioned for a future that will
almost certainly be less dependent on our individual driving machines.

Savannah's dark days also illustrate, however, that as much as our infrastructure shapes our cultural perspectives, our perspectives also shape

the infrastructure that we build. During those middle years when Atlanta was exploding with car-dependent growth 250 miles to the north, and the River Seine in Paris was lined with highways, a generation with a similar cultural mind-set also emerged in Savannah. They imagined a future very different from the city's tidy street grid, and they organized themselves around a different physical structure. Like virtually every place in the West, the decision makers and cultural momentum in Savannah built a new infrastructure for a new way of life and continued to reinforce it through decades of supporting policy, public investments, and private development. This included Oglethorpe Mall—yes, that's actually the name of it—which opened five miles south of downtown in 1969. And until recently, and by almost any measure, the new world that they created would be defined as highly successful.

TODAY, HOWEVER, WE CAN BEGIN to see things differently. The limitations of car-dependent physical growth patterns are becoming more apparent. Even Banana Republic has found a home on Broughton Street, not out at the mall. And no matter if this is a deliberate decision or just another uncertain sign of our current new interest in cities, it helps make the case that if we want our local economies to take advantage of shifting economic conditions, we need to be honest about the future of sprawl. We need to reconsider policies like free parking and cheap oil that prioritize cars over people as they shape the world around us. Of course this is already happening organically in many places, but if we want change that is more intentional and geographically comprehensive, then we need to be deliberate about our role in shaping national cultural conditions.

The sprawling edges of metropolitan Atlanta or any place that came of age under heavy influence of the automobile, including the fringes of cities with a more urban reputation like New York, Boston, or Savannah, have taken on a physical form that is not exactly wrong but is fundamentally different from the older parts of town. These places function differently, and as people live and work there—as entire generations of people like me and my cousin were born and raised there—they shape the way we think about the world. As a result, they influence and inform the decisions we make about other policies and investments.

Of course this is also true in urban or rural places. If people like the place where they live, they support it with other policies, regulations, and investments. If they don't like it, and if they are empowered to do something about it, they usually find a way to change their circumstances. They may simply move to a different place that is more in sync with their interests or values—think of the massive suburbanization in the second half of the last century when people with mobility left the city and created an entirely new lifestyle for themselves. Or they may stay where they are to work and vote for change—consider the seven women who fought to protect Savannah's historic district, built a strategic revolving fund for preservation, and later passed meaningful legal protections.

In both cases, physical changes are reinforced by shifting cultural expectations. This kind of synergy can become manifest incrementally through reforms in policies, regulations, and investments, or it can take a more disruptive course through spectacular transformations, protests, and even revolution. Today, as we look into our future at what is likely to be a dramatic, perhaps even radical reorganization of urbanized regions in the United States in the next half century, it is essential that we understand how we can shape that future and help determine whether this will be a thoughtful or a chaotic transition. To do this, it is important for us to understand both the way that infrastructure shapes our worldview and the way that our ideas about the world shape the infrastructure that we build.

From the 1940s through the 1960s, for example, as cities made incremental shifts toward an exciting modern lifestyle led by automobiles, buses, and truck-based freight, the older infrastructure networks and the land associated with them became increasingly undesirable and eventually obsolete. As a new collective vision for the future emerged, citizens, businesses, and governments built an amazing new infrastructure and an entirely new economy organized around a new way of doing things. They also discarded their old ways, often abandoning them both physically and emotionally. Their lack of interest and attention to older communities led

The Los Angeles River from the 7th Street Bridge, Los Angeles. (Ryan Gravel, 2011)

to decades of disinvestment in the systems and economies that they had once sustained.

Take the case of the Los Angeles River, which gave the city its original reason for being and nourished its early cultural life and economy. Today, many people don't even know Los Angeles has a river. By the time local industry began shifting from rail to trucks for the shipping of goods and supplies, the once-wild river had been hemmed in by railroads and industrial zones and channelized to control flooding for its full 51 miles from the San Fernando Valley to the port at Long Beach. The public had largely forgotten about it, and their indifference allowed the ugly concrete "river" to disappear from consciousness and become further degraded by highways, high-power transmission lines, and other transgressions.

Of course, today things are different. Fed up with traffic and sprawl, people are rediscovering their river and are fighting to reposition it as a central part of a more sustainable vision for Los Angeles. They are proposing significant changes to the physical infrastructure of their river, but more importantly, they are inserting the river back into the public consciousness. In the process, they are challenging their fellow citizens to rethink the decisions they make about the places where they live, work, and play. It is in this national story about our finicky oscillation between what is useful today and obsolete tomorrow that we can begin to see clearly the intimate relationship between infrastructure and our way of life.

CYCLES OF CHANGE

I GOT MY FIRST GLIMPSE OF THE ROLE THAT HUMAN motives play in the dynamic construction of cities when I moved away from my suburban childhood home to the middle of Atlanta to attend college at Georgia Tech. I lived in a dorm on the then-gritty west side of campus. I didn't understand at the time that that grittiness was recent history. The place I was living had been laid bare by a national cultural movement that prioritized civic "progress" over the communities of urban poor people, and the still-unhealed scars of its 1960s-era urban renewal program blended seamlessly with the west side's down-and-out industrial aesthetic. I distinctly remember collecting random bricks and garden plants from the gravel lot on Eighth Street where I parked my car and thinking how that must have once been somebody's home.

It was. Following its 1965 master plan and backed by the threat that it could condemn private land, Georgia Tech rapidly and dramatically expanded its campus westward into the mixed-race Hemphill Avenue community, which was "a vibrant neighborhood, but it was also poor."[1] The area had previously become famous for its Pickrick Cafeteria, owned by the segregationist Lester Maddox, who decided to close it rather than integrate its dining area in compliance with the Civil Rights Act of 1964. He became governor of Georgia in 1967, and his term coincided, coincidentally perhaps, with the primary time frame of Hemphill Avenue's buyout by Georgia Tech.

Most of the neighborhood was gone by the time I arrived, so even though it was the first time I had lived in an urban environment, that term should be qualified because anything truly "urban" about my immediate surroundings had been erased by the university's expansion. This included the Pickrick, which by that time had morphed into the school's parking office, but that didn't matter. I didn't know any better. I had no idea where I was.

This was also the first time I was conscious of living in a community of sharp contrasts. The mostly middle-class students with new cars and credit cards were on campus, and the blighted communities forgotten by much of metropolitan Atlanta sat just over its western fence. It was the early 1990s, well before the west side's trendy restaurants and apartments began transforming the Howell Mill Road corridor. My memories from that time are mostly of liquor stores, broken sidewalks, and unremarkable vacant buildings—a mental slideshow of poverty and discarded land collected from my exploration of the forgotten sides of the city.

Even Piedmont Park on the east side was worn and bare. Midtown was drab. The small-scale buildings that had supported a vibrant hippie culture in the 1960s and 1970s had been almost completely demolished by the time I started college. Relative to their stronger position today, most in-town neighborhoods were lifeless and tired, but they had at least stabilized from a generation of physical destruction and social turmoil at the hands of highway building, depopulation, redlining, and white flight. These conditions were real and devastating for many people, but for better or worse, they had also begun to establish an appropriately fertile environment for the reimagination of the city's future.

Of course I did not recognize that opportunity at the time. I was just a loner student mesmerized by the railroads that entangle those communities and connect them directly but discretely to the more affluent sides of town. Just as the river gave Los Angeles its reason for being, Atlanta's founding purpose was that of a railroad junction, and I found railroads everywhere I went. My first memory of physically standing on any of them was during my junior year of college, just before going to Paris. I had moved from the west campus dorms to an apartment in a now-demolished 1960s faux–Tudor style complex called Yorke Downs at the end of 26th Street in Brookwood. My two-story unit backed up to an active railroad that had been built a hundred years earlier as the Seaboard Air Line Belt Railway. It sliced across the rolling terrain that had been bloodied by the Civil War Battle of Peachtree Creek. It now divides Collier Hills from Ardmore Park, two neighborhoods developed primarily in the 1940s.

I remember late nights standing by that railroad, watching streams of railcars rumble by. They labored with endless loads of oil, grain, automobiles, and containers of unknown cargo as my friend Joe and I engaged in long conversations about God and purpose and other things. We watched the trains move through the night like shadows until they screeched to a slow stop a mile or so away just short of Howell Junction. And as they continued south through Atlanta's forgotten west-side neighborhoods, the adventure of their unknown destination had an effect on me. Along with the different environment I found myself living in, my curiosity about their destination engaged me in an academic tradition in architecture that teaches students not only to challenge assumptions but also to develop creative, even unconventional solutions to problems. It cast a new perspective for my understanding of the physical and social structure of the city.

ATLANTA'S RAILROADS WERE NOT always hidden by the dark shadows of night. In fact, they originally played a central role in the city's development. In pursuit of economic opportunities offered by the state's abundant natural resources, early European settlers moved north from Savannah into the Piedmont region of Georgia, and by the early 1800s, they were establishing towns and county seats like Decatur and LaGrange. The city that would later become Atlanta was founded in 1837, seven miles to the southeast of Fort Peachtree, a strategic crossing of the Chattahoochee River and a meeting place for the Creek and Cherokee people. It was named "Terminus," and its singular purpose was that of a railroad junction. With a direct route to the river crossing, the town was built on a large, reasonably flat pass on the subcontinental divide, the ridgeline between the watersheds leading west to the Gulf of Mexico and east to the Atlantic Ocean. It grew in anticipation of the Western & Atlantic Railroad, a strategic investment by the taxpayers of Georgia that connected them to the northern trade markets of the Tennessee and Ohio River valleys. The railroad's southern endpoint was the Zero Mile Post, a short stone marking the city's conceptual birthplace, which has now been moved several blocks east, buried under a parking garage, and encased in a small brick building.

Terminus was renamed "Marthasville" in 1842 after Governor Wilson Lumpkin's daughter, and then renamed again and incorporated as "Atlanta" in 1847, a feminine reference to the Western & Atlantic Railroad, which finally arrived in 1851. By many accounts the town was never expected to amount to much, but it quickly grew into the most strategic railroad hub in the South. It joined lines following ridges from the east, south, and west, including the Georgia Railroad (1845), the Macon & Western (1846), and the Atlanta & LaGrange (1854), and it connected them to the state's northbound investment. By 1860, on the brink of the Civil War, railroads had made Atlanta a crucial link in the logistics of the fledgling Confederacy for the transportation of food, goods, and troops, and therefore a key target for the Union army.

On September 1, 1864, after months of fighting along the route of the Western & Atlantic south from Chattanooga, Union General William Tecumseh Sherman captured Atlanta and delivered the city to President Lincoln just in time to seal his reelection. As famously dramatized in *Gone With the Wind,* the Union army burned Atlanta to the ground, destroying its railroads and sparing only its churches and hospitals. With Atlanta fallen, Sherman began his devastating "March to the Sea," delivering Savannah to Lincoln before Christmas. The South was split in half and the close of the war was in sight, ending just a few months later.

Atlanta had never really been the stereotypical city of the Old South as portrayed in the movie. It was more akin to a frontier town that was leveraging its railroads for business development. Metaphorically, however,

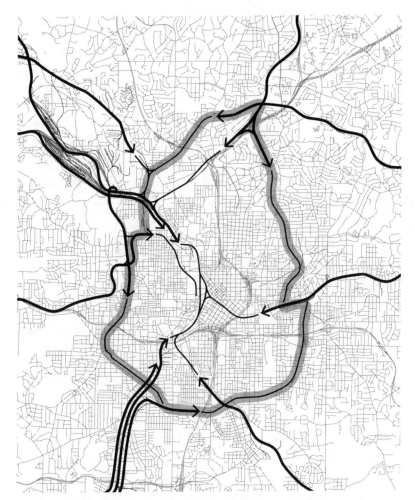

Railroads converge to form Atlanta. (Ryan Gravel/Perkins+Will, 2015)

the city compares quite well to the story's central character, Scarlett O'Hara, who manipulates her many suitors and effortlessly cuts her losses with the cultural associations of her past in order to find a modern, profitable way forward. She's not entirely superficial, but she's driven. And when her back is against the wall, she comes out swinging.

This survival skill has served Atlanta well. In the postwar era, the city's overtly conciliatory position toward reunification of the United States and its decidedly forward view toward business and economic progress enabled the rebuilding and significant expansion of both its economy and its physical extents. By 1870, Atlanta's population had more than doubled from the prewar period, and railroads remained central to this rebirth, defining growth patterns well into the next century. In addition to the restoration of the original lines, several new main-line railroads joined the system, including the East Tennessee, Virginia & Georgia (1882), and the Atlanta, Birmingham & Coast (1908).

The main lines provided access for both passengers and freight into the central business district from anywhere in the country, and as the city flourished during Reconstruction, the original rail junction became increasingly congested. In response, four different railroad companies built four new railroads around the outskirts of the city, repurposing farmlands, crossroad settlements, and the former battlegrounds of war in order to expand the city's industrial base.

These "belt lines" aligned to form a rough circle, and even though they never operated as a loop route, some accounts refer to them as the "circle line" or the "railroad cordon." Their circumferential routes meant they were unable to follow the ridgelines. Instead, the belt lines sliced across the hilly Georgia Piedmont, constructing embankments, deep cuts, tunnels, and bridges that could provide flat conduits for trains around the city. As industries lined up along these routes, they further flattened hilltops and piped up the waterways that drained the central, uphill part of Atlanta.

The first of the four belt lines was Southern Railway's Decatur Street Belt, which entered the city from the northeast in 1871, only a year after Georgia was readmitted to the Union. It was originally built as the main line for the Atlanta & Richmond Air-Line Railway; of all the belt lines, the Southern has played the most visible role in the life of the city. Railroad construction workers, for example, are said to have discovered Ponce de Leon Springs, which later became a popular resort. The Southern carried the funeral train for Jefferson Davis, the former president of the Confederate States who died in 1889, the same year Georgia completed its new capitol building in Atlanta. It also carried people to see the

Liberty Bell, which arrived just a few years later on a reconciliation visit from Philadelphia to the Cotton States and International Exposition in 1895. These festival grounds were also the site of Booker T. Washington's famous "Atlanta Exposition" speech and were later converted into Piedmont Park, for which Southern's belt forms the long eastern boundary.

By the late 1920s, the spring at Ponce de Leon Avenue had been covered by the mammoth Sears and Roebuck store and distribution center (now Ponce City Market). The building expanded over the years into one of the largest buildings in the southeastern United States. Across the street, Southern's railroad embankment became a unique feature of the city's baseball stadium. It served as the rowdy, racially integrated outfield, where along with "gambling and whisky drinking,"[2] fans watched both the minor league Atlanta Crackers and Negro League Black Crackers, including the integration of Atlanta professional sports in 1949 by Jackie Robinson of the Brooklyn Dodgers. Two magnolia trees on the Southern's embankment remain today as the only vestige of the ballpark. A ball hit into the trees was considered an automatic home run, but the only two players to accomplish this 462-foot hit were Babe Ruth and Eddie Matthews. Other baseball icons to play at "Poncey" included Lou Gehrig, Mickey Mantle, and Phil Rizzuto. In 1954, Crackers home run record holder Bob Montag hit a 450-foot home run that landed in a passing train. A few days later, the train fireman met Montag to present the ball, which had traveled in a coal car on a 518-mile round-trip to Nashville.[3] This sparked local lore that retold the story as "the home run that went around the world."

Histories of the other belt lines are not as well recorded, but certainly the businesses they supported provided an expanding economic base for growth in Atlanta. The Seaboard Air Line Belt Railway made its way around the northwest side of town in 1892, past Peachtree Street and the old battlefield that a century later would be home to my college apartment. In 1899, the Atlanta & West Point Belt Line plowed around the southeast, crossing the fading Civil War trenches of the notorious Battle of Atlanta. Finally, sometime around the turn of the century, the

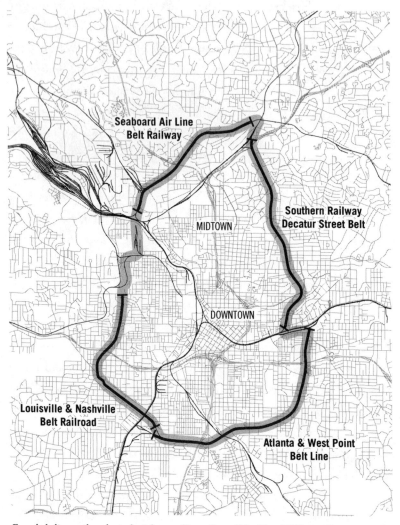

Four belt line railroads circle Atlanta. (Ryan Gravel/Perkins+Will, 2015)

Louisville & Nashville Belt Railroad slid down the city's west side, criss-crossing the remnant city barricades and the front lines of the Battle at Ezra Church.

Meanwhile, the booming economy supported by the city's railroads drove significant growth of residential and commercial districts in every direction from downtown, enabled largely by the advancement of the

The Atlanta & West Point Belt Line, Atlanta. (Ryan Gravel, 2015)

streetcars that were revolutionizing urban expansion around the world. Entrepreneurs and real estate developers established an extensive private streetcar system in Atlanta by linking new residential development like Inman Park (1889) to the central city. Most of the neighborhoods that were built between the late Victorian era and the 1920s were constructed in this way. As growth jumped across the belt lines and the industrial zones that followed them, neighborhoods built on one side of the tracks or the other were often significantly differentiated by socioeconomic conditions.

An example is Pittsburgh, a thriving African American working-class neighborhood founded in 1883 that expanded south from downtown along McDaniel Street to the Atlanta & West Point Belt Line. Across the tracks to the south, Capitol View Manor was established in the 1920s by a streetcar line along Stewart Avenue (now Metropolitan Parkway) as a middle-class white community. Over 40 neighborhoods developed in similar pairings along the belt line railroads. While not dense by northern standards, these communities developed with physical attributes that any good urbanist would pine for today. They were characterized by relatively compact residential districts with sidewalks, mixed-use clusters around streetcar stops, a variety of housing types, and neighborhood-oriented parks, schools, and churches.

Many of these neighborhoods were both politically and institutionally reserved for whites during the Jim Crow era, but increasing black voting power led to significant changes that would lay the groundwork for powerful social change in the second half of the century. These include the designation of Washington Park as the first recreational park for blacks in 1919, breaking the west-side "color line" that had been held at Ashby Street (now J. E. Lowery Boulevard), and providing new residential districts for blacks that eventually spread well beyond the Louisville & Nashville Belt Railroad that borders Washington Park. The surrounding Washington Park neighborhood became Atlanta's first new community built specifically for blacks, and in 1921, a bond referendum passed enabling construction of several new black schools.

African American history in Atlanta may be better known by the exuberance and symbolism of "Sweet Auburn" Avenue, which stretches east from downtown to the Southern Railway's belt line. It was the birthplace and pulpit of Dr. Martin Luther King Jr. and was once described by *Fortune* magazine as the "richest negro street in the world."[4] Atlanta's notable black middle class, however, actually resided more substantively on the city's west side, anchored by the colleges of the Atlanta University Center, which had consolidated their campuses there by the 1940s. Rising political power allowed the negotiation for black residential expansion west beyond the Louisville & Nashville belt along corridors like Cascade Avenue, Hunter Street (later Martin Luther King Jr. Drive), and into other communities that white flight would eventually leave behind. While the belt line railroads likely played only background roles in this shift toward an expanding black middle class in Atlanta, the communities alongside them became the origin and anchor of a new African American west-side prosperity, helping to define an era of opportunity and eventually a more equitable, if still imperfect, capital of the American South.

THE NETWORK OF PRIVATE TRANSIT LINES that originally brokered the development of Atlanta's oldest streetcar suburbs like Inman Park and West End were consolidated into a more cohesive system owned by the Georgia Railway & Electric Company in 1902. By the time neighborhoods like Capitol View Manor were platted 20 years later, the system's peak ridership had access to hundreds of miles of track with routes all over the city. By the postwar 1940s, however, increasing automobile ownership resulted in plummeting demand for streetcars and generated traffic congestion in many city streets. These and other factors led to the decline of the streetcar system, which was completely dismantled by the end of the decade.

The streetcars were initially replaced with "trackless trolleys," which kept overhead electrical service but could maneuver through street traffic more easily on rubber tires. By 1963, as entire demographics of former transit riders fled to the suburban frontier, the wires were removed and the vehicles were replaced with diesel buses, which allowed easier adjustments to routes to reflect changing geographic demands. The in-town neighborhoods along their routes, which ranged "in character from new and luxurious Sherwood Forest to badly blighted close-in sections in need of redevelopment,"[5] experienced mixed results as they competed against the exodus of Atlanta's white working and middle class during this time of dramatic transition.

In tandem with the destruction of Atlanta's streetcar system was the swift decline of Georgia's statewide passenger rail network. Once-heralded streamliner routes like the Nancy Hanks to Savannah or the Dixie Flagler from Chicago to Miami could no longer compete with automobiles out on the open road. Eight years after the extraordinary public outcry that followed the demolition of New York City's beaux arts Pennsylvania Station in 1963, Atlanta nonchalantly razed its handsome Terminal Station, a monumental shed cloaked in a picturesque Renaissance Revival façade that had been built in 1905. A few blocks to the east, Union Station was demolished the very next year, and major stations in other cities across the state were also razed or shuttered, including those in Savannah, Macon, and Columbus. Today, the only passenger rail service that serves Atlanta is Amtrak's Crescent line from Washington, DC, to New Orleans, stopping once a day in each direction at the formerly suburban Brookwood Station three miles north of downtown.

Around the region, the small-town stops that had once been portals to the economic engine of Atlanta, including Decatur, Marietta, Chamblee, Norcross, East Point, College Park, and Acworth, also closed their doors. The trains that gave Atlanta its reason for being no longer represented the future for its citizens, businesses, or government. The tracks, which by this time rumbled invisibly below the downtown streets and out of town along blighted backyards and industrial zones, were relegated to competing freight operators who then worked with roadway builders to more fully disengage the tracks from city life through line abandonments and grade separations.

As for the belt lines, their fate was also sealed by the national movement toward an automobile-dominated lifestyle. As long as local industries used these rail routes for shipping and receiving, they lived in relative harmony with the growing city around them. But just as individuals abandoned trolleys and streamliners, industry soon began to abandon rail in favor of truck-based freight, which could more effectively service the region's increasingly dispersed population, especially for short-haul trips.

This was devastating for both the communities along the belt lines and the economic viability of their industrial territory. Their streets were not suited to the heavy truck traffic coming to service their confined industrial zones. As early as the 1950s, city planners could see the effects. "Large-scale truck traffic on inadequate local streets has resulted mainly from the lack of effective land use planning. Business and industry have been developed in locations which encourage the movement of trucks over residential or shopping streets, thus blighting many miles of good development. Only a fraction of the total frontage on these streets can be occupied by business and industry; the rest threatens to become the slum areas of the future."[6] Shipping to and from these sites was challenged by "narrow streets, steep grades, sharp turns, and short sight-distances [that] combine to slow trucks and add to general traffic congestion."[7] An earlier study noted "the nearness of slums and the lack of future expansion land for individual firms" as "negative factors" for the re-use of close-in industrial sites.[8]

As freight shifted to trucks, adjacent neighborhoods became increasingly battered—literally—with physical damage like broken sidewalks and street trees, as well as worsening air and noise pollution. These conditions contributed to blight and, ironically, blight was used as a prime reason for the construction of more highways, which only further ensured the neighborhoods' decline. A 1954 plan emphasized that "highways designed to accommodate trucks—expressways and limited access boulevards—are urgently needed to relieve residential and shopping streets of the harmful effects of heavy trucking."[9]

Highways may not have been the best answer, but those harmful effects were real. As early as 1952, planners acknowledged the blighting effects of truck traffic,[10] but their solutions remained focused almost exclusively on moving trucks more efficiently. There was essentially no assistance for the close-in industrial sites that were struggling to adapt to the changing world. "There has been little effective planning to improve, protect, or more fully develop the centrally located industrial districts in Atlanta. As a result, a great deal of good prospective downtown space has fallen into disrepair."[11]

These challenges were compounded by the changing demands of industries, most of which eventually left the central city altogether. They were attracted to the region's new periphery where large tracts of land with better truck access were plentiful.[12] Departing companies took good working-class jobs away from the city and left behind abandoned lots, vacant buildings, and degraded environmental conditions. And while the main-line railroads retained their value for long-range freight operations and for the service of large regional industrial zones, prospects for the belt lines grew worse. They had relatively limited utility as through routes, and their small service areas put them at a clear disadvantage compared to the big new industrial sites being developed on the outskirts of the region.

Underutilized and forgotten, much like the Los Angeles River, the belt lines became vulnerable to additional degradation by unscrupulous remaining industries, illegal dumping of trash and tires, the installation of high-power transmission lines, electrical substations, and the criminal or otherwise offensive activities that often take place in vacant and invisible places. Even as late as the mid-2000s when I lived in southwest Atlanta and our movement for the reimagined Atlanta Beltline was fully underway, illegal dumping, drugs, prostitution, and petty theft comingled with nefarious business practices in the forgotten land along Atlanta's in-town railroads. I remember a particularly notorious example of a company burning cars and pouring their visibly toxic fluids into storm drains that led directly into the creek that runs through the neighborhood park.

Most vulnerable, perhaps, was the Louisville & Nashville Belt Railroad on the west side of town. It was the youngest of the belt lines and therefore it never had much of a chance to develop a strong industrial user base before industry shifted to trucks. The land along its northern half was instead developed with residential neighborhoods, presumably due to declining industrial demand and the rising market for housing. Ashview Heights, Washington Park, Mozley Park, and Hunter Hills were all built alongside the tracks, and their backyards peered into the corridor as trains continued to rumble by for another half century. By the time the trains disappeared and the west side had transitioned to become almost exclusively African American, the utility of the railroad as a through route was physically broken by the construction of a new transit line to Bankhead, which opened in 1992.

Similarly, the controversial construction of a new intermodal freight transfer facility at Hulsey Yard in the poor white community of Cabbagetown and the poor black neighborhood of Reynoldstown severed the southern end of Southern Railway's belt in the 1980s. It also broke off the northern end of the Atlanta & West Point Belt Line, which was used to build a new interchange with I-20 and provide trucks better access to the yard. Now, along with the southwest belt, both the northeast and southeast lines could no longer operate as through routes. And while the Seaboard Air Line Belt Railway in the northwest remains in operation today, it works exclusively as a through line for CSX, having lost its local customers in favor of long hauls and faster trains.

This story of Atlanta's belt lines illustrates how our national interest turned away from the rail-based economy of our past and toward a new, modern vision for our future. As it did so, the old infrastructure, along with the communities it once supported, suffered severe disinvestment and decline. By midcentury, the belt lines had been undermined by policy and public investments. They were physically broken and saddled with small, obsolete, contaminated industrial properties with limited highway access. They were abandoned by businesses and families who could choose to move away from the city for a brighter future and economic opportunity. Following their departure, schools, parks, and the public realm were degraded. Jobs left. Much of the loop became characterized by unmaintained corridors lined with abandoned buildings and overgrown vacant lots. Perhaps most poignantly, however, this obsolete ring of infrastructure sat helpless, no longer able to help Atlanta defend herself against the powerful consequences of dramatic regional transformation taking place in the second half of the twentieth century.

Southern's belt line looking south toward North Highland Avenue. (Ryan Gravel, 2004)

Every city in America was struggling with similar challenges. As Atlanta tried to resist, or at least to manage this change, the city greatly expanded its limits in the 1950s through annexation, including that of affluent Buckhead to the north. But with so many incentives for leaving the center, like restricted home loans, increased automobile ownership, highway construction, and cheap suburban land, further fueled by the delayed racial integration of Atlanta's city schools, nothing could slow the net exodus of white residents from Atlanta. The city became politically landlocked, weakening its ability to benefit from the region's ongoing and unprecedented expansion. The city's population peaked in 1970 with nearly 500,000 residents, but then it plummeted for the next two decades. By the 1990 census, around the time I was starting college at Georgia Tech, the region had grown to 3.3 million, but the city had shed 100,000 people—a fifth of its population.

In addition to the loss of their neighbors, for the people who stayed behind, the physical cityscape was altered dramatically. A locally infamous plan by the H. W. Lochner Company out of Chicago had set the stage for this transformation, claiming in 1946 that "the present street system is entirely unsuited to the needs of modern automotive travel." It laid out new expressways that would sever downtown from its neighborhoods. It also narrowed sidewalks throughout the city to accommodate the increasing volume of cars. Other changes to streets included the "elimination of jogs, separation of grades and preferential treatment in traffic control" and the introduction of a one-way network across Atlanta's tangled downtown street grids.[13] Beyond roadways, massive urban renewal projects demolished many poor neighborhoods, including Buttermilk Bottom, site of today's Civic Center; Lightning, where the Georgia World Congress Center now stands; Hemphill Avenue, where I later lived on the west campus of Georgia Tech, as well as a dozen others.

These physical changes reflected larger cultural preferences for the people of Atlanta—beyond just suburbanization, highway construction, and urban renewal. Even attendance at the Atlanta Crackers' games declined. Abandoned by baseball, the once-beloved stadium that sat on the embankment of the Southern belt line was demolished in 1966, the same year the Braves franchise moved south from Milwaukee. The Black Crackers, along with the rest of the Negro Leagues, also declined steadily after the integration of major league baseball. And, unable to compete with regional malls and suburban warehouse space, the mammoth Sears and Roebuck store across Ponce de Leon Avenue shut its doors in 1979, keeping office space open until completely closing down in 1987.

When I arrived at Georgia Tech four years later and discovered garden plants breaking through the gravel parking lot at my dorm on west campus, the city was raw. Downtown had survived, if barely, but it came at a price to average citizens. Blank walls, loading docks, and parking garages were the new view for most people walking along the street, while the professional classes crossed along new skyways and malls that connected Peachtree Center and other buildings high above the street.

Survival also came at great expense to old Atlanta, which was increasingly demolished by a real estate industry eager to clear blocks for surface parking and the speculation of new skyscrapers, and a cultural perspective—not dissimilar from that of Scarlett O'Hara—that rather callously dismissed the past with a view squarely on the future. It allowed the city's mayor at the time to famously declare a historic landmark as a "hunk of junk" with little political consequence.[14] Ultimately, however, the cut-your-losses tactics modeled so well by O'Hara failed to fully protect downtown from the relentless flow of business and wealth north to Buckhead, Perimeter Center, and beyond. Atlanta spread horizontally into the Georgia Piedmont at an unprecedented pace, consistently topping national growth charts and earning its reputation as a poster child for sprawl.

The region's extensive investment in highways and car-oriented infrastructure was not purely bad news for the city. The world, not just Atlanta, was changing. And like Scarlett O'Hara, she was trying her best to set the past aside and focus forward on a new day and a new route to prosperity. The region moved swiftly and aggressively to take advantage of the opportunities that were presented to her. The era of highways injected a sense of modernity and progress for a region that had previously been "shackled to the prostrate Southern economy while the industrial revolution pushed other great US cities ahead."[15]

Atlanta's success came at the height of America's motor age, fueled by a powerful outward migration from central cities generally, and nationally toward the South and West. The new infrastructure of highways and arterial roadways that enabled this growth powered one of the strongest economic growth engines in the country over the second half of the twentieth century. The Atlanta region was inflated from a region of 1 million in 1950 to nearly 6 million people today.

Throughout it all, whether active or abandoned, the belt line railroads remained witnesses to the overlapping chapters of Atlanta's history, acting as barriers that supported segregation, as political boundaries that defined constituent allegiances, and as conduits for remnant industry and infrastructure. As belt line trains became less frequent and their adjacent land sat idle or abandoned, the tracks took on a more passive role in the life of the city. They were connecting routes for homeless and other forgotten people. They were hangouts for drug addicts and kids escaping their parents' supervision. And for visionaries who were so inclined, they became an inspired structure for new ideas about the city's future. As in most of urban America, things may have looked bleak, but the stage was being set for a new kind of city to emerge.

THERE'S NOTHING WRONG WITH SPRAWL

A KID GROWING UP IN THE DEEP SOUTH CAN NEVER RE-
ally believe in the possibility of a white Christmas. In fact, the best you
can hope for, realistically, is a nice sheet of black ice dusted with flurries,
somewhere around mid-January. Schools close without hesitation. And
since my childhood home was midway up one of the longest, steepest, and
straightest hills with no cross streets, on the occasion that its surface was
icy, our street was a destination for the neighborhood. Dads on sleds were
piled high with all sorts of kids on their backs, and we spent the morning
hours in our own sort of winter wonderland. Usually by lunchtime the
hill had turned to unsledable slush, and after an ice-ball fight and a cup
of hot chocolate, everything had melted away.

In the summer, we spent our days at the neighborhood pool, whiling
away our time with friends and eating flavored potato chips and candy.
We explored the woods in our backyard, including a polluted drainage-
way and kudzu-covered embankment that buffered us from the industrial
park beyond. When fall rolled around, our friends would drop by for
snacks after school and spend the late afternoon swinging from a rope tied
high to a tree in our front yard. In characteristic form for the emerging

Generation X, my twin brother and I spent the latter half of the 1980s as latchkey kids with free range of the neighborhood.

Our quintessential suburban American life revolved around this seasonal rhythm of mild winters, springtime pollen, homegrown tomato sandwiches in the summer, and high school football games every autumn. I never imagined there was anything wrong with the place of my childhood. I didn't know that the construction of my neighborhood played a bit part in a national drama that undermined urban communities. I didn't know that suburbs and sprawl were different, or that "sprawl" even had a name. Despite today's suppositions about life in sprawl, I don't have a single memory of being stuck in traffic, or of my friends having asthma, or of my neighbors driving dreadful commutes to downtown. In an interesting twist, however, I only recently realized that my own family's history helps to illustrate the story of sprawl.

My father's sister Gerry describes their mother, Geraldine, as a "feisty young woman" who had moved from her tiny hometown of Palmetto to the big city of Alexandria in the 1930s to attend business school. She met my grandfather, a downtown banker named Samuel Gravel, while waiting at the bank with a friend. The staunchly Catholic Gravels of central Louisiana "weren't at all sure about this Baptist girl from the country who had captured the heart of their primary breadwinner."[1] They married on a rainy day anyway, and in 1941, she became pregnant with my aunt, the first of four children.

To prepare for their growing family, a loan officer at the bank where my grandfather worked convinced him to purchase a home on Northview Drive in a new housing development on the edge of town. It was in Northview Annex, an extension of an older neighborhood, and our family photos resemble those classic images of postwar America where Levittown-style houses line streets without sidewalks. Each house had a driveway, a fresh lawn, and a little live oak in the front yard. My grandparents later upgraded to a three-bedroom house next door where they rented rooms to servicemen and their wives who were stationed at the military bases surrounding Alexandria.

*Geraldine Keller Gravel with daughter Gerry on Northview
Drive, Alexandria, Louisiana. (Gravel family collection, 1942)*

As wartime innovation shifted to the private sector, a mechanized economy emerged that, aided by the G.I. Bill and other federal policies, would
enable many Americans to leave behind the tragedy of war and, along with
it, the sooty, crowded conditions and social complexity of cities. Countless
soldiers who had fought for freedom abroad sought the prosperity promised
by economic growth to support their growing families. Technology and
policy supported the mass production of housing and automobiles that not
only helped recast our sight to the edge of town but created an entirely
new way of life in the process. In this sense, Northview Annex was a local
variation of a national movement that would form the foundation for what
today we call "sprawl," but at that time we simply called "the future."

Nearly three decades after the war, my parents bought their first
house in a neighborhood called Huntley Hills in Chamblee, a small community swallowed by the metropolitan growth of Atlanta. It was built
on the fringe of town, and its physical layout, architectural range, and
public amenities were consistent with new communities organized anywhere in America between the late 1950s and the early 1970s. It was built
around my elementary school, which had opened at the center of the

new neighborhood in 1964. This school-centered arrangement represents a logical next step in neighborhood design, following Northview Annex.

While the streets immediately surrounding the school had narrow sidewalks, most of the neighborhood had none. Houses were exclusively single-family, but their size ranged from small postwar modern ranches to much larger split-levels from the 1960s, including a handful of classic "California contemporaries." The least desirable lots in the neighborhood were at the bottom of that long sledding hill, and the handful of houses that finally got built there were big, multilevel structures in that modern 1980s style with diagonal cedar siding.

Huntley Hills had a single bus route that still serves the neighborhood, passing along its central drive on the way to other places. I only rode that bus once—for a field trip to the central library in downtown Atlanta that was led by an eccentric teacher in a class called "Discovery." Eccentric old ladies were, I later imagined, the only people riding that bus. The rest of us chose automobiles to go anywhere beyond our community's boundaries. In contrast to the sprawl of today, however, the neighborhood street plan had a loose network of interconnected streets with few true cul-de-sacs, and it had more than one exit to the world beyond. Even though most of the streets lacked sidewalks, I grew up walking or biking to school, and I had multiple routes to get there. Chamblee Plaza was also within a reasonable walk from most houses, and along with a couple of small office buildings, it was also on the bus line. "The Plaza," as we called it, offered two major supermarkets, a Woolworth's, Hancock Fabrics, and at least a dozen other stores. I don't ever remember walking to buy groceries, but as a kid in the 1980s we made that half-mile journey almost daily to play video games at Razzle Dazzle or to get ice cream and Cokes at Sugar Bear.

The construction of Huntley Hills corresponds exactly with the large social, cultural, and political shifts taking place in Atlanta and across America, including the desegregation of public schools, white flight out of central cities, growing dependence on two cars per family, and massive public investment in highways and other roadway infrastructure. In fact, the development of Huntley Hills was almost certainly incentivized by the concurrent construction of I-285, Atlanta's now-infamous perimeter expressway, which opened as a four-lane highway in 1969. When my parents moved our family to Georgia from Louisiana in 1974 following my father's service in the Air Force in Vietnam, they were attracted to metropolitan Atlanta's skyrocketing economy. My dad took a job with an engineering firm that prepared the infrastructure for that economy— wastewater treatment plants, pump stations, and dams that supported massive expansion well beyond the perimeter highway.

While the central city was just beginning to lose population, having peaked in 1970, the metropolitan region swelled by well over a million, taking the white suburbanizing middle and working classes from Atlanta, as well as migrants like us from all over the country and immigrants from around the world. There was no doubt at this time that the future of growth was out at the edge of town. In one direction from our house along the perimeter highway was Perimeter Mall, which opened its doors in 1971 with two anchor department stores, a movie theater out in the parking lot, and one of those Chick-fil-A's stuck in a corner because the concept of a "food court" had not yet been invented. In the other direction, one of the very first Home Depots opened down the road from my father's office, so we no longer needed to go to the lumberyard or hardware stores in order to fix up our house. These kinds of destinations meant that except for an occasional ballgame, we rarely needed to venture beyond those few exit ramps, and we rarely did. We lived our lives almost exclusively on the northern edge of the region. Like thousands of other communities across the nation, we were settled quite comfortably in the marriage between suburban life and automobiles that was characterized by Huntley Hills.

In retrospect, the reason that living on the edge was so comfortable at that time was that we weren't stuck in traffic. When I was a kid, the full force of sprawl was not yet in effect. The roadways were not at capacity because the region was always building more of them. During my child-hood in the 1970s and 1980s, the region grew by a little over a million people, and I-285 more than doubled its width from its original four lanes to ten near Perimeter Mall. In the years since I left for college, however, only a single lane has been added in each direction to that same stretch of highway while the population of the metropolitan area has swollen by nearly 3 million. We built plenty of highways elsewhere, of course, spreading our neighbors over more than 8,000 square miles. So with almost no viable alternative to driving these great distances, we made Atlanta into one of the most sprawling regions in the world.

In addition to the greater burden of cars funneling onto corridors like I-285, the configuration of local roadway networks has also changed in ways that heighten congestion and define a truly new condition for living. Huntley Hills represents a midpoint in this transition, which did not happen overnight. It took time and was physically expressed in the layout of neighborhood plans as American cities evolved slowly from compact, transit-oriented, walkable urban districts at their centers to sprawling and isolated subdivisions around their peripheries. By the late 1980s, when the last houses in our neighborhood were being built on those undesirable lots at the bottom of the hill, somewhere out in the next county, at the new fringe of growth, the refinement of sprawl as a highly compartmentalized and fully car-dependent physical growth pattern was essentially complete.

A comparable neighborhood built there in the 1990s, for example, would most likely have only one connection to the arterial roadway, preventing cut-through traffic by avoiding direct links to adjacent communities. It would have houses of more uniform size and price point, increasing the isolation of people with different family incomes. There would be nothing at all within walking distance except neighbors, so sidewalks, even where they existed, would not likely take you anywhere. And rather than winding through the community on its way to somewhere else, if there was a bus at all, it would speed by an empty stop out by the subdivision entrance.

It's hard to imagine not having the freedom that Huntley Hills offered me to roam around as a child. More refined versions of sprawl are marked by physical, social, and often cultural isolation, illustrating not only a fundamental difference in the way we build these communities, but also in the way that we live in them. They have unsettled that comfortable marriage between the car and Huntley Hills, defining an important nuance between communities that accommodate automobiles and those that are consumed by them. The difference from older urban districts is even more stark.

Sprawl has not only changed the way we build new places, however; it has changed everything. Our growing reliance on cars also destroyed the transit systems that had evolved to create and support older cities, suburbs, and towns. It facilitated population loss in virtually every central city across the country. And it contributed directly to the decline of communities that were bypassed by new highway construction or that struggled to adapt to the changes brought by the automobile, or that were simply out of fashion because they lacked big lawns and wide driveways.

Locally and nationally, as the private market began providing people with the auto-oriented communities they wanted, and as governments supported that development with subsidized home loans and publicly funded roadways, we began an astounding new chapter of city building in this country that has resulted in, among other things, the majority of Americans being dependent exclusively on automobiles not only for their jobs, but for their very existence. In this transition we gave up more than just an outdated or unfashionable transportation network. We gave up a way of life.

I had never experienced that way of life until my senior year in college when, within weeks of my arrival for that year abroad in Paris, I had lost fifteen pounds. I was eating fresh food from the local market, and I was walking wherever I went—two blocks to the Métro; two more from the station to school; four blocks to the grocery; two to the laundromat; seven to my friend's apartment (split by a transit ride with one transfer); six more to dinner; four more from there to the Champ de Mars; fifty-two more for an evening stroll simply because I was living in the most beautiful city in the world. Suddenly I was in the best shape of my life, and the connection between our built environment and my personal health and well-being was undeniable.

What was less apparent was how much more connected I was to people, in a way that had not been conceivable for me in Chamblee in the 1980s. On an average commute from my apartment near the Gare de Lyon to my school near La Villette, I would watch strangers interact, catch someone's eye, or overhear a conversation that I could at least partly understand. Leaving our building, my roommate and I would often encounter the building supervisor sweeping out front and children on their way to the school next door. The streets were full, but many were familiar faces. There was the owner of a big German Shepherd waiting at a café door, the man behind the counter at the *tabac,* the guys setting up tables at the seafood restaurant that faced the train station's tower, and the women at the ticket counter in the Métro station underground. There were musicians and mimes on the train. There were kids gossiping about friends, men in suits reading *Le Monde,* women with small dogs and dark hair, artists, couriers, lawyers, teachers, salespeople, and tourists.

When we departed the Métro at Corentin Cariou, we would buy a piece of bread or small quiche at the boulangerie with the clerk who had a higher tolerance for the American students, rush along a sidewalk past the rank smells of strange meats and urine, and finally step through an anonymous door into the courtyard of the school. The trip was not only healthy, affordable, and efficient, it was a social experience. Even though I rarely spoke a word on that commute, I participated for nine months in a social construct that included acknowledgment of and empathy for strangers. Upon later reflection and experience, I see how those feelings, sustained over many years, would consistently translate from the subway to the voting booth.

The lesson is not about the French or about big cities or subways. The lesson is that transportation infrastructure does more than move people. It builds communities, and it constructs our way of life. In short, it matters what kind of infrastructure we build, so we should think carefully about how we would prefer to live and make sure that the policies and projects we invest in are supporting those lifestyle goals.

When I got home from Paris in 1995, I lived with my parents for the summer and took an architecture job with a commute across the "top end" of I-285. The office was on an anonymous road in a virtually windowless office park, and my job was to design similar office parks in similar parts of town. Relatively speaking, the drive wasn't bad, partly because I was going against the primary flow of traffic and partly because traffic is just something that I had grown to expect. In fact, before Paris, I never knew life without highways and parking lots, but having just returned from a year without cars, the contrast was jarring.

I found myself sitting in traffic, immobile even when my car was moving. My commute took about the same amount of time as my trip to school in Paris, but I barely had to move my body to get there. I wasn't getting exercise and I had no connection with strangers. I would leave my house having acknowledged my parents at breakfast. The next person I connected with was the receptionist when I walked in the door at the office. That's it, even though I-285 carries over 250,000 vehicles a day.[2] We don't look each other in the eye while we're driving, and we can't overhear each other's conversations. In a lifestyle dominated by sprawl, there is little shared experience, only similar experience with the traffic jam du jour—often the topic of chitchat with coworkers around the coffeepot or on social media, where our personal connections are more likely than not to be with people of similar income, education, and background.

These kinds of social, cultural, and physical barriers matter for a lot of reasons. They separate us from each other. They divorce housing from retail from office from recreation and worship. They divide people living in apartments from people living in houses. They even separate people living in expensive houses from people living in moderately expensive houses. They create a world where we spend the majority of our time living, working, shopping, and playing with people who are more or less like us, and where it is nearly impossible to live through each stage of our lives—as a child, college student, parent, and aging senior—all within the same community. In the process, they minimize the need for various groups of people to come into contact with each other day to day.

In this way, sprawl—or, more accurately, the free market framed by policies that deliver sprawl—favors social isolation and heightens our sense of difference between groups of people. And because we interact less as we move along our publicly funded infrastructure networks and do not experience each other's lives, much less look each other in the eye, I believe that sprawl also contributes significantly to political polarization—to a lack of acknowledgment of and empathy for people who are different. This is true looking across any of our divisions and it reinforces stereotypes about income, race, ethnicity, educational attainment, and even political party affiliation. It is also true across the geography of a region, heightening the perception of difference between urban, suburban, exurban, and rural populations. Looking ahead at the shifting demographics across our metropolitan areas, the assumptions we make about groups of people may change, but the reality of those physical dividing lines will remain, and as a result, we will continue to build a substantially degraded social construct.

This is what drove me back to school to study city planning. After I had lived in Paris, the kind of compartmentalization created by sprawl didn't seem like a very interesting way to live. What did seem compelling was the challenge of transforming these anonymous suburbs of sprawl into anything remotely as diversified as my neighborhood in Paris, which was actually a rather ordinary collection of people and streets, businesses, homes, and schools under the watchful eye of the Gare de Lyon's monumental clock tower.

I was naïve and thought I might make a difference, but I never imagined that my formative years growing up in a kind of transitional sprawl, combined with my year abroad in an almost opposite kind of environment, would serve me so well professionally. Together they offered a moderated view, one able to recognize the real dangers and costs of sprawl without knocking it blindly as a total failure, a malicious conspiracy, or a cultural vacuum. I couldn't ignore the fact that somehow sprawl works just fine for millions of Americans, including many of my own friends and family.

For many people, and by many measures, sprawl has real and clear advantages. It is easy, especially in comparison to the logistical challenges of living in cities that have suffered decline and might no longer offer essential services like grocery stores or reliable transit. Families can usually find larger and newer houses for less money in sprawl, and sprawl is often the location of better public schools. Because it tends to isolate people who are different from one another, sprawl also largely avoids the uneasiness of

Gwinnett County, Georgia. (Ryan Gravel, 2011)

social and economic disparity. Not everyone wants the hustle and bustle of the city or the anonymity and confined energy of dense urban living. Where sprawl resembles the countryside, it can be quite peaceful. Long scenic commutes, if you actually have one, can even help moderate stress and depression by allowing you to decompress from the workday before engaging in family life.[3]

The point here is that like any place, communities defined by sprawl have both advantages and disadvantages, both good and bad consequences, and we do ourselves a huge disservice if we don't consider everything in this discussion. Love it or hate it, there is no denial that sprawl has been a successful physical structure for unprecedented economic growth in this country, and that, like my own family growing up in Chamblee, a large proportion of Americans were lifted by that prosperity as a direct result of our nation's investment in it.

Besides, it's hard to argue against the open road when the windows are down and the traffic is flowing fine. Culturally, our notion of the "open road" has embraced the mobility of the automobile to generate a distinctly American identity. And even though it is increasingly unrealistic for most people, the freedom that idea represents has immense value. It connects us with an earlier narrative, a kind of cowboy, pull-yourself-up-by-your-bootstraps brand of rugged individualism. Reflections of it can even be seen in some aspects of today's hip-hop culture, creative capitalism, and empowered immigrant communities, suggesting that our interest in it is not likely to go away.

Nor should it. Our auto orientation has made many valuable cultural contributions. Sprawl set the stage for American life today as much as our vibrant downtowns did for generations before. Who can deny its influence on modern culture—in movies, music, food, travel, and the refreshing horizontality of midcentury architecture, furniture, and industrial design? The early stages of sprawl, much like my neighborhood of Huntley Hills with its International Style schools, modern-ish houses, and open roads, became the backdrop for an inspired future that for many people was brighter than the old, crowded, dirty city it left behind.

It's important to remember that we were experimenting with this new way of living at the very same time that science was curing disease, exploring new energy, and lifting us to the moon. The sexual revolution was breaking down barriers and the civil rights movement began its steady march toward the fulfillment of our nation's promise. As the growth of new automobile-oriented suburbs exploded through subsidized highways and home loans, and as downtowns skinned over their old-fashioned façades and scrapped their trolley networks for wider roadways and free parking, the American dream was made manifest in an incredible array of cultural icons—forms that now, with a hint of sentimentality, have taken on the mantle of a forward, transformative, yet thoroughly concluded era.

Ensuring that conclusion, of course, is the destructive nature and obsolescence of sprawl. Its advantages, like cheap land and cheap houses, were also built on a less robust and less efficient network of infrastructure, leaving them now at a clear disadvantage. As the true costs of sprawl are being realized, characteristics like geographic isolation, demographic homogeneity, and visual uniformity that previously were considered advantages are now threatening the economic value of real estate stuck in sprawl. This territory is going to have a hard time adapting to new market conditions. The negative economic, health, and environmental consequences of sprawl are well documented elsewhere, as are the ways in which we subsidize it. Similarly, the demographic and generational shifts that suggest sprawl is not likely to be a competitive structure for our future economy are duly noted.

In light of these arguments, it is important that no matter how nuanced our view of it, we need to stop building sprawl immediately. We need to change regulations like zoning and land subdivision that actually require sprawl to be built in most jurisdictions, and we need to end the policies that subsidize it in capital improvement budgets and policy at all levels of government. This will not be easy, but it will also not be enough. We must figure out what to do with the vast regions of sprawl that already exist before they become an unmanageable burden.

These challenges for sprawl exist across almost immeasurable territories in every city and small town and in every corner of this nation. More than that, and at least for the foreseeable future, much of our current population and economy depend on its successful maintenance. If they are to survive and thrive in the long term, we'll need to discover and invest in constructive strategies that can maintain a reasonable quality of life and economy in the face of what will almost certainly be the complete upending of regional real estate conventions.

As we do that, it's critical for those of us who care to concede that there's nothing wrong with sprawl. Really, I mean it. Across the vast geography of this celebrated democracy and within broad legal bounds, we get to choose how and where we want to live. Sprawl works just fine for millions of people. If I'm comfortable with a future where I drive an hour or more each way to work in traffic, losing time with my family and years of my life so that I can have a home so far removed from the store or park that I have to get back in my car to go there, that's my choice, and America offers me that sweet freedom. Other kinds of tradeoffs are made every day by people who live in downtowns, small towns, and rural areas.

The problem isn't sprawl. The problem is that we go so far out of our way to incentivize and even subsidize virtually every aspect of sprawl as our dominant growth strategy—an investment that is clearly not in our best interest. Our addiction to sprawl is degrading our health and environment and is straining our financial and natural resources. It is undermining the very set of social constructs that America was founded on. But while it's important to understand these challenges, the fact remains that we are stuck with many of their consequences. We made those decisions a long time ago. We're already vested in this way of life, and we can't pretend it doesn't exist. The future of this country is tied directly to the destiny of sprawl. We need to stop arguing about whether it is a good idea or not. We need to do something about it.

TOUGH LOVE

NEIGHBORHOOD PLANNING UNIT X (NPU-X) USED TO meet in the dingy community room of a chaotic mini police precinct on the commercial strip stretching south from downtown Atlanta. From the point where sidewalks and bungalow neighborhoods give way to early sprawl, Stewart Avenue in its prime opened to a gleaming new landscape of the modern city built for cars. Its showcase included dealerships filled with all the latest models, a bowling alley, motels, and even a drive-in theater. Later the home of strip clubs and seedy motels, the corridor today is mostly vacant and has been renamed Metropolitan Parkway. The police precinct where we met was one of only a handful of unlucky tenants in the otherwise broken-down shell of a formerly fabulous open-air mall that, like the rest of the corridor, had fallen victim to the economic, social, cultural, and demographic forces that devastated much of in-town Atlanta in the second half of the twentieth century.

I once dreamed of saving a 25-foot-tall Vegas-style neon sign across the road from the former mall that announced the entrance to Atlanta Trailer City, one of the last trailer parks in the city. It was a bold beacon and a lonely remnant of Stewart Avenue in its prime. It wasn't long, however, before a small crowd, bolstered by the enthusiasm of city leadership, toppled the sign at the groundbreaking of a low-density, suburban-style apartment complex surrounded by faux–wrought iron fences.

Historically, the NPU system has been a remarkably effective method of formalized community engagement. NPU-X is one of 25 NPUs across the city, each drawn around clusters of four to six neighborhoods. Its northern boundary is the Atlanta Beltline and the streetcar-era, gentrifying neighborhoods of Capitol View, Capitol View Manor, and Sylvan Hills, where my wife and I bought our first home. Following southward along the commercial strip of old Stewart Avenue, the NPU boundary stretches past two other neighborhoods before reaching the Hapeville city limits. Just beyond that is Atlanta's portal to the world, the behemoth Hartsfield-Jackson Atlanta International Airport, which has become the busiest air passenger terminal on Earth.

Not long after moving to this community in 2001, Karen and I started attending NPU-X meetings because we wanted to make a difference. I learned about this kind of community service while working for an architecture firm converting old industrial buildings into lofts and adapting their sites with new mixed-use development. One project was a 20-acre site in Inman Park that would start a public dialog about the Atlanta Beltline. Its rezoning process required us to meet with affected NPUs, and in doing so, I met a lot of people who were volunteering their time for their community. Many were architects, planners, and other professionals, so when Karen and I bought our house in Sylvan Hills, we took on similar roles in our neighborhood.

Along with community cleanups and other initiatives, Karen served for two years as NPU secretary, and I joined and later chaired the Land Use Committee, which builds consensus and makes recommendations on local issues related to zoning, code enforcement, and those sorts of things. For example, we recommended that the new owner of Atlanta Trailer City restore that old sign and that his buildings front the avenue with street-level retail instead of fences. Other committees at NPU-X tackled public safety, parks, and youth programs.

Alongside older, established community organizers, newcomers like us offer fresh energy to staff committees, volunteer for cleanups, support forward-thinking candidates, and eventually advocate for all the benefits promised by the Atlanta Beltline. We met dozens of people from all walks of life, and that old open-air mall provided us with an enormous and fertile site for big ideas about what our future might look like. The developers who began attending our meetings gave us confidence that such a vision was possible, and it's important to note that active redevelopments under way all over the city at that time had put everyone under a binding spell of optimism that cannot be overstated. This included both a physical and a cultural transformation, and the NPU system offered a structure for the integration of our vision with those of other communities.

In plan after neighborhood plan, that broken-down mall was marked as the catalyst site that would make everything else come together. Combined with two other large strip malls, it totals over 50 acres. Its skyline view and interstate access make a strong case for redevelopment, and the gentrifying neighborhoods to the north continue to attract residents with more buying power. Even so, the mall's prospects remain thin. The site is too big, and the building is too far gone structurally for incremental change. It will require a much higher return than the improving demographics can muster in order to justify the overhaul required to achieve the community's dreams. And so it waits.

In economically stronger parts of town like Virginia-Highland and Inman Park, it is curious and relevant that the first cycles of revitalization came primarily to the small sites and existing buildings within the older, walkable parts of the neighborhood. Change started with individual homes, workshops, and neighborhood retail—small buildings that adapt more easily over time. This organic and incremental change by many homeowners, entrepreneurs, and investors has built some of the strongest real estate markets in the state. It has also justified the subsequent redevelopment of larger properties like the one in Inman Park that started our conversation about the Atlanta Beltline.

So it is noteworthy that many sites along the car-oriented commercial strips in these now high-dollar communities still resemble Stewart Avenue. There are probably many reasons for this, but in any case, it should be no surprise that in communities where far weaker economic conditions prevail, properties like that giant old open-air mall remain all but abandoned.

When we see this financial reality for large, broken, car-oriented strips within a regional sea of competition, Stewart Avenue begins to foreshadow a similar fate for the next generation of sprawl that was built out beyond the perimeter highway. The mall on Stewart at least has the advantage of proximity to downtown, the airport's economy, and adjacent communities that are now likely to grow. In contrast, the vastness and ubiquity of outlying sprawl offers much less hope for a turnaround. Endless competition from dozens of similar corridors and too few market differentiators will hinder the chances of meaningful redevelopment. In this context, it's easy to imagine a new set of entrenched forces in many parts of the region that, like the forces stacked against urban communities in the late twentieth century, will increasingly be stacked against sprawl.

I'm not suggesting that all of sprawl is necessarily headed for decline. What I am saying is that we should take the challenges there seriously and be honest as we look for solutions. The end of sprawl-building practices would not only be good for cities. It would be the best thing that sprawl could do for itself. We should consider it an act of self-preservation.

We'll get back to that point later. For now, it is important to see existing communities of sprawl as integrated parts of an inclusive and sustainable vision for our future. We can start by acknowledging that despite the national narrative about the revitalization of urban centers, cities are also far from perfect and they are unable to accommodate our entire population anyway. Issues like raging traffic, crumbling infrastructure, failing schools, rampant displacement, spiraling inequity, and entrenched poverty still define tremendous challenges there. These are familiar topics in the public dialog, however. They are real, but they aren't the full story.

If we want to develop a fair and comprehensive approach to our future together, it is essential for us to bring the unique challenges facing sprawl into our discussion. If we want to thrive, this won't be an optional exercise, and the solutions will not be easy. After six decades of building cities for cars, however, we've actually learned a few things. Four observations bring to light critical topics that should be added to any future dialog. Consider them tough love from a constructive point of view. Communities defined by sprawl (1) are sparsely occupied by segregated groups of people, (2) are highly dependent on automobiles, (3) do not adapt easily to change, and (4) eventually choke on their own success.

SPRAWL SEGREGATES LOW DENSITY

Perimeter Mall is just over three miles from my childhood home in Chamblee. Like most of America, rather than driving almost 20 miles to the dying department stores in downtown Atlanta circa 1979, whenever we went shopping for clothes, housewares, electronics, or almost anything other than groceries, we went to the mall. My memory of it begins when it was surrounded by farms and forests. Literally, there were cows across the street. As I grew older, I watched one of America's original "edge cities" grow up around the mall. "Perimeter Center" replaced a nearly rural landscape of ranch houses with shiny glass office towers, national-brand stores, hotels, and parking lots.

The irony of such a name—a center that sits on its own perimeter—perfectly describes the fuzzy approximation of a city made of sprawl. Perimeter Center is a non-urban city named after the expressway that generated it and, like me, this new organism was shaped by the car as its primary mode of expansion. It transformed those farms and woodlands, and it changed the way that we lived, eventually growing into one of the region's leading commercial submarkets, but cast over a geography that is more than six times the size of downtown.

This kind of sparse habitation or low density is what introduced the term "sprawl" in the first place—a simple physical concept conveyed by the word itself. It is a city spread across the landscape, and in doing so, it contradicts the very idea of what a city is about. The word, however, didn't need to enter the lexicon of urban planners until our investments in automobiles and highways turned it into an economic powerhouse and spawned a hundred Perimeter Centers all over the country, dominating American growth policy for more than a generation.

Low density is the simple and often pleasant condition of not having a lot of stuff in a defined amount of space. While the concept fuels public commentary on sprawl, by itself it is not a problem. A host of other characteristics combine with low density to make it both powerful and destructive. Chief among these is the segregation of land uses through zoning, which originated from a dispute about the expansion of noxious things like slaughterhouses and lumberyards into residential areas. Ever since the 1926 Supreme Court decision in *Village of Euclid v. Ambler Realty Company,* however, which made this commonsense separation legally possible, our commitment to separation has been taken to an illogical extreme. It has become so fine grained, in fact, that now, simply as a matter of course, we essentially separate everything from everything else.

By the late 1980s, our refined compartmentalization of uses, combined with low density, had completely destroyed any expectation for the integration of land uses on which virtually every city and town in the country was founded. It had also co-opted America's small-town cultural identity even while it bore little resemblance to the actual places where that character was formed. And where relative concentrations were permitted, they came only in loose clusters like Perimeter Center—visually denser than other areas, but unfolded along highways with no regard for the human dimension of walking.

Take a small town in south Georgia, for example, which is also low density, but which might include a church or corner store on the same block as a house. Those relationships were a natural result of our desire and need to walk from one to the other. They defined the very notion of "community," exemplified by the term "neighborhood," which has both physical and social connotations. They also articulated an enduring American cultural identity—the flag-waving, porch-sitting, momma's-apple-pie-baking character of this great nation.

Yet given the same program—a house, a store, and a church—sprawl denies any possibility of the physical relationships that created that character. It segregates distinct zones for each use by common practice and also by law through a set of regulations that are loose in every way except for this rigid commitment to separation. The result is a very different model for the physical plan of a community, one that devalues walk-ing and one defined by a very different nomenclature. A new neighbor-hood built today more often takes on the legalistic term "subdivision," and rather than downtowns or districts, we have commercial "strips" like Stewart Avenue and "edge cities" with names like "Perimeter Center."

Laws regarding zoning, future land use, and the subdivision of land now enshrine the concepts of separation so thoroughly into our regula-tions that it is actually illegal in most places to follow traditional growth patterns that respect the human dimension of walking. Even though there are anomalies in more forward-thinking jurisdictions and in his-toric places that are already compact, the vast majority of America is al-ready built in such a way that it cannot be reasonably retrofitted. This is because sprawl not only separates distinct uses into zones; it then orga-nizes those zones within a hierarchical system of roadways that ensures even greater distance between them. It further articulates that separation with physical barriers like wide roadways, landscaped buffers, fences, and the deliberately disconnected ends of cul-de-sac'd neighborhoods. The result is an essentially permanent and segregated low density.

The condition of segregated low density matters for a lot of reasons. These include time and productivity lost to traffic jams, the environmen-tal impact of unprecedented land consumption, the inefficient distribu-tion of utilities and public resources like water, sewers, police, transit, and schools due to long distances, and the destruction of the natural beauty, wildness, and agricultural bounty of this country that inspired the origi-nal American dream. Perhaps more urgently, it has segregated us from each other, and this social and cultural isolation has dramatic impacts that go well beyond the physical plan of our cities.

SPRAWL IS DEPENDENT ON CARS

If you have ever tried to walk the Las Vegas Strip, you understand intui-tively the challenge of walking in an environment designed on the scale of the automobile. Its spectacle of lights was a mirage when I first made an attempt in 2003. It somehow diminished the Strip's overwhelming dimension and tricked me into thinking that walking was a reasonable idea. The Strip actually runs about 4.3 miles from the Stratosphere to Mandalay Bay, traversing approximately 19 blocks, or about an hour and 20 minutes for an average walking human, assuming you don't have to wait at crosswalks. That makes every block a whopping 1,195 feet long on average, with well over four minutes required to walk each one.

For comparison, the same 4.3 miles in Manhattan would take you roughly 85 blocks down Broadway from Columbus Circle to Ground Zero, with an average block length of 267 feet. That's just under a minute to walk each block. With every minute comes a choice to change direction—to follow the smell of fresh bread, to drop in on a friend working the late shift, or to avoid congestion near a theater letting out after a show. With a lot of choices comes a great walking environment, providing easy access to sites that are off the main route. Longer blocks like those along the Strip limit options, limit access to sites that are not directly on the Strip, and in any place other than Las Vegas, they also tend to be boring—another deterrent to pedestrians.

Places designed on the scale of cars are fundamentally different from those designed on the scale of people. They are not reasonably walkable. While Manhattan also accommodates millions of cars every day, it is first and foremost designed for people, utilizing a robust transportation network of buses, bikeways, subways, and taxis to extend the reach of pedestrians across a larger land area. That network generates an incredible range of economic activity along its sidewalks. From the small bodega to the corporate skyscraper, this active and fertile environment accommodates an amazing volume of activity while maintaining a robust economy and a very high quality of life.

Most urban districts are organized around a similarly walkable street grid because, like that town in south Georgia, they were built at a time that required them. A simple grid of streets provides multiple routes to any destination, and because most urban street grids were built before cars, most are designed on a scale suitable for walking. This is important because the dimensions of city blocks are critical factors in the creation of a vibrant walking district.

Humans are a certain size. Our legs allow a particular stride and speed. We are only willing to walk so far. Grids built for walking have blocks measured in hundreds of feet, while grids built around cars are measured on an almost regional scale. It's not that smaller blocks necessarily make you walk farther, as if you might walk the entire Las Vegas Strip if only it had smaller blocks. Rather, they compress life into a smaller footprint, meaning that there is no need to travel so far. Instead of spreading its three dozen or so casinos along 4.3 miles of the Strip, a more efficient arrangement would fit them into the dozen or so blocks surrounding Times Square.

Sprawl is essentially the everyday version of the Las Vegas Strip, exploded over a much larger area and less centrally located. Its physical environment is defined by the scale of highways, driveways, and parking lots, which is a direct expression of a car's dimension, its speed, and the time a reasonable person is willing to spend getting from place to place. This measure is no different than cities organized around walking, except that the distance permitted by automobile travel ensures that walking and biking are unrealistic for most people and for most trips. While a walking distance still works for cars, the opposite is never true. And while distance alone is less of a problem for transit, the spread-out, low-density, disconnected nature of sprawl makes transit so inefficient that it is often prohibitively expensive to operate at a reasonable service schedule and trip time. In most areas dominated by sprawl, transit cannot reasonably compete with automobiles, even in near-gridlock conditions. For all of these reasons, people in such areas are highly dependent on automobiles.

The consequences of car dependency start with those who are most dependent. Chamblee Plaza was no substitute for a walking commercial district, but its proximity to our neighborhood did offer kids a level of independence that is hard to come by in more contemporary sprawl. It allowed unchaperoned exploration of a consumer playing field that included a music store, pet shop, video arcade, and soda shop, not to mention bubble gum cigarettes at Woolworth's. My brother and I talked to strangers, frittered away our allowance, flirted with girls, got in fistfights, and generally horsed around. "The Plaza" provided a transitional place for learning about the world before we moved off to college a few years later. We gained an appropriate measure of independence, walking not only to the Plaza, but also to school and other places. Beyond that, if we were going to church or to the mall, somebody had to drive. In communities that are even more car dependent, driving-age adults must chauffeur children, elders, and other people who are unable to drive to virtually every place they need to go.

Unlike even early automobile communities like Huntley Hills, modern sprawl really has no alternative to driving. Our elementary school was the center of the neighborhood, but schools today are more often built far away and buffered from neighborhoods. Our fear of the traffic impact of a school outweighs our desire for our kids to be able to walk or bike there. The same is true for stores, hospitals, churches, and office buildings. Except for the dog walk or pool that is financed by homeowner association fees, even parks are typically not an integrated part of neighborhoods in sprawl. They are conceived instead as large recreational facilities or large passive landscapes and designed for arrival by car. For the vast majority of people, they are not within a reasonable walk for a quick playdate after school or an evening stroll before bed. So a significant consequence of car dependency is diminished mobility for those who are unable to drive. Without access to drivers, these groups find fewer options, leaving bored teenagers to their own devices and seniors to isolation and loneliness.

For drivers, of course, there are additional consequences to car dependency. Not only do they have to haul kids around, they waste a lot of time stuck in traffic. This lost time for family or lost productivity at work is not a huge revelation to anyone who commutes by car during a typical workday rush. But it is important to understand that this traffic congestion is a direct result of the way in which sprawl is organized, and after decades of doing it, we should have no expectation that more highways or wider roads are going to solve our problem—even with vehicle automation. The larger roads of sprawl create a grid of sorts on a metropolitan scale. But the system breaks down at the neighborhood level. The roadway network is highly disconnected locally, composed of cul-de-sac'd subdivisions, gated campuses, and dead-end parking aisles around shopping centers and office parks. There is no localized grid that would have developed naturally in a traditional town plan in order to provide options and disperse traffic.

Local roads in sprawl create traffic congestion by funneling everyone toward very large roadways. Widened roads may ease traffic for a while after construction, but by not also connecting local streets into a network, not adapting regulations to change development patterns, and not providing alternative transportation, the new capacity only attracts more of the same kind of development, which pushes even more traffic onto the same roadway. Not only have the new lanes not solved the problem, they have created an even less desirable condition for everyone.

For those who enjoy the time alone in their car and need more convincing of the downsides to car dependency, the evidence of negative health outcomes that result from an environment of sprawl is irrefutable. It includes a whole set of chronic diseases and a long list of new public health challenges. For example, high blood pressure is the most obvious side effect of commuting by car in heavy traffic every day—a unique kind of stress captured perfectly by an article I read in the *New Yorker* about the culture of the American commute. "The trip wears him down—with its toxic blend of predictability and unpredictability—tedium broken by episodes of aggravation and despair."[1] Studies show that people who consistently drive in heavy traffic have significantly higher blood pressure than people who don't drive or who don't drive in traffic.[2]

Beyond stress, the easiness of driving allows us to move across town while barely flexing a muscle. As a result, people who live in car-dependent communities have significantly lower rates of physical activity. So unless we're driving to the gym, we're at higher risk of being overweight, a condition that has reached epidemic proportions in the United States. In fact, "the risk of low physical fitness is comparable to, and in some studies greater than, the risk of hypertension, high cholesterol, diabetes, and even smoking."[3] People who are overweight are at greater risk of "high blood pressure, osteoarthritis, high cholesterol and other lipid abnormalities, asthma, ischemic heart disease such as angina and heart attacks and gall bladder disease."[4] As if that weren't enough, "obesity increases the risk of type 2 diabetes by as much as fortyfold."[5]

Of course the threats to public health from a culture of car dependency are not borne only by drivers. By prioritizing the convenience and safety of cars over people, sprawl creates an especially hostile environment for anyone not in a car. Air quality is a major concern. Particulate matter shortens life expectancy by two or three years, and in fact, more people die premature deaths due to exposure to particulate matter "than die from motor vehicle crashes and homicides combined."[6] Both adult and childhood asthma continue to rise steadily. Still, because the general public typically doesn't connect this to increased driving and car dependency, there is little sense of urgency to address the problem. And even if automobile technology solves our air-quality problems before we develop that urgency, the threat to non-drivers remains high for many other reasons. These include diminished social capital, strained mental health, and increased injuries and deaths from traffic due to the inadequate design of roadways and road networks.

An example is the tragic story of Raquel Nelson, a carless 30-year-old mother of three who jaywalked with her children across five lanes of traffic on a typical boulevard of sprawl outside Atlanta in the summer of 2011. This stretch of roadway is interchangeable with virtually any in America—it could just as easily be suburban Las Vegas or Chicago. Nelson had finally arrived at her bus stop after missing a bus transfer on the way home from grocery shopping. Her children were restless and tired. She was faced again with the decision to cross the street illegally or to walk over half a mile out of her way to the nearest signal and back. That day she did what any reasonable person would do—she jaywalked. So when her son ran ahead and was killed by a hit-and-run driver who had had a few beers mixed with painkillers, it was Nelson instead who was charged with vehicular homicide. David Goldberg asked in the *Washington Post*, "what about the highway designers, traffic engineers, transit planners and land-use regulators who placed a bus stop across from apartments but made no provision whatsoever for a safe crossing?"[7] They were not even on trial.

Beyond the obvious personal tragedy and the appropriate challenge to planners and engineers to make better roadways, there's an even more complex and profound cultural dimension to Nelson's story. Even if the non-bus-riding jurors[8] did not want to convict her, they were interpreting laws within a political, economic, and cultural context that has stacked the deck against Nelson and her kids. And even though the charge of vehicular homicide was eventually dropped, it is hard to imagine that we can ever solve the problem that put her in that position in the first place. We are unlikely to come up with enough money to substantively transform that corridor and the thousands of others just like it across the country into hospitable places to live without a car, where the physical environment expresses a legal structure and set of social values that place a higher value on Nelson's son's life than on a driver's convenience.

To be clear, the direct negative health and social impacts of increased driving and a culture of car dependency are borne by everyone, not just by those who live in sprawl. People who live in small cities, older suburbs, or urban neighborhoods may also be dependent on cars, especially where they no longer have effective transit service and where destinations like grocery stores, barber shops, and clothing stores that were once walkable may no longer be in business. As we are developing solutions, however, these places fall into a different category from sprawl because under different economic and policy conditions, they could with relative ease be refitted with those services again. It is the horizontal separation of sprawl that sets it apart from these places, making it unsuitable for reasonable retrofits and preventing it from adapting incrementally to change over time.

SPRAWL IS INFLEXIBLE TO CHANGE

In a letter to the president of the Board of the New York City Department of Public Parks in 1876, lauded American landscape architect Frederick Law Olmsted and engineer J. James Croes wrote, "Such distinctive advantage of position that Rome gives St. Peter's, Paris the Madeleine, London St. Paul's, New York, under her system, gives to nothing."[9]

It wasn't a compliment. Olmsted was recommending against the expansion of Manhattan's unfinished street grid into the 23rd and 24th wards. As a result of his and others' efforts, the otherwise uncompromising grid yielded to topography and other considerations as it marched north of Central Park. Thankfully, however, this moderation of the grid's original vision came late to the island, and today we still have what is otherwise the clearest representation of democracy made manifest in a street plan anywhere in the world.

By design, the Manhattan grid offers neither the subtlety of Savannah nor the monumentality of Washington. In fact, its relentless pattern of 13 uptown avenues and 220 crosstown streets offers almost no hierarchy at all. Anything can happen here, and no parcel is favored over its neighbor. This was one of Olmsted's criticisms: "If a building site is wanted, whether with a view to a church or a blast furnace, an opera house or a toy shop, there is, of intention, no better a place in one of these blocks than in another."[10]

This impartiality offers the private land within the grid a kind of democratic equality, meaning that no parcel is given a privileged position over another by the government structure of streets and public spaces. The grid is also neutral in regard to the use of the land. It simply provides ample access to the larger systems and districts of the city and allows private owners to adapt their property to meet changing market conditions. If someone wants to convert an apartment block into offices that have different needs for space, access, and utilities, or if they want to replace it entirely with a mobile home or with a skyscraper, the grid is agnostic to their actions, but it works for virtually any use.

In this way, the public realm does not protect the original use of the land. Instead, it protects the long-term economic viability of the land by embedding the flexibility for its use to change over time. Blocks that originally accommodated houses with gardens and later brownstones and corner stores are now occupied by great towers like the Empire State Building—unimaginable feats of occupation when the grid was conceived and drawn in 1811.

An urban grid works no matter if it is rigidly orthogonal like Manhattan, or if it is a less formal composition as in Boston. Private property, including both land and buildings, changes its use over time—a shoe store becomes a church and later a dentist's office and then a shoe store again. Whether through minor additions or total reconstructions, it adapts relatively easily within the grid because the grid works well for virtually any use—a house, a brownstone, a skyscraper. Regulations like zoning provide a mechanism for the orderly transformation of private land across an entire district over time, allowing for both very strict regulation, which might be appropriate in a historic district, and very loose regulation, which might better incentivize growth or innovation.

In a similar fashion, the public way—the grid of streets themselves that provide access to private land—also adapts and changes over time. The surface level originally used by horses was eventually paved to accommodate streetcars, buses, bikes, and cars. Its subterranean way remains an evolving mess of utilities, pipes, and subways. Its aerial way changes with overhead wires, lights, traffic signals, signs, and tree canopy. The public way also changes through the course of day and night and can be closed for special events. Some of the more interesting city transformations today reclaim traffic lanes for people where a generation ago that same space had been claimed by cars. Broadway, for example, is now closed to cars as it passes through Times Square and Herald Square in order to expand pedestrian space as well as slow and improve traffic flow.

So the use of both private land and the public way are always in flux. But what doesn't change as easily is the relationship between the two—the invisible lines drawn between what is owned by you or me individually and what is owned by us collectively. Not insignificant, the configuration of these simple lines is the very framework on which the city operates. They can make a city highly adaptable to change, or they can ensure that it is very resistant to change.

On one end of the spectrum is the relentlessly open grid of Manhattan that offers almost infinite possibilities. On the other end is the closed and protective cul-de-sac of sprawl, which severely curtails the usefulness of the public way and restricts the private parcel's access to the larger systems and districts of the city. More durable than zoning, the configuration of the invisible lines between what is public and what is private is actually much more important than what we each do with our individual plots of land. These lines are critical to an individual's or to a community's ability to respond to changing political, market, and regulatory environments.

In this way, sprawl stands in stark contrast to a democratic, adaptable urban grid. Its disconnected structure offers strict limitations on the utility of the public way and therefore limits the options for retaining economic value of private property over time. As long as people want what this structure has to offer, no other system in the world is better positioned to create that vision. Sprawl does a great job building that one very specific condition, but it does a poor job of supporting its value over time. It is unable to adapt in any meaningful way when conditions change beyond its control—whether through additional growth that strains shared infrastructure systems, or when its lifestyle or its geographic position is no longer considered desirable. Combined with segregated low density and car dependency, the structure of sprawl is stifling and unresponsive to innovation, experimentation, and small, incremental change.

In an increasingly competitive marketplace, this kind of inflexibility is a big disadvantage. Consumer demands and market conditions are constantly changing. Younger generations today are looking for something very different. Demographic shifts and new economic realities suggest that the traditional real estate conventions that have guided us for the last 60 years are in flux. Urban districts, made more agile and responsive by their adaptable physical structures, their compactness, and their suitability to car-free living, will meet these changes more quickly, more effectively, and more durably. In contrast, areas locked into an inflexible physical structure will have a difficult time adapting. Many will find themselves struggling in a context of economic decline and political disinvestment, which brings us to the final observation on the challenge of transforming sprawl.

SPRAWL EVENTUALLY CHOKES ON SUCCESS

Barring traffic, oceans, and mountain ranges, driving allows us to go as far as we want in virtually any direction, offering us amazing mobility. But that freedom is a double-edged sword, and it turns sprawl into its

own worst enemy. While our personal mobility is high, the value of any
particular parcel of land is diminished by the ease with which we bypass
it for the next one—past the next traffic light, after the next exit, beyond
the next county line. Once you're in your car, you might as well drive a
little bit farther to get exactly what you want—a better-priced gas station,
a slightly newer apartment, a jurisdiction with lower property taxes. New
growth keeps sprawling down the road because the inflexible nature of
sprawl means that the parcels that are already developed are more challenging to redevelop. Their buildings rarely have any intrinsic value for
re-use in place, and so it's almost always cheaper and easier to build something new on a site uncompromised by old standards—not enough parking, only one drive-through, outdated brand architecture. As consumer
preferences or business practices change over time, rather than adapting
or rebuilding existing sites and structures, the unconstrained ease of driving enables and promotes an unprecedented consumption of land, often
followed by a wake of depreciation and sometimes significant decline.

In this cycle of change, the private market is only doing what the private market always does. It builds things and provides services within the
constraints of both regulatory controls and the consumer marketplace.
A doll company, for example, makes and sells dolls that kids want their
parents to buy. They don't use lead paint because it is against the law, but
the safer paint adds to the cost of the doll. The same is true for buildings. Developers build offices that companies want to lease or houses that
families want to buy. They don't make them into firetraps because it is
against the law, but the fireproofing and egress routes add to the cost of
the building. So the construction of the world around us is framed both
by the consumer market and by regulations that are at least theoretically
in our best interest.

This is a great way to build cities, and it has worked especially well
in America since its inception. But sprawl offers an essentially unfettered
regulatory environment. It requires things to be separated from each
other, but otherwise it allows the consumer market to call all the shots.
There is no balance. And unlike regulations, which are intentionally written by humans to shape the world under an oath to the public interest, the

consumer market has no ethic—no standards or guidelines—no intent. There is no one *in charge* of the market. It is indiscriminate.

So unlike the private market construction of nearly every single historic town and urban neighborhood in America, private investments in sprawl contribute very little to the larger public good simply because neither the regulatory controls nor the consumer market requires it to do so. It does not form an expanded street network or an improved public realm over time. In fact, other than conforming to sprawl-minded zoning and perhaps a minor transportation improvement or two like a deceleration lane or a traffic light, sprawl requires essentially nothing of private-sector development. Therefore, sprawl contributes essentially nothing to the public realm. It takes and never gives. In sprawl, if we are talking about a strip mall, an apartment complex, an office park, or a housing subdivision, none of them will contribute substantially to an interconnected network of streets that provides public access, infrastructure, and mobility to support a larger or growing city structure. Yet all of these developments rely completely on access to publicly funded arterial roadways and utilities, channeling their burden of cars, schoolchildren, and sewerage onto an infrastructure built almost exclusively by the public sector.

That wasn't always so. In older parts of town, the development of land over time by many developers would have resulted in an interconnected, resilient, adaptable, and walkable grid. Along with its streets and sidewalks, it also offered a network for citywide water, sewer, and utility lines, as well as through-routes for school buses, transit, and emergency vehicles. Private market developers created new infrastructure that benefited their project but also contributed to the larger public good by creating a flexible system that can adapt for future generations. Sometimes we built according to an official city plan, but in later streetcar suburbs, like Atlanta's Virginia-Highland, developers assembled walkable grids because that is what the market demanded. Residents wanted access to streetcar stops, and landowners near those stops captured value there with modest commercial clusters.

In sprawl, by sharp contrast, the kneejerk reaction has been to solve the problem by "fixing" the public realm—by adding more lanes to the roadway. Of course this asks even more of the public sector, which must now fix the problems that the unregulated private market has created. And since the solution of more lanes, unbound from stringent land-use regulations, only promotes more sprawl, the problem can only get worse. The public sector is always in a defensive position, always playing catch-up, and always paying more. Citizens wonder why the costs of maintaining free-flow on all these roads is growing so much and blame government ineptitude rather than the freeloading consumer market.

It is not only the public sector that loses, however. Private land and property are often devalued by traffic congestion or by new competition down the road. The only consistent winners are those who play the game: (1) Make a quick investment in cheap land and inexpensive buildings; (2) Sell before their life cycle is over; (3) Move down the road and repeat.

The kind of blight that can be found in the wake of this cycle is most often associated with the devastated town centers and urban neighborhoods that were left behind late in the last century. But sprawl also indiscriminately cannibalizes older sprawl, decimating the economies that once supported early commercial strips and their companion postwar neighborhoods. As it turns out, compared to urban neighborhoods, early sprawl has only a thin safety net of midcentury nostalgia, and more contemporary sprawl has even less protection than that. In response to new sprawl, old sprawl has a much harder time adapting.

BACK IN SOUTHWEST ATLANTA, where I lived for twelve years as the Atlanta Beltline sprang to life, Stewart Avenue proves this point exactly. It was once a vibrant corridor of classic midcentury sprawl, a shiny beacon of modernity in the 1950s and 60s. It seduced shoppers and families away from the trolley-congested, soot-covered central business district and the aging neighborhoods that surrounded it. But when construction of a parallel interstate highway colluded with white flight to steal away its middle class and saddle Stewart Avenue with a burden of strip joints and now-seedy motels, the surrounding neighborhoods fell into a generation of decline.

In light of that, my nostalgic view of the Atlanta Trailer City sign and other embellishments of that era always framed Stewart Avenue as a static symbol of urban decay. On my last visit to Chamblee Plaza, however, I realized it was one of many victims in the dynamic and endlessly destructive wake of sprawl. I was astonished to discover that the commercial strip of my youth had been mostly drained of life. All four of the anchor tenant spaces and much of the rest of it was empty. I saw a small group of cars parked in front of Last Chance Thrift Store—a far cry from it's heyday with Big Star, Winn-Dixie, Hancock Fabrics, and Woolworth's anchoring a dozen or more smaller shops. I guess the kids in the neighborhood today may never know the wonders of the Plaza in its prime. Already well beyond its third cosmetic overhaul since the old days, Chamblee Plaza is a tired shell of its former self.

Meanwhile, the city of Chamblee is growing. It is well positioned regionally, has good schools, and decent infrastructure. It even has a rail transit station, which is attracting a lot of new development. So there could be any number of reasons why the Plaza looks eerily analogous to the old mall down on Stewart Avenue. It has been a tough economy and there is a lot of competition. But as long as the strip mall can find some new tenants— perhaps an auto dealership, a megachurch, and a trendy new bowling alley—Chamblee Plaza will hold its own. After all, the inability to adapt only matters when adaptation is required. Otherwise, it's going to sit in limbo, peddling its "Last Chance" efforts until the market value of its land can justify the wholesale redevelopment of its nearly 20 acres into something more suitable to today's market demands. With so much competition from so many competing, underutilized sites, that could take a while.

Now take Chamblee Plaza—aesthetically tired, materially beyond its life cycle, economically obsolete, and hammered by competition—and multiply it across 20 counties, or across the nation. The ubiquity and accessibility of similar corridors generates so much competition that each has a hard time maintaining long-term economic sustainability. Every site undercuts the value of the others. By preventing walkable concentrations that would more likely hold their value because they are more resilient and adaptable to changing market conditions, and by continuously offering new competing sites of equal value just a little bit farther down the road, sprawl creates a vicious cycle of suburban cannibalization.

Chamblee Plaza, Chamblee, Georgia. (Ryan Gravel, 2012)

Along with segregated low density, car dependency, and inflexibility, our understanding of this tendency is essential. And if we combine these challenges with the more familiar ones facing downtowns and urban neighborhoods, it seems like we should be sufficiently prepared to crack open some ideas about our shared future. The following chapters will do this, but it is important to note that ideas will not be enough. We will also have to act. And the communities that are honest and strategic about their challenges ahead won't accept the difficulty of action as an excuse for inaction. They'll act on a growing ambition to experiment with answers and develop new prototypes for what a better future might look like.

AN IDEA WITH AMBITION

IN RETROSPECT, THE STORY OF THE ATLANTA BELTLINE is bound so closely to the blistered nerves of the city's soul that sometimes I wonder myself where it must have come from. It is simultaneously obvious and invisible. It is both emphatically simple and unbearably complex. It is a thing and also a place; a project and also a movement. It has emerged from our history in such an authentic way that it somehow doesn't seem possible that it could also be so relevant to our future. Yet, like the most refreshing summer wind, it has humbly embraced the scars of our past, and then, with a slight and effortless drawl, revealed an unexpected and honestly inclusive new voice for our city that is compelling and vibrant and bold.

The vision it describes has surfaced as the receding roar of the twentieth century fades into a soft night, and its fresh energy brightly and impatiently nudges us forward. It takes what were once conduits for industry, barriers, boundaries, and later, symbols of what the future left behind, and it redefines them with a new ambition for our lives. While unexpected, this new role for the belt line railroads has not come suddenly. There have always been people who eyed them as uncertain pathways to a better future, and their ideas—all pragmatic—have been percolating for half a century.

Where the story of the Atlanta Beltline begins, therefore, remains open to your interpretation. It depends on what you want to see because, as a magnet for ideas, it is littered with old plans, rolls of drawings, and amateur maps stuck in the dusty attics of other times. In the 1950s it was an idea to protect the viability of industrial land; in the 1960s it was for public transportation; in the 1970s it was to remedy blight; in the 1980s it was to generate new business; and in the 1990s it was to spur cultural connectivity and economic development. It also has political roots that reach beyond each idea by several decades. Most accounts, however, mark its origin more recently, with my graduate thesis in 1999, and I tend to start there too. That was the moment when those individual, partial, and pragmatic ideas were put in service to something bigger. They became more than an idea. They became a vision for what we wanted our future to become.

Anybody can love the undeniable beauty and utility of the Atlanta Beltline without believing in every aspect of that vision. There is an inherent understanding, however, that a larger ambition is part of the deal. The thesis that first framed it this way is a set of ideas just like the others, but it also very deliberately describes that larger purpose. It proposes more than simple utility. It says that if we build this thing, we will create the kind of Atlanta where many of us want to live, and this intention to change the way we see our future is what sets it apart from other ideas.

Another essential physical and conceptual aspect of the proposal is its manifestation in a full geographic circle that very deliberately links places with names like "Cabbagetown" and "Blandtown" together. These forty-plus neighborhoods each have their own history, culture, and politics, and the Atlanta Beltline connects them across the tracks and down the line, making historic barriers into a new public meeting ground. It creates a physical space for people, but it is no ordinary place. It is a 22-mile linear place that links back up to itself.

This loop formation is as important metaphorically as it is pragmatic. It is an inherent part of the project's egalitarian appeal and its ability to bring people together around ideas. It also taps into our innate desire to repair the wrongs of our past and become a more equitable and unified city. As we will see, its circular form has also become a powerful framework for the expansion of the thesis proposal.

Before we get to that, it is worthwhile to describe the context and creation of the original thesis itself. Following that year abroad in Paris and my graduate school obsession with the cultural role of infrastructure, I began looking for a thesis project that could satisfy the requirements for both a Master of Architecture and a Master of City Planning. I found advisors from each program to work with me and a lead advisor, Randy Roark, who could bridge the gap between the two disciplines.

Atlanta was my laboratory, and I knew that I wanted to tackle the region's sprawling car dependency with new transit. My first idea was a plan for the downtown railroad gulch that would incorporate the city's main transit hub with a new terminal for regional and high-speed rail. My second idea was to take the loop of old railroads that I had discovered in my wanderings around the city and put them to better use. I knew the neighborhoods along their routes and I liked the idea of linking them together both physically and conceptually in ways that they had not been connected before.

I found more inspiration searching through the graphic archives of the main library on campus. I discovered a provocative rendering by Swiss architect Walter Hunziker showing the historic Sears and Roebuck building on Ponce de Leon Avenue with a spectacularly modern transit line running along Southern Railway's belt line in the foreground. With classic midcentury optimism, a station and glassy office building stand across the street on the site of "Poncey," the old Crackers baseball stadium, which would not yet have been demolished when the drawing was done in 1961. I was captivated.

With the encouragement of my advisor, I went with the second idea, and I developed my thesis paper over the course of the fall semester. It proposed a new public use for the belt line railroads that would spur private market development of the industrial belt and revitalization of the old streetcar neighborhoods surrounding downtown. This would improve the city's tax base by putting underutilized land to better use and also create diverse and vibrant communities where even more people would want to live.

The specific physical proposal for the Atlanta "Belt Line" thesis was straightforward. The four lines would be strung together for the first time as a 22-mile loop of light rail transit that would also link to the existing MARTA (Metropolitan Atlanta Rapid Transit Authority) rail system at each of its crossing lines. Stations and service would be frequent enough to achieve the proposal's redevelopment goals and make sure people could walk to the stops from both the historic neighborhoods and the new higher-density districts. Appropriate land use, zoning, and urban design strategies would ensure that the project's implementation over time would respect land values and ridership needs, as well as community assets and context. The thesis included precedents from Paris and Chicago, and I even made a pilgrimage to the city-planner mecca of Portland, Oregon, as part of my research to see firsthand the seemingly exotic, but successful and proper, correlation between modern transportation investments and land use.

It was a sensible and interesting, almost obvious, proposal, and more importantly, it satisfied my degree requirements. I found additional support from two other advisors, Richard Dagenhart and Arthur C. Nelson, but of course none of us ever thought the project would actually get built. The idea, however, had resonated with Roark, at least partly because he had a history with two of those earlier proposals which provide some context for what would come next.

Roark's role in this story started in the 1970s, an exciting time of progress and fresh energy in downtown Atlanta. This included new landmark buildings like the 73-story Peachtree Plaza Hotel and the construction of MARTA, a visionary new symbol of our modern metropolis. A sister to Metro in Washington, DC, and BART in San Francisco, MARTA's construction helped put Atlanta among a national league of cities that were investing in modern transit systems. Sprawl, depopulation, and urban blight notwithstanding, a city of the future was being constructed downtown, and, importantly, this included the groundwork for a political structure to match its modern vision.

At that time, several neighborhoods east of downtown were fighting for their future against two proposed urban freeways. One would slice north-south from Morningside to Reynoldstown. The other would cut east-west from Druid Hills and the Old Fourth Ward into the heart of the city. The two routes would intersect at a point on Southern's still-active belt line, and the railroad's industrial fringe comingled with much of the contested land. After a decades-long battle, the result was a partial win for neighborhoods. The freeways were stopped by a powerful grass-roots movement, but huge swaths of the city had already been cleared. This epic and bittersweet drama demonstrated the community's potential for political action and helped launch a progressive new era of leadership from Maynard Jackson, Atlanta's first African American mayor.

We'll discuss that more later, but suffice it to say that Jackson's election electrified City Hall. City planners called on Georgia Tech to help repair the highway scars, where former yards and streets had lost their homes and pavement. They tapped Randy Roark, a professor and local architect, who, along with others, developed a plan they called the "Great Park." It proposed to stitch the edges of the scar back together with modified streets and new houses in a way that would front a wide, rolling linear greenspace. The team carried the idea door-to-door and to neighborhood leaders, building sufficient momentum that an organization was formed to oversee it and communities were activated in support. Their efforts, however, were undermined by the state's control of the land, and their idealized plan morphed with compromise. Along the way, secondary notions for what to do with Southern's belt and its associated land also fell away.[1]

As the controversy continued, the world roared toward the end of the twentieth century, and Atlanta was destined to go out with a bang. The 1990s not only provided the time frame for my post-secondary education at Georgia Tech, they allowed Roark's ideas and those of others regarding the belt line railroads to simmer in an environment of constant change. In fact, every idea for the city's future became swept up in an enormous distraction that claimed all of the region's attention for the better part of the decade. A truly unprecedented time for Atlanta opened up, amplifying her ambition and further loosening restraints on what kind of future seemed possible.

ALONG WITH THE REST of the region, on September 24, 1990, virtually the entire senior class of Chamblee High skipped school to participate in a ticker-tape parade through the heart of downtown Atlanta. We were celebrating the announcement just six days earlier that our city would host the 1996 Summer Olympics—the centennial of the modern games. Instantly, a new era of optimism unfolded across the region and the state, mounting through the next several years as I graduated and moved downtown to study architecture at Georgia Tech. It seemed that every week a new urban scheme or proposed landmark structure was on the cover of the local paper. Almost any suggestion seemed possible—new stadiums, streetscapes, parks, and hotels—anything as long as it fulfilled the city's self-conscious desire to be worthy of Olympic stardom. While ideas like a new train station and an aquarium didn't pan out in time for the games, many others did, including Centennial Olympic Park, which at the time was said to be the largest new urban park in the country.

Around the same time that the early whirlwind of Olympic preparedness began, the nonprofit PATH Foundation came together in 1991 in response to the lack of good regional trails. Led by Ed McBrayer, the group began working with the Bureau of Planning at City Hall to identify the best opportunities. PATH's work built on a draft report from the previous year by the Rails-to-Trails Conservancy and in 1992, it culminated in the "Atlanta Greenway Trail Corridor Plan," which outlined a network of greenways throughout the city. One of their proposals ran the length of Freedom Park, the at-grade parkway that had evolved as a bitter compromise between the two failed highways and the more life-affirming concept of the Great Park.

PATH's plan was expanded by the city the next year into the "Atlanta Parks, Open Space and Greenways Plan." Noting that "the City has no greenway trail system,"[2] it incorporated 17 proposed trails from PATH's plan, including four along portions of the belt line railroads. The plan anticipated both quick abandonment of the three sections of railroad that were still operating and a flood of Olympic-related development to pay for the trails. Additionally, the plan identified a "Cultural Ring" as a special event site built out of the two northern belt line railroads. "Imagine a cultural ring around downtown and midtown, which is a circular greenway park with a pedestrian/bicycle trail and which coincides with more than 20 cultural facilities and historic districts and sites. Regional and national arts events are held annually in and around the cultural ring, which contains numerous historic sites and structures for staging art shows, craft shows, sculpture displays, theater, dance, concerts, lectures, conferences and other special events."[3]

The circle route as illustrated would follow Seaboard's belt counterclockwise, turning south through downtown at Underground Atlanta before returning north along Southern's belt. It included some notion for a train that had seven stops for tourists at locations like the Jimmy Carter Presidential Library and Piedmont Park. It also allowed Amtrak to run along Southern's belt, a logistical requirement of the proposed downtown station. With even less description, a second phase would incorporate greenways proposed for portions of the two southern belt lines.[4]

Conceptually, this idea for a Cultural Ring is an expanded version of the Great Park. It is organized primarily around greenspace, trails, and cultural destinations. Simultaneously, however, and apparently with only a little cross-pollination, a distinctly separate effort by the same name also emerged. This one had a different objective, but it came with a familiar face.

During the years leading up to the Olympics, while I was figuring out who I was on some lonely street in Paris, Randy Roark was leading an older cadre of students to support CODA, the Corporation for Olympic Development in Atlanta. Along with its goal of deploying new streetscapes, artwork, plazas, and revitalization efforts before the games, CODA had come up with a very different idea for the Cultural Ring. Following the belt line railroads and a couple of other corridors, it focused primarily on the economic potential for cultural sites and events that could "facilitate and speed up private market conversion of obsolescent railroad and industrial properties."[5] Their plan proposed "a collaborative economic development effort among various public and private entities with common interests in promoting the growth and importance of Culture as a key component of Atlanta's history, economic viability and social stability."[6] In the process, CODA proposed that the Cultural Ring would contribute significantly to the revitalization of in-town neighborhoods by creating an enduring arts-related economy. Retrofitted industrial buildings, like the century-old cotton warehouse on Southern Railway's belt line that would soon be converted into StudioPlex, would provide "Atlanta's arts community with needed affordable space for offices, rehearsal, performances, storage, exhibitions, residences, and live/work uses."[7]

While re-use of the still-active railroads for some sort of transportation was mentioned as a "long term consideration,"[8] the group supporting CODA determined that it was not feasible at the time because the route did not directly access many of its target Olympic destinations. They focused instead on a "more realistic . . . rubber tired vehicle on existing roads. This has the benefit of being able to penetrate the city core where much of the ridership will originate," like the hotels and event venues downtown.[9] Georgia Power partnered with CODA to propose two electric bus loops along city streets, but with the uncertain battery technology at that time, the project was scrapped.

The greenway-oriented Cultural Ring mentions economic development incidentally, but not as a priority goal. The economic-development-oriented Cultural Ring makes barely a mention of parks or greenways. Ultimately, by the summer of 1996, neither version was able to make sufficient progress to be implemented in any form in time for the Olympics. And at the end of the closing ceremonies, Atlanta let out an almost audible sigh of exhaustion—relieved that the games were over and that they had been a relative success. Everybody took a nice long nap, setting aside the Cultural Ring for another day, alongside a few dozen other unrealized ideas. The greenways were incorporated into the city's official plans, but CODA was dissolved almost immediately. Without momentum, funding, or a political champion, the concepts were essentially shelved. In the words of Scarlett O'Hara, "I can't think about that right now. If I do, I'll go crazy. I'll think about that tomorrow."[10]

Tomorrow came soon enough. Just as Georgia's coastal plain had given Oglethorpe a raw setting for the design of a physical place to match a new social paradigm, by the end of the twentieth century, the belt line railroads provided the opportunity for a new way of life for Atlanta's residents. The world was changing, and Atlantans were hungry and ready for a compelling new vision for their future.

WITH THIS KIND OF HINDSIGHT, it's easier to see how the thesis for the Atlanta Beltline tapped into the soul of the city. It connected directly and intuitively to a deeper history that I was largely unaware of and that we'll explore further in the next chapters. In 1999, however, I was just a naïve graduate student, intoxicated by my experience in Paris. I found myself in the rich laboratory of post-Olympic Atlanta where anything seemed possible, and while I wasn't familiar with most of the previous belt line proposals, I had a good advisor and a basic understanding of the city's history. I also knew enough about the potential pitfalls of urban development and infrastructure to be careful about what I proposed. The city had an interesting story and lots of potential, but somehow that wasn't enough. It needed a new paradigm. I wrote a thesis declaring that the kind of infrastructure we build matters to our lives, and I went further to propose that if we built this particular set of ideas—transit, community revitalization, and redevelopment around a 22-mile loop—it would strategically reposition the city to compete in the new century.

I honestly believed in the proposal, but my primary motivation was to graduate. The months that passed as I developed the thesis were gratifying but academically uneventful. I dated my future wife. I skipped my graduation ceremony. And I carried my 109-page dark green hardbound thesis up "the hill" to the library where it belonged. That was the easy part, and perhaps the least exciting episode of this story. My more turbulent journey since has obviously been worth the effort. It has also been fun—animated with intriguing details and amusing anecdotes, like the story of an unusual loop route into Atlanta for the Ringling Bros. and Barnum & Bailey Circus train in 1947, the first (and only) annual "kudzu caper" in 1973, and a ride I took to lunch in a Lamborghini in 2004 with a guy who looked exactly like Al Pacino in *Scent of a Woman*.

Perhaps the most relevant story to share is an anonymous fax I received in 2010. It's a copy of a typewritten letter dated December 15, 1980, from an engineer named James Grant to Frank Jones, chairman of the Great Park Authority. He writes that in 1974, he walked the Southern Railway's belt line with W. W. Westerman, superintendent of the railroad's Atlanta operations. "At that time Mr. Westerman told me that Southern Railway would be open to the possibility of closing that rail line, if appropriate compensation were forthcoming." Grant goes on to suggest that the section of that belt from the Great Park north to Piedmont Park "could be redeveloped as an urban bikepath, or small scale bus/light-rail trolley line to connect these two major urban parks."[11] He says it might extend all the way to the then-proposed Lindbergh MARTA station—a prophetic idea. Even though Hunziker's drawing had illustrated the region's original plan to put transit on Southern's belt in the 1960s, Grant's letter is the earliest proposal I'm aware of that includes both transit and trail along any of the belt line corridors.

A couple of years later, an employee at CSX proposed a new short-line railroad that would operate along a version of the loop to develop new industries and grow the city's tax base. Later, an excursion train took dinner guests on a somewhat different circle through the city. Alongside Hunziker's drawing, the Great Park, and the Cultural Ring, these and other early proposals describe the belt line corridor as a compelling magnet for ideas about the future.

Timing was part of what made the thesis different, of course, because the city was starting to grow. What really set it apart, however, was its ambition to change our lives. The particular ideas of its proposal were put in service to a vision that would accomplish more than basic infrastructure, and as we will see in the next chapter, that's how it was proposed to the public at large. It would change our lives, we said, and also the way we think about our lives. The thesis went so far as to suggest that "Atlanta can seize this chance to redefine itself with a new understanding of city form and redefine urban life in the 21st century South."[12]

The fact that the Atlanta Beltline came from an academic paper with no notion that it could actually be built permitted such bold statements to be made, and this notion should not be underestimated. In contrast to the Cultural Ring, the thesis proposal had the advantage of being unfettered by reality. For example, it ignored many facts of the day—that some of the railroads were still operating; that the city didn't own any of the land; that regional funding for bicycle and pedestrian infrastructure was pitiful in those years, and for transit essentially nonexistent; that the state at that time had a stranglehold on MARTA's ability to improve or expand service; and that local politics were notoriously rife with naysayers, infighting, and lingering racial tensions. It didn't concern itself much with other priorities that were competing for both funding and political attention, and it looked beyond the constant and seemingly more-immediate need to address issues like crumbling sewers and failing schools.

Politically, the weight of those other demands never translated into a force powerful enough to shake the Atlanta Beltline from the public's imagination. The bell had been rung, and nobody could un-ring it. As our small group of believers took our vision to the public starting in the summer of 2001, the project's innocent origin allowed people to suspend their disbelief and focus first on whether it was a good idea before getting lost in the challenges of details.

Broad public opinion coalesced around an aspirational view of our future. The proposal developed a powerful following of residents and organizations that began to require that any nuts-and-bolts debates about details like competing priorities and funding be put in service to the project's realization, not the other way around. In this way, the idea was not only remarkably refreshing conceptually, it was able to break through any disbelief that such a big vision was possible. It was attainable, so we could believe in it. And if it was doable, then we should do it.

The project's innocuous origin as a graduate student thesis played another role in these politics of possibility. It was an ambitious vision, but somehow it wasn't threatening. It gave community activists something to fight *for*, not against. It represented neither a public-sector transportation agenda nor a private-sector plan for real estate development, even though it satisfied both outcomes. At the same time, it was not an edict coming down from City Hall, which would have carried political baggage. While we did get essential early leadership, it would be a few years before the weight of the political establishment got fully on board and started to make the Atlanta Beltline a priority. The proposal's ability to generate these unusual alliances was at least partly due to its academic origin. It could be trusted and evaluated on its merits without causing speculation about ulterior motives.

Described in this way, our success so far makes a powerful case for academic environments everywhere to be nurseries for ideas about the future. Unrestrained by budgets, politics, physics, or technology, students are empowered to be inventive and to develop big ideas that solve real problems. They are free to make proposals without knowing all the answers; actually, not knowing is a key to their strength because they are able to imagine things that many of us rarely see anymore. Outside of academia, it is easy enough to find excuses for not being ambitious—not enough money, lack of creativity, political or corporate bureaucracy, voter apathy, or the general inertia of the status quo. Inside academia, however, with all of the problems facing our world today, there's little excuse for not taking advantage of such valuable time to explore. In fact, there may be no better place to take risks, develop ideas, or articulate a larger ambition for our lives or for the world. Who knows, a curious and unassuming thesis might happen to go further than anybody ever thought possible.

A WIDE-OPEN PLACE

REID BETZ WAS WORKING AT HIS DESK NEXT TO MINE IN the studio one night during graduate school when we decided to name the stations on the Atlanta Beltline. It was just for fun, of course. There was absolutely no chance that these stations would ever become real. What was real for me at that time was a need to inject some smart references into my thesis project, creating an entirely new set of place-names for a largely abandoned and nameless territory that was previously not a place, but a space in between.

Reid had gone to Grady High School, which stands near a station we named "Kanuga" after the least well-known of several very well-known intersecting streets that include Tenth, Monroe, and Virginia. He had a similar sense of geeky humor about it all, and we distracted ourselves for a few hours late one night with names like "Exterior Line" and "Piggyback." We imagined the train's intercom announcing, "The approaching station is *Jail. Jail* is your next station. Exit here for the Fulton County *Jail.*"

On other nights over the course of that fall semester, Reid and I speculated about how the idea might come to life. We thought that maybe if we just talked about it enough, people would think it was real. Eventually it would show up on the city's capital-improvement list and then somehow it would spontaneously materialize. It's a stretch, of course, to say that's what happened. But the engine that carried the Atlanta Beltline along its journey toward reality, and that still keeps it running today, is in fact a long, organic, expanding conversation about how it might improve our lives. The project wasn't the result of some grand scheme. It wasn't a comprehensive plan that proposed to solve all of our problems. It was just an idea. Anyway, there was no reason at all to believe that it could really happen.

The conversation that would evolve into a city-changing movement started this innocently. We finished graduate school in December 1999, and I left the idea for an Atlanta Beltline behind on a shelf full of other hardbound ideas in the main campus library at Georgia Tech.

After the holidays, I took a job with an architecture firm drawing apartments and mixed-use master plans for Atlanta's growing in-town population. By that time, the central core of Atlanta was experiencing a rapid influx of new residents in search of a more urban lifestyle. The demand generated a flood of construction that, following national trends, was beginning to create new, compact, mixed-use, walkable, transit-oriented communities.

Tower cranes loomed over midtown and Buckhead. The pace of change and speculation across the city was palpable. In the industrial belt and similar districts, developers easily snatched up large tracts of land in some of the city's most newly desirable neighborhoods and sailed through rezoning to support medium-density residential and mixed-use redevelopment. Under particular pressure were the east-side communities that stretch along the Southern Railway's old belt line from DeKalb Avenue north past Piedmont Park. Early adaptive-use projects like the Ford Factory Lofts (1987), the Telephone Factory Lofts (1996), and StudioPlex (1999) had already proven the market demand. The firm that I worked for, along with half a dozen other firms, was feverishly working on similar transformations, and it was impossible not to see an entirely new future taking shape in the central city.

As early as the late 1990s, City Hall was increasingly under pressure to respond to concerns brought about by all this new growth. The construction of new apartment buildings like Highland Walk, which rose five and six stories across the street from single-family houses, was taking residents by surprise. The Inman Park neighborhood, eager to both protect its prized residential enclave and shape growth coming to its industrial fringe, embarked on a historic district zoning overlay that would include its belt line frontage. The idea was to protect the neighborhood from oversized development and to leverage private-market growth to build public improvements like connectivity, greenspace, and sidewalks that would be needed to support the growing population. Eventually, this led to a new set of Quality-of-Life zoning districts that would create a new baseline standard for growth in the city.

In a more targeted response to the redevelopment of industrial land along Southern's belt line, the City of Atlanta's Bureau of Planning, along with the District 2 city councilmember at the time, Debi Starnes, completed the "District 2 Rail Corridor Inventory and Assessment" in early 2001. It confirmed the community's concern that "the piecemeal manner in which industrial land is converting to residential and commercial uses has a potential negative impact on the long-term quality of the urban environment both in the Assessment Area and the surrounding neighborhoods."[1] Aaron Fortner, a friend of mine from planning school who was familiar with my thesis and had gone to work for the Bureau of Planning, helped write the District 2 plan. His boss had attended my final thesis review and I had interviewed other people on staff while doing my thesis research. We certainly discussed the "Atlanta Parks, Open Space and Greenways Plan" from 1993 that was otherwise gathering dust, and I kept in touch with Fortner and other staff members after graduation.

Back at the office, the new developments breaking ground all over town were generating increasingly intense discussions. I often debated the latest changes to our city over lunch with my colleagues, including Sarah Edgens and Mark Arnold. It seemed like almost anything was possible—every week there was news of some bold new project or some tragic demolition. By 2001, we had embarked on a master plan for the 20-acre Mead Paper Company distribution facility on Lake Avenue in

Inman Park, and we had met with Councilmember Starnes. The Mead property, which would later become Inman Park Village, was on the chopping block for over 600 housing units and would significantly increase the population of the neighborhood. We were trying to decide whether to shove the parking garage up against the old abandoned railroad or orient the project toward the corridor as the draft historic regulations suggested. Over lunch one day, I told Edgens and Arnold about this idea that I had had in school. I guess because it connected the neighborhoods they lived in (Midtown and Virginia-Highland, respectively), with a lot of new development and destinations like Piedmont Park, they were excited by the concept. They were as frustrated as I was with Atlanta's underwhelming transit network and its inadequate public realm, and they were as naïve as I was in thinking that we might actually make a difference.

There was some fortuitous comingling of ideas at this time. We incorporated the multiuse trail into our thinking about the corridor, and the District 2 rail study included a concept for transit. It was mentioned almost as a side note with only a map and a few sentences, and it was muddied by the political and logistical realities of the long-hoped-for reuse of Southern's belt line for Amtrak and commuter train service. But it was still the first suggestion in any official city-sponsored document that transit and trail within the rail corridor might be used jointly to address the pressures of development.[2]

The three of us started talking to anyone who would listen. When we pitched the idea, people responded enthusiastically, and their energy motivated us to keep talking. Then, on July 30, 2001, we mailed a letter describing the concept:

Dear [regional leader]:

Everyone agrees that Atlanta has a traffic problem. While many transit proposals have been submitted to move people in and out of the city, a necessary component that has not been adequately addressed is how to effectively move people around within the city.

We submit for your consideration a synopsis of a proposal for a light rail system weaving through the city on exiting railroad rights-of-way and connecting to five MARTA stations. This proposal is certainly not the only answer to Atlanta's traffic problems, but it does lay out a strategy for public policy and accomplishes the following goals.

This proposal is affordable.

This proposal is comparatively easy and quick to implement.

This proposal requires a minimum number of impact studies.

This proposal emphasizes the important relationship between Atlanta's historic neighborhoods and urban centers.

At the heart of this proposal are Atlanta's historic rail lines which already weave through the city connecting Atlanta's historic neighborhoods and urban centers. This proposal advocates the re-use of these lines to protect and revive historic neighborhoods, facilitate access to affordable housing, accommodate an influx of new residents, redevelop available land, and provide alternative and desperately needed means of transportation.

Sincerely,

Sarah Edgens

Mark Arnold

Ryan Gravel

We borrowed a map from my thesis and included a more detailed description of the project. Importantly, in addition to transit, this included the greenway and trail, "creating a thin necklace of green that connects several major city parks."[3] We mailed the letter to all the regional leaders we could think of at the time—the governor, the mayor, all the various transportation and planning agencies. We sent out about 50 letters and mostly got no response. We did receive a handful of notes on letterhead saying basically, "Nice idea—good luck with that." And then we got one reply that would change everything.

"I called Ryan, and he and some colleagues came in, and we started talking and they described the plan, and I thought, eureka!"[4] recalls Cathy

Woolard a couple of years later in a pro bono promotional video narrated by Jane Fonda, who lived adjacent to the corridor. At the time we sent our letter, Woolard was a pragmatic freshman city councilmember from District 6, which covered Virginia-Highland, Poncey-Highland, Druid Hills, and Candler Park. She was the first openly gay elected official in Georgia when she won that seat in 1997, and she had worked in public advocacy efforts related to LGBT rights in Washington for the Human Rights Campaign. When she returned to Atlanta, she ran for District 6 and won and was later appointed chair of the City Council's Transportation Committee, which is why she got our letter. Usually that committee deals with our mammoth airport, but Woolard was interested in public transit. She had just hosted a meeting of all the regional transportation agencies to better understand what they were doing for people in the city of Atlanta.

The city proper comprises only a fraction of the metropolitan land area but is by far the densest part of the region. Its daytime population swells far above its residents, making it the most suitable and logical target for transit. Yet at this meeting, Woolard's council committee was only presented with proposals for moving people from the far-flung, low-density fringes of the region into downtown and back home at the end of the day. She saw nothing in those plans that seriously addressed the needs of people living in the city. There was nothing for her constituents who were more likely to want transit and more willing to pay for transit; nothing to support city residents who had helped build MARTA, the region's only rail transit system; and there was essentially nothing for the residents who depended on transit to get around because they couldn't afford a car. She was frustrated by that meeting and went back to her office.

That very day, our letter landed on her desk.

Woolard was instantly taken with the idea, and she called us down to City Hall to learn more. She asked us to do a public presentation to see if her constituents would be receptive to the proposal. On August 15, 2001, just two weeks after our letter went out, she held a town hall meeting in a church basement in Virginia-Highland. The same regional proposals that had been presented at her council committee meeting were shared by representatives of those agencies along with PATH's plans to run a trail alongside future commuter rail on Southern's belt. We followed with a short slideshow of the Atlanta Beltline. The neighbors were intrigued. They had already been complaining to Woolard about the vagrants and suspected thieves that reportedly roamed the old railroad behind their homes and apartments along the long eastern edge of Piedmont Park, and there were fears about reactivating the line for Amtrak. We held a handful more of these meetings in her district, and people started sharing the idea with their neighbors. In September, our presentations to Woolard's Transportation Committee and the Atlanta Planning Advisory Board were both televised on the city's public-access channel.

We gained instant momentum, and with Woolard's leadership, her staff, PATH, and a growing number of volunteers and partner organizations who began hosting meetings, cleanups, letter campaigns, and bus tours, our proposal emerged as a strategic response to the ongoing transformation of the city—a catalyst infrastructure that was a relief valve for growth as well as its generator. Our proposal could upcycle the entire city, recycling not only the railroads but also the vast vacant land of the industrial belt for a more productive purpose. In the process, it would provide an amazing new public amenity, improve the city's tax base, attract jobs, and breathe new life into our communities, economy, and cultural life. With a relatively modest investment by the public sector, the city would be transformed with multiple positive outcomes.

The private sector would play an enormous role in the actualization of this thesis, and Atlanta's in-town real estate market was red hot in anticipation of that challenge. The public's embrace of the Atlanta Beltline, especially the transit component, was in fact at least partly a response to this mounting development pressure. With an "anything is possible" mind-set, the revitalization of in-town neighborhoods caught fire, fueled by their solid stock of late Victorian and Craftsman-style homes, walkable streets, small commercial clusters, adaptable industrial buildings, and proximity to the center city.

WITH THAT KIND OF ENERGY, the notion that the Atlanta Beltline was real continued to gain momentum. More people wanted to hear
about it, motivating us to talk to more people. Within a few months,
Woolard was elected City Council president, and we took our conversation citywide. Over the course of three years we spoke to anyone who
would listen, including hundreds of neighborhood organizations, business groups, church groups, schools, nonprofits, and clubs, as well as local
government agencies and committees, and even state legislators down at
the Gold Dome. The people of Atlanta fell in love with a vision for their
future. They understood its value intuitively. Woolard described our early
momentum in 2003: "It's amazing to go out to neighborhood groups and
hear people talk about it. They get it, instantly."[5] More recently she told
Atlantic's *CityLab*, "When they could see the rail line as something positive, it changed everything."[6]

Conveniently, Atlanta's unique Neighborhood Planning Units
(NPUs) provided a political framework to support our growing movement. Like the Great Park, the NPU system was originally drafted with
support from Georgia Tech and implemented under Mayor Maynard
Jackson in the 1970s. It began primarily as a community process to access
federal grants, but by the early 2000s, its role had expanded to provide
officially recognized input on just about any public endeavor. NPUs enlist
resident professionals and other volunteers into active community service,
and initially, each of the 24 NPUs (now 25) across the city was assigned a
dedicated planner on staff within the Bureau of Planning.

By the time Karen and I were volunteering for NPU-X and a larger
group of us were taking the Atlanta Beltline vision to NPUs across the
city, however, the system was struggling. It had been stripped of funding and dedicated staff at the very time that increased growth pressure
was mounting. Still, the Atlanta Beltline brought a fresh wave of volunteers, and the NPU system gave us direct access to community leaders
in every corner of the city. Traveling across the city's racial, geographic,
cultural, socioeconomic, and educational divides, we found people everywhere working hard to improve their communities. Older generations
were showing the ropes to newcomers, who in turn were bringing revived

energy to many long, protracted battles. Good, committed community organizers of all stripes were working through the messy process of democracy to effect change in their neighborhoods by considering liquor license requests, reviewing zoning and development proposals, questioning public safety performance or code compliance, and highlighting challenges for local schools, parks, and libraries.

Before NPUs make recommendations on these issues to the City Council, the four to six individual neighborhood associations that make up each NPU meet to determine and offer their position on current issues, so we also sought their support and involvement. I remember a particularly contentious zoning proposal that was being made to the association in Reynoldstown, just before my spot on their agenda. It generated a loud and decisive conclusion from the audience. I worried that my much more impactful proposal was going to be met with a similarly negative and high-volume response. But because we had already met with the community a couple of times, and because we had true believers who lived down the street, the reception in Reynoldstown was overwhelmingly positive.

It is possible that Reynoldstown would have embraced their part of our proposal without the political framework of the NPU system. However, the coordinated support of over 40 neighborhoods, tied together along a continuous corridor of transit and trail that is so enmeshed in the daily life of the city, on such a grand scale, at such cost, and with such a significant physical, social, and economic impact could not have been obtained without the political structure provided by the NPUs. It allowed the Atlanta Beltline to quickly become integrated as part of the solution for leading issues of that time—mobility, density, crime, and the scarcity of city parkland, to name a few.

Woolard's background in community advocacy gave her a unique understanding of the role the public would play in this kind of support and momentum. In anticipation of a June 2003 meeting at StudioPlex, she emailed our Action List, "Public advocacy is the key to making the Belt Line a reality. I am planning a strategy meeting to bring all of the Belt Line Action List members together for the first time to hear updates, to help plan our next steps, and to provide input on this important project."[7] Other messages encouraged public comments in response to articles or op-eds in the local press, and in official public hearings at MARTA and the Atlanta Regional Commission. Woolard had a knack for engaging the public with the project, leveraging willing partners like the Sierra Club to help generate volunteer opportunities including community cleanups, letter-writing campaigns, a speaker's bureau, and a self-guided driving tour.

Woolard's staff provided additional fodder for the public dialog, such as reports that over 21 percent of the enrollment in Atlanta Public Schools was within a half mile of the route.[8] Led initially by Helen Robinson and later by Matt Hicks, her staff also made sure that the project was included in both transportation and economic development studies, proving the project's merit by those metrics and, in the process, building even more arguments for our cause. With support from PATH, they got trail segments prioritized for transportation funding. With the support of civil rights legend and US Congressman John Lewis, they got transit inserted into a feasibility study conducted by MARTA. With back-of-the-envelope support from Invest Atlanta and friends in the private sector, they found that the economic impact of the Atlanta Beltline would provide enormous benefit to the city and that a tax increment finance district was an appropriate and feasible tool to help fund it. Woolard met biweekly with Mayor Shirley Franklin, and her perseverance and passion for the project caught the mayor's attention.

Over time, with the support of a widening array of constituencies—including hundreds of volunteers, a dozen nonprofit organizations, and "moles" providing advice from within many of our most relevant public agencies—the Atlanta Beltline took on a life of its own. Our grassroots movement led to political support from the rest of the City Council, the mayor's office, all the city departments, and eventually even the Georgia Department of Transportation.

The intensity of the public's response was especially exhilarating, and it was easy to get distracted from work by the energy arriving almost hourly by email. I remember one particular message that came from the Poncey-Highland Neighborhood Association, an east-side community that had been physically fractured by the demolition for those two unbuilt highways. It sits to the north of Copenhill, a neighborhood that had been erased for the proposed highway interchange. Like Hemphill Avenue, Lightning, and a dozen other neighborhoods, Copenhill had been wiped off the map in the name of "progress." By the time I wrote my thesis, any remaining fragments had been assumed by neighboring Poncey-Highland and Inman Park, and the scar left by demolition for the failed highways had healed into the deceivingly bucolic Freedom Park-way. When Reid Betz and I were naming transit stations in studio that night in graduate school, we named the station there "Copenhill" in its memory.

The email from Poncey-Highland began with two questions that were directed to me, but they were forwarded atop the body of a much longer email that contained a lengthy debate among several community leaders. Starting from the bottom of the email and reading up, I learned that there was initially some fear about the idea of the Atlanta Beltline and what it would do *to* the community. The Copenhill Station as pro-posed at Ralph McGill Boulevard was just a few hundred feet from the Jimmy Carter Presidential Library, right smack in the contested area where the highways had originally been proposed, so some hesitation was understandable. But further up, the email's back-and-forth comments shifted from trepidation toward excitement. As more details were shared, that excitement escalated to enthusiasm. By the time the conversation was forwarded to me, there was no reference to any of the association's origi-nal concern. Instead, they were asking me two simple questions: "Can we rename the station from 'Copenhill' to 'Copenhill/Carter Center'?" And, "What color is the bridge going to be?"

That kind of quick understanding of the project's advantages and the public's early buy-in to our movement was both typical and conta-gious. From the summer of 2001 to the summer of 2004, a true grassroots movement grew in support of the Atlanta Beltline. It was constructed organically around three core groups, each one focused squarely on the dramatic changes that were coming to in-town Atlanta. The first were neighborhood activists—people who had been working to improve their communities for a generation. The second were developers—people who recognized the opportunity to make a buck by catering to the influx of new residents who were defining that change for in-town neighborhoods. The third group I collect loosely as environmentalists—people and organizations who saw the potential for the Atlanta Beltline to strengthen and sustain positive change for the urban environment. It would catalyze more efficient and compact growth patterns, for example, which would result in a more sustainable built environment, improved air quality, and reduced regional land consumption. It was unusual, if not somewhat uncomfortable, to have these three groups at the same table demanding the same outcome, but there we were. And the exchange we were having was fun, challenging, mutually supportive, and forward thinking. We knew it would be hard, but we were also optimistic that we could figure it out.

Recognizing the need for the project's advocacy efforts to live outside the political environment of her office, Woolard and I founded Friends of the Belt Line (FBL) as a 501©3 nonprofit corporation in February 2004. A few months later, hoping to bring more focus on transit and transportation funding to the state's congressional delegation, Woolard left her position for an ultimately unsuccessful bid for the US House of Representatives. With her departure, FBL took the responsibility of chief advocate for both the project's vision and the 40-plus communities that were so essential to its progress. Like Woolard, FBL was aspirational and direct. "Friends of the Belt Line aims to change the way we think about Atlanta. Instead of accepting our role as the poster child for sprawl, we want to see a brighter future. The Belt Line is certainly not the only answer to building a more sustainable region, but it's a pretty good start. Thanks for joining Friends of the Belt Line and for your support for this bold project. Please help spread the word by forwarding this newsletter to your friends and neighbors."[9]

People did get the word out, and that note captures the spirit of our movement. It was a socially driven initiative well before "social media" was even a term. We met with people face-to-face in official public meetings, at conference room tables, in hallways, and on barstools in places like Manuel's Tavern. We wore through a lot of shoe-leather. I was going to several meetings a week for three years, and Woolard, her staff, and many volunteers were doing the same. We relied on the email listserv originally created by Woolard's council website and expanded under Friends of the Belt Line to disseminate information and communicate with our growing and engaged base of support. I was drawing architectural plans for apartments by day and going to neighborhood meetings and other events in the evenings and on weekends. Eventually, I was able to work full-time in an advocacy role for FBL.

Our astonishing momentum attracted more partners to our table and opened the door to a dramatically expanding vision for the project that included things like expansive new parks and affordable housing. For people on the north and east sides of town, the Atlanta Beltline promised to protect their quality-of-life in the face of new density and traffic. For people in the south and west, where generations of disinvestment had left food deserts, abandoned buildings, and blight, it promised to rebalance growth in the city, bringing access to jobs, stores, and other economic activity. For the city's array of nonprofit organizations who were advocating for pedestrians, bikes, transit, housing, trees, art, or other things, the project offered the opportunity to actively engage on mission-central topics with their core audience and also with the broader community.

When Woolard re-engaged with the project as an active board member of Friends of the Belt Line in 2005, Invest Atlanta was hosting regular meetings with all the project partners, including FBL, MARTA, the PATH Foundation, the Trust for Public Land, and half a dozen others. The table was open to everyone involved in the joint effort to shape the project's future. Ironically, when the Atlanta BeltLine Partnership was formed later that year and absorbed FBL, those meetings stopped, and the sense of collaboration faded for awhile. The loss of FBL's community-focused advocacy has been a challenge for the project, and in many ways I think we're still recovering. The decision to merge the two organizations was tough, but we made it anyway so that we could achieve our larger goal of building the Atlanta Beltline. As a result, the project's momentum has grown in ways that it couldn't have otherwise. It was difficult, but we kept it alive.

I mention that only because I don't want you to think our efforts were easy. The Atlanta Beltline took knocks from every direction, and there was always disagreement and drama. Case in point: in 2005, a developer bought the Southern Railway's old belt line from Norfolk Southern. It was the same year that we kicked off the Redevelopment Plan in support of our first major source of public funding, and residents were already antsy about density. The developer proposed two 40-story towers that would be built on the railroad overlooking Piedmont Park. The train would be buried under the buildings, and the trail would be kicked into the park. Additional towers would form 20-story walls between Poncey-Highland and the Old Fourth Ward, destroying the physical space of the corridor. I was worried that the neighborhoods, angered by his proposals, would kill off the entire Beltline concept with more skill and speed than they slayed those unbuilt highways. They did come out swinging, but it wasn't against the Atlanta Beltline. They were actually fighting *for* the vision that we had built together. They wanted to protect it. And they won.

The reason that win was possible is that the public believed in this vision before anyone else. They own it. It is theirs. They empower city leadership to make it happen, but they aren't willing to give up all control. Their expectation is not just that the Atlanta Beltline gets built, but that it happens in the best possible way. And when things go wrong, they get loud. The city's early interest in accepting the developer's offer for a narrower, highly compromised alignment was eventually squelched by the volume and stamina of their response. Other experiences like the somewhat controversial passing of the tax increment district later that summer, a late proposal by Amtrak in January 2009 to reactivate Southern's belt, and Grant Park's unsuccessful battle over an ill-conceived big-box store starting in 2013, all help to illustrate the public's attention to the project's progress and their high expectations for its delivery. Together, they also demonstrate very clearly that the Atlanta Beltline's political durability remains mobilized by the public's ownership of a broad, inclusive vision.

NOT TOO LONG AFTER that email about the name of the station and the color of the bridge, I met Anna Foote up the street in a booth at Manuel's Tavern. It's a legendary watering hole that sits right at the northern edge of Copenhill where countless similar encounters have no doubt shaped the future of Atlanta. At that time, Foote was an emerging community leader from Poncey-Highland and an ardent and early supporter of the Atlanta Beltline. She was raising her son in her childhood home, a large rambling house on Linwood Avenue where her parents had been central figures in the fight against one of those two unbuilt highways. She told me about sneaking away in the summers as a teenager to walk along the old kudzu-covered belt line to Piedmont Park and smoke cigarettes with her legs dangling from the bridge over Ponce de Leon Avenue. She told me the story of houses being torn down behind her family home to make way for the highway, and of her sense of betrayal at Mayor Young for his compromise that would result in Freedom Parkway.

In subsequent meetings over several years, and with an expressive, liberal, southern determination, Foote introduced me to other figures in the epic drama that had unfolded in those east-side neighborhoods. We also started a discussion that we still continue from time to time about the political context within which the Atlanta Beltline came to life. In the summer of 2001, I had naïvely entered the civic life of Atlanta at age 28. Over the next several years, we built a grassroots momentum by engaging community leaders through the NPU system, which was set up perfectly for such an undertaking. It provided a political framework for change, but until my discussion with Foote, I had no idea that the system itself was so special. I learned that it connects our story back to Atlanta's civil rights legacy and that its development had required quite a measure of vision itself. As a result of our conversations, I am convinced more than ever that the Atlanta Beltline could not have happened at any other point in time.

Under the slogan "the city too busy to hate," Atlanta's attention to its future in the third quarter of the twentieth century reinforced the city's Scarlett O'Hara–like reputation for facing unpleasantries only when doing so leads to the most profitable way forward. The realization that a negative national reputation on race relations would be bad for business helped build and maintain alliances between the white business elite and public officials with Atlanta's growing black middle class. As described in Clarence Stone's eye-opening book *Regime Politics,* these efforts were both intentional and effective in bringing about change. Stone explains how concessions in practices like neighborhood redlining and additional resources for new public housing created a valuable platform for negotiation between these parties. "This habit of biracial bargaining and cooperation could then be applied to new areas of conflict as they arose. Several factors thus converged to maintain the coalition, and individual incentives in particular helped to preserve the overall group bargain. Repeated interactions in dealing with issues that were both concrete and controversial served to cement the coalition and promote cooperation across racial lines."[10]

This brand of highly negotiated peacefulness was both cause and result of Atlanta's role as the cradle of the American civil rights movement. The relationships held together even as political power shifted from white to black with the election of Maynard Jackson as mayor in 1973. Through the next decade, he provided a framework through which a progressive vision for the future city could be realized.

And it was. Along with improvements like the expansive growth of our airport into the busiest in the world and the groundbreaking for MARTA's rail system in 1975, Atlanta launched itself well beyond other southeastern cities to become the uncontested capital of the South. And importantly, even as whites abandoned the city limits in droves toward the end of the twentieth century, the cultivation of a political framework for social and cultural change in the city was well under way, laying the groundwork for the current chapter of Atlanta's story.

There was a symbolic aspect to the progressive political environment created by Mayor Jackson's first two terms, but it was also real, and it played a critical role in shaping the city's future. On one of those nights at Manuel's, Anna Foote introduced me to Panke Miller, who had been a key leader in the now-legendary highway fights. She was also appointed the first woman on the Board of Alderman just prior to Jackson's election and later ran the Bureau of Planning. She reflected on the political climate of the time. Much of the suburbanizing white middle and working classes, she said, was made up of natives who had been resisting integration. As they left, they took their intolerance with them, and "outsiders" with more progressive views began moving in. As a result, the local political representation in the east-side neighborhoods was "shifting toward hippies and women." She describes the new atmosphere in the city as "a wide-open place," when she moved to Atlanta in 1969. Anything, it seemed, was possible.

Miller describes how the highway fights, which were already under way at the time she arrived, "swept people into the community organization," providing a range of high-caliber professionals to support the cause, including lawyers, economists, architects, and researchers from Georgia Tech and Emory University. They blasted the highway project with data and examples from other cities, challenging the project leadership's status quo position on "progress." They leveraged the MARTA referendum of 1971 to support their cause, arguing that federal money should not be spent to undermine the transit system that the federal government had just approved.

Maynard Jackson held no allegiances to the state-led effort in support of highway construction when he started his bid for mayor, and he became a supporter of what many describe as "the neighborhood movement" that was organizing against it. He connected with the primarily white east-side highway fighters and included them in a broad alliance of interests with an empowered and expanding black middle class. Following his election, Mayor Jackson led this coalition toward a progressive vision and new city charter that abolished the Board of Aldermen, in which each official was elected citywide—a common tool for holding down minority voters in the South. In its place, he installed a district-based City Council, and for community input on their activities, he established the NPU system. Both improvements provided unprecedented and officially sanctioned platforms for passionate, expert, or otherwise-engaged citizens who were willing to work for their communities and interests.

These groups did what they could to protect the city during the largely destructive era of the late 1970s and 80s. By the 1990s, the political reorganization of Atlanta was finally met by a growing desire for urban lifestyles, which unleashed the private sector to fuel the city's physical and economic revitalization with new apartments, restaurants, and stores. The singles, young couples, and empty-nesters who began gentrifying the in-town neighborhoods surrounding downtown did not represent a complete reversal of regional growth trends, but they were sufficient in number to have a positive impact on the in-town housing market. For the first time since the 1960s, they helped generate net population growth in the city of Atlanta. By the end of the decade, bolstered by the energy of the Olympics, growth had become physically manifest in neighborhood revitalization, especially on the east side. A booming construction industry also provided work for the young architects of my generation, and as these emerging real estate market trends evolved into a formidable force, we saw the central city literally changing before our eyes. Anything was possible. It had once again become "a wide-open place."

THIS OPENNESS IS IMPORTANT, especially when it is made visible and vocal. The Atlanta Beltline's early naysayers were loud, but they were drowned out by a more resonant voice from the public at large. We were undeterred in our efforts because we could see that the naysayers operated at the fringes of public momentum. The ordinary people of the city wanted the vision that they had created and that they believed in, and without question, their vocal and active support is the reason that we are building it today.

I remember the very moment when I first understood the power of those politics and the role they would play in the realization of our vision. It came in a rather ordinary setting—a public meeting of the Atlanta Regional Commission in 2003. Woolard had sent an email to our Action List asking people to attend and advocate for the project as a priority for regional transportation funding. I got there early, and the room was already crowded. While I nervously prepared to make a public comment on the record, I was eavesdropping on two middle-aged women standing in front of me. Over the low murmurs of the crowd before the meeting began, they were talking about how "our project" would loop around the city, connecting over 40 neighborhoods to MARTA, and detailing what "our project" would mean for the city. It had become "our project," not mine or Woolard's. They had taken ownership of the Atlanta Beltline, even though I had no idea who they were.

Before that moment, I hadn't been so confident that we could ever pull it off. The proposal had seemed far too ambitious. I kept talking to people about it simply because I was enjoying the discussion. At that moment, however, I realized that the proposal's daunting politics and project costs could, and likely would, be overcome by the powerful will of the people. Six years later, in the city elections of 2009, this revelation would be illustrated by the simple fact that you couldn't be a viable candidate for mayor if you didn't support the Atlanta Beltline and have some kind of plan to implement it even better and faster. Politically, that's a pretty powerful position.

So as we look ahead today at our much larger regional problems of traffic, pollution, blight, and sprawl, I remain undeterred by those who think a truly honest conversation about the region's future is naïve or premature, or that bold solutions are politically unpalatable. If our success answering these questions with the Atlanta Beltline proves anything, it's that ideas are really persuasive and that naysayers are usually wrong. The problem is not that we can't come up with the answers. The problem is that our expectations are set too low. But even for those of us with a higher aim, another problem remains. In many places we don't have a viable political framework like the NPUs to affect change at the grassroots or community level. As a result, we find it difficult, if not impossible, to act on our ideas. Our vision for the future remains trapped by our obstinate politics, which instead of aspiring to solutions, are focused squarely and comfortably on maintaining the status quo.

To get out of that cycle, we can't just talk about ideas. We're going to have to engage—each in our own way—with the messy and uncomfortable politics of change. I found myself doing this over the years, I guess, because of my desire to make a difference, the unbelievable opportunity presented by this journey, and the commitments I had already made to people along the way. I didn't always know where we were going, but I certainly understood intuitively that Atlanta was a wide-open place and that I wanted to be a part of it.

AN EXPANDABLE VISION

IN THE LAST CHAPTER, I TOLD THE BONA FIDE FAIRY tale of how average citizens became custodians of the Atlanta Beltline's ambitious vision. That story, however, is intertwined with a related but somewhat separate narrative about what their sense of ownership has meant for the idea—for the fundamental question of what the Atlanta Beltline is. From its beginning as a relatively simple proposition for a transit loop that would catalyze neighborhood revitalization and economic development, it has grown exponentially and become conceptually much richer.

The greenway trail was the first expansion of its vision, and also the most important because it perfected the core proposal and proved that the concept could grow. It was formalized by a short email to my coworker in the late summer of 2001, just five days after our first town hall meeting. The note came from Ed McBrayer of the PATH Foundation on August 20, 2001.

Sarah:

I enjoyed your light rail presentation last week. I am willing to modify my vision to a greenway corridor for light rail and a trail in a heartbeat. Imagine having a continuous bike/ped trail linking stations to neighborhoods and destinations along the corridor. Can you go along with my idea of a landscaped, wildflowered greenbelt for the rail and trail? I don't think it's been done in this country.

With MARTA already allowing bikes on trains and (soon) busses, our rail-trail corridor would be accessible from anywhere through the MARTA connections.

Give me a call if you are interested in "piggybacking" our ideas.

Ed

McBrayer's offer to scrap the unrealistic leftover Olympic legacy idea of a trail following Amtrak in favor of a new, equally unrealistic but fundamentally more ambitious and community-minded idea of sharing a larger loop corridor with light rail was a monumental step forward. We had met McBrayer at Woolard's town hall meeting where he also presented his concept following Southern's old belt line past Piedmont Park. We were excited by his attention because he brought experience, private funding, and an almost fearless need to act and build.

The new concept that PATH became a part of had a greatly expanded geographic range and program, intentionally pairing urban-scaled mixed-use redevelopment in the old industrial belt with conservation efforts in over 40 neighborhoods along the way. It developed a clarity and energy that would quickly compel a broad and powerful constituency to want it, to believe in it, and further, to fight for it.

Likewise, the greenway trail offered the project something more immediately tangible, and PATH's partnership lent the effort a proven track record of getting things done. Together, the concept's fresh, simple logic allowed people to imagine their individual futures as an integral part of a much larger story about the future of their city that was rapidly changing. The ability for ordinary people to participate in the formation of the concept and our need for their assistance in the advancement of its politics as described in the last chapter translated into a legitimate claim of citizens as co-owners and co-authors of the Atlanta Beltline's ambitious vision. As that sentiment spread, not only did we become obligated to actually start figuring out how to build it, but the set of ideas that define the Atlanta Beltline itself expanded well beyond what any of us could have imagined in the beginning.

With hindsight, I'm not sure any of us understood the power of what we had done. That strategic combination gave us a robust, wonderful, successful physical proposal that focused and motivated a broad citizen movement and political leadership to get something done. In the process, the project also became an amazing magnet for other ideas about our future.

The greenway trail firmly established the concept's ability to expand programmatically, so by the time the Trust for Public Land and Invest Atlanta got seriously involved in 2004, the project was capable of accommodating their program along with related dialog on challenges like affordability and health. Remarkably, as its scope continued to grow, its overarching vision and momentum somehow protected it from getting bogged down by the additional load. New ideas, in fact, seemed to only fuel the project's fire, making the process of upcycling our city that much more productive and certain. In this way, the Atlanta Beltline has proved itself to be a perfect framework and testing ground for ideas about the future of the city.

NEIGHBORHOOD CONSERVATION (1999)

Neighborhood conservation is the core of the proposal for the Atlanta Beltline. From the beginning, the NPU system and grassroots movement framed the project in community interests. Almost every discussion started with a map and a detailed orientation between the railroad corridor and individual homes. The protection of single-family houses in particular was of paramount importance, and starting with our original proposal to Woolard, we promised that residential areas "would be protected from high-density development through zoning, but reinvigorated with infill housing on vacant land and commercial and cultural districts in appropriate areas."[1]

That promise resonated. In fact, the basis of the public's early enthusiasm for the Atlanta Beltline was this essentially protectionist position toward change. They had seen a generation of active destruction and passive disinvestment. They had fought highways, blight, and declining schools and population. As they saw change coming once again, they took a powerful, if subconscious, position not to protect themselves against change altogether, but to protect their opportunity to leverage that change to their advantage.

TRANSIT (1999)

The signature instrument for the protection of quality of life was always transit. Community support for transit was fervent from the beginning because it directly addressed the public's primary concerns about growth. Unlike many proposals, however, transit on the Atlanta Beltline takes an unorthodox approach. It does not justify light rail according to current ridership projections. It proposes that if the land associated with the Atlanta Beltline is redeveloped appropriately, future population and employment growth on those sites will support it.

This runs contrary to much of conventional contemporary planning practice, but it taps into a more intuitive understanding about city building. An excerpt from Atlanta's "Rapid Transit" plan of 1961 captures the same sentiment. "Thoughtful planning will recognize transportation as a 'tool' for shaping the region, instead of forever using it to catch up with its own inadequacies."[2] Rather than having transit chase after growth that is fundamentally organized around automobiles, the Atlanta Beltline incentivizes private development to make better decisions. It avoids a future problem of traffic gridlock and car dependency by re-concentrating growth into areas where multiple infrastructure networks, and existing cultural and social institutions, can support it more effectively and efficiently.

From a technical perspective, there have been a few modifications from the original proposal, including new infill MARTA stations for better connectivity and an unfortunate west-side detour along Marietta Boulevard. Thankfully, the idea of more stations and slower speeds instead of faster trains and reduced local service has been protected by ongoing public engagement. The public also secured a commitment to rail, which has been the preferred mode since the beginning. Today, plans call for a seamless integration with the Atlanta Streetcar, which opened its first segment downtown at the end of 2014.

To make this integration, the loop route on the Atlanta Beltline has become one of a much larger network of streetcars proposed across downtown and midtown. Along with other benefits, this allows the city to move incrementally forward with transit before it has control over the entire 22-mile corridor and before it has the money to address some of the project's most costly physical connections. My only caution with this approach is that we remain determined to finish the job. Transit on the Atlanta Beltline—in its continuous and traffic-free splendor—is critical not only because it is the core of what we promised to deliver, but more importantly, because it is required for the rest of our vision to work.

ECONOMIC DEVELOPMENT (1999)

There are more than 4,000 acres of underutilized and redeveloping urban land following the belt line railroads and within walking distance of their tracks. These sites include not only the old industrial belt but also adjacent obsolete, disconnected apartments and car-oriented commercial strips. On the east side of town today, the economic potential for new apartments, coffee shops, and jobs to support the day-to-day lives of residents is undeniable. It is difficult to remember, for example, while looking at the crossing of North Highland Avenue, that just a few years ago it was the barren backside of remnant industry, a broken-down landscape of kudzu-covered obsolescence. For the other parts of town that haven't yet seen such revitalization, the Atlanta Beltline brings hope.

The in-town-minded developers who were already working along North Highland and similar corridors in the early days of our grassroots movement understood the economic potential for the project immediately. It was given life, after all, as a response to the projects that they were building. Ultimately, this development pressure and our desire to capture its value supported a tool that could help fund the cost of the project itself. It also brought in a new partner, Invest Atlanta, which was called the Atlanta Development Authority at the time. They joined discussions with Cathy Woolard, Alycen Whiddon, and others as early as 2003 to hatch an idea for a tax increment finance district, which Georgia law calls a tax allocation district or TAD. The TAD would leverage the incremental increase in property taxes paid by landowners as a natural result of redevelopment to help pay for the public amenity. After 25 years, the Atlanta Beltline would be built, and the tax increment would go back into the general fund. Since Invest Atlanta administers the city's other TADs, it took the lead in this effort, eventually spinning off Atlanta BeltLine, Inc. in 2006 as the city's official implementing agency for the project.

The idea for an Atlanta Beltline TAD garnered steam from Mayor Franklin's administration after an initial feasibility study projected that it would contribute substantially to the estimated $2 billion to $3 billion cost of the project. By state law, the TAD required an extended planning process to confirm its purpose and intent. This "Redevelopment Plan" was approved by the end of 2005, and the effort demonstrated very clearly that the grassroots pressure for the Atlanta Beltline was a critical part of achieving such approvals. It offered political cover and urged city, county, and school board members to make decisions of support for the project's first major source of public funding.

The TAD, however, is just a mechanism to capture some of the value that the Atlanta Beltline generates in order to help fund its own cost. The more important story is the larger economy that the project is building. Even while TAD revenues did not meet original projections because of the Great Recession, by the end of 2014, the private market response had still generated over $2.4 billion in investment.[3] Most visible was the renovation of the gargantuan Sears and Roebuck building into Ponce City Market, which began opening its doors in 2015. Even that kind of very tangible development, however, doesn't tell the whole story of what is happening.

By investing in this kind of catalyst infrastructure, adjacent sites become better positioned for today's market conditions. Older areas are revitalized and obsolete districts are redeveloped, providing opportunities for lifestyles that have been lost from Atlanta for over a generation but are now in increasing demand. When Athenahealth, a health-care-oriented technology company, decided in 2013 to move from a car-dependent suburb 25 miles outside of town down to Ponce City Market, the larger potential impact for this kind of change became clear. A vice president of the company offered *Georgia Trend* magazine a sort of testimony for the move. "We were considering other states and other cities, but decided that Atlanta is a great place to grow our business, and the Ponce City location really reflects our corporate culture." Suggesting that the building and location would help with recruiting young talent, he continued, "It just feels like the type of company that we are."[4]

TRAIL AND GREENWAY (2001)

When the thesis project expanded to include a greenway trail, it became a central hub connecting trail spokes in every direction. Many of PATH's existing trails already connected to the loop. Proposed extensions

The Atlanta Beltline's Eastside Trail. (Valdis Zusmanis, 2014)

to others, including the Silver Comet Trail, which reaches the Alabama state line, would link it further afield. Inspired by that idea, new spurs have been conceived in every other direction, following creeks, railroads, power lines, and roadways, including the PATH400 trail leading north into Buckhead, the South Fork Conservancy trails leading east toward Emory, and the Proctor Creek Greenway connecting west to the Chattahoochee River.

NEW PARKS (2004)

Our original pitch for the Atlanta Beltline included existing parks as important destinations along the corridor, totaling about 700 acres at the time. The idea was that if you don't have a pool or a basketball court in your neighborhood, the Atlanta Beltline would connect you to one that does. It could also link you to large regional parks and small neighborhood parks, along with historic sites and cultural destinations like the Atlanta Botanical Garden, the Jimmy Carter Presidential Library, Zoo Atlanta, and the King Plow Arts Center. This new connectivity, however, only partially addressed Atlanta's larger problem with parks.

The region's remarkable tree canopy as seen on your arrival by air is misleading. Atlanta is severely under-parked per capita. Almost all of those trees are in backyards and on other private property. In 2004, Atlanta had only 3.8 percent of its area devoted to parks—the same as Oklahoma City and Toledo, and only one-fifth the percentage of top-tier cities like San Francisco, Washington, DC, and New York.[5] The deficiency is made worse with population growth because most newcomers are living in more densely packed conditions, so there is a growing need for new parks and public space.

The Trust for Public Land (TPL), a national land conservation organization focused on protecting land for use by people, began looking at the corridor as early as 2003. They had already been working to help address the city's parks deficit. When TPL's Georgia office director Jim Langford saw the Atlanta Beltline proposal, he immediately understood the project's opportunity to link those new investments to create a continuously connected greenspace circling the city. He brought TPL in as a partner in the project with the ability to snap up property for new parks faster than the slower-moving public agencies. In 2004, TPL commissioned a study by New York City planning consultant Alexander Garvin to help shape his vision. Garvin's interest was more broadly in the successful integration of the public realm into the life of the city; for this reason, the report also gave meaningful attention to transit and private development.

By that time, I was trying to make a job out of our fledgling Friends of the Belt Line, and I leapt at the chance to work with Garvin as part of his on-the-ground team. We engaged in fieldwork and mapping and developed concepts for a string of parks along the corridor. The project's climactic moment came during an aerial tour in a police helicopter when Garvin spotted Bellwood Quarry, a 45-acre, 350-foot-deep granite pit. We drove down into the bottom of the quarry. It sizzled in the summer sun—a bright gray machined version of the rocky canyons of the American Southwest. Garvin envisioned a new park designed around the 150-acre, then-active quarry land, expanded across adjacent properties to a proposed total of 579 acres, over three times the size of Piedmont Park.

When some leaders at the time resisted including such an audacious proposal in TPL's final report, Langford insisted. The bigness of the vision for the new Westside Park alone got immediate positive attention from the press, the public, the county that owned it, the company that leased it, and the city's Department of Watershed Management, which saw its value as a reservoir for the city's drinking water system. Within months the stars were aligning for critical land acquisitions.

The document that TPL delivered by year's end was wildly ambitious—it proposed carving 1,400 acres of new greenspace out of the industrial belt. In the process, it brought an entirely new constituency of support for our vision. It reinforced the role of both the greenway trail and transit by proposing that "a connected park system that unites a city's great parks is something most cities can only dream about. When combined with the transit and development opportunities, the continuous Beltline provides a 21st century public-realm framework around which Atlanta will grow for the next 100 years."[6]

BROWNFIELDS (2004)

The mitigation of environmentally contaminated industrial land, or brownfields, was always an inherent aspect of the Atlanta Beltline. It incentivizes the private market to remediate adjacent minor brownfields, providing a valuable public benefit at no direct cost to taxpayers. This is especially important for communities where a history of "relaxed" environmental regulations has contributed to disinvestment and blight.

Brownfields became a more intentional part of the Atlanta Beltline's case in 2004 with the citywide Sustainable Brownfields Program, which focused early efforts toward sites along the loop. This continued in the context of the Redevelopment Plan the next year when brownfield conditions helped the project qualify as a "redevelopment area" under Georgia's Redevelopment Powers Law. The plan also made brownfield remediation an eligible expense for TAD funding, but recommended that this should be used only in areas where the Atlanta Beltline's public amenity is still not sufficient alone to provide an incentive for the desired private-sector cleanup.

The project's potential for meaningful remediation has also attracted regulatory agencies to support more aggressive cleanup efforts. Both the federal Environmental Protection Agency (EPA) and the state Environmental Protection Division (EPD) offered early assistance, bringing our story to the forefront of discussion in these circles nationally. It even won the EPA's Overall Smart Growth Project of the Year in 2013 because in addition to cleanup efforts, the project then puts those reclaimed land assets in service to a significant community purpose.

AFFORDABLE/WORKFORCE HOUSING (2005)

The positive response to the Atlanta Beltline was almost universal, but many communities had concerns about economic displacement. People with lower incomes had fallen in love with the vision, too; they just wanted to be there when it was built. This was an especially strong fear in communities where promises about the benefits of stadiums and highways had been broken in the past. This time would be different, we promised. And it is.

Because at-risk communities were part of the movement, advocates made sure that some financial tools were put in place to offset financial pressures. The first official attempt to tackle affordability was through the inclusion of housing subsidies in the tax allocation district (TAD). Legislation protects 15 percent of TAD revenues to support housing affordability. It is put into a trust to help fund grants for the preservation and development of affordable housing, for land, and for down-payment assistance. While modest in the context of the extraordinary need, this commitment of 5,600 units is substantial for Atlanta. The ongoing dialog around it also supports the possibility for action on other strategies like mandatory inclusionary zoning.

PUBLIC REALM (2006)

The large parcels of industrial land that flank the old freight rails create an obstacle between neighborhoods and the Atlanta Beltline. A series of urban design studios at Georgia Tech from 2004 through 2006 provided a detailed exploration into how these sites should be subdivided with new streets and public spaces. They were led by David Green, one of my professors in college, and the idea was to draw a new street grid across these big tracts much like the one Oglethorpe drew for Savannah or the Commissioners Plan made for Manhattan. This would ensure connectivity with adjacent neighborhoods, frame a more robust public realm, and create appropriately dimensioned city blocks for walking.

By the end of 2006, we had assembled the students' work into the Atlanta Beltline Street Framework Plan. The plan was incorporated into the new overlay zoning district, and later refined through the local area planning process. Through negotiations with developers, it offers some leverage for communities trying to improve their connectivity to the corridor and ensure they get the vibrant, walkable public realm that we have always envisioned.

PUBLIC ART AND CULTURAL FACILITIES (2006)

Existing artwork, galleries, and cultural facilities were always envisioned as important destinations on the route, but the arts community did not quite coalesce around the project in the early days as other advocates did. There were valiant efforts, including an unsuccessful push for the city's percentage for arts funding to be applied to the TAD bonds. Artists did get representation on the TAD advisory council, and in 2006 a "Cultural Impact Study" by artist and arts consultant Danielle Roney was completed. Without an external partner organization that has funding and staff able to focus strategically on the Atlanta Beltline, however, public art advocacy efforts languished.

When a formalized arts initiative finally began several years later, it grew out of a guerilla effort that put informally painted artwork at every street crossing. It quickly reorganized as Art on the Atlanta Beltline and grew into the city's largest temporary public art exhibition. Its signature story is the Lantern Parade, led by the Krewe of the Grateful Gluttons. This citizen parade of homemade lanterns grew exponentially from a couple hundred people to well over 60,000 revelers by its sixth year. It illustrates the pent-up and otherwise untapped demand for a cultural life on the Atlanta Beltline, and it has drawn the public's attention to the potential for public art.

While artwork, performances, and related events have finally taken root, however, it is ironic that ideas about artist housing and work spaces that were such a critical component of CODA's Cultural Ring back in the 1990s have been lagging. As Roney also concluded, in addition to great public art, an improved curatorial process, more funding, and design integration, it is essential that the Atlanta Beltline be protected as a welcome place for artists and for cultural experimentation.

PRESERVATION (2006)

Unlike Savannah, the state's post-Reconstruction capital has not made a priority of historic preservation, which has been advocated by only a

Hanson Motor Car Company, Atlanta. (Ryan Gravel, 2005)

passionate minority. As if to underscore the city's ambivalence, while 16 students from Georgia State University were producing a thick compendium and database of historic assets along the Atlanta Beltline in the spring of 2006, the important but crumbling Hanson Motor Car Company buildings were demolished. Known as the "Hanson Six," these were the first automobiles built in Atlanta, yet the entire block was razed with almost zero public response. After witnessing far more challenging renovations in cities with a stronger interest in preservation, it's hard to accept Atlanta's nonchalance regarding its physical history.

There are also wonderful restorations, of course, and the historic elements in the corridor—the bridges, tunnels, and landforms—are similarly meeting mixed results. Like the city at large, the project's implementation has seemingly taken no consistent position or policy on their preservation. The artifacts that survive do so mainly by chance or for utterly pragmatic reasons like high replacement costs or impacts to construction schedule. Lost in the process is a rigor and respect for an honest and inclusive reading of our physical, social, and cultural history. In a larger sense, at least, the Atlanta Beltline does support a kind of preservation concept for the city's identity by memorializing its origin as a railroad town and adapting those railroads as a reclaimed framework for an inspired new vision for its future.

PUBLIC HEALTH (2007)

I happened to attend a panel discussion in 2003 that included Dr. Andrew Dannenberg, then an associate director at the National Center for Environmental Health at the Centers for Disease Control and Prevention (CDC). In the middle of his talk he put up two slides with the title "Public Health Benefits of the Beltline." He made several key points: "Opportunity for Recreational Physical Activity," "Exercise Easily Incorporated into Daily Commute," "Obesity Reduction," "Cleaner Air," "Fewer Traffic Injuries," and "Brownfield Redevelopment."

Dannenberg argued that communities with walkable access to transit and trails are inherently healthier. They encourage people to increase physical activity, which helps prevent obesity, which is associated with an increased risk of overall mortality, heart disease, diabetes, hypertension, and some cancers. I posted a related article on our website and started incorporating health benefits into my talks, but it wasn't really until a couple years later that the connection between health and the Atlanta Beltline became formalized.

Under the leadership of Dr. Catherine Ross, director of the Center for Quality Growth and Regional Development at Georgia Tech, along with technical assistance from the CDC (including Dannenberg), a health impact assessment (HIA) of the Atlanta Beltline was conducted in 2007. Its purpose was to include public health in decisions about project implementation. A wide range of recommendations included everything from obvious health benefits like physical activity and access to jobs and healthy food to more abstract goals like social capital and equity.[7]

ARBORETUM (2007)

Greg Levine from Trees Atlanta first pitched the idea of a linear arboretum along the Atlanta Beltline in 2007. I'll admit I had to Google the term: "a botanical garden devoted to trees." In addition to supporting their goal of restoring the tree canopy, the arboretum would become a focus for the nonprofit's educational programs about tree planting and care, invasive species, and other urban ecological issues. It might also become a civic attraction and contribute to neighborhood identity.

I was easily convinced, but when Levine introduced the idea to the Atlanta Beltline's leadership at the time, they weren't so sure. There was concern about adding to the scope of the project and elevating the public's expectations. Levine, however, had already been supporting the project for many years. He knew it would require a lot of trees, and he wanted to make sure Trees Atlanta was at the table for decisions that would be made about them. He wanted his organization to claim its share of ownership in the project's success alongside other partners like PATH and TPL and to more fully support the in-town communities in which they were most engaged. He pushed hard, even hiring a consultant to deliver a concept plan. It put the idea of a 22-mile linear arboretum into the public dialog, and effectively into the public's expectation.

By the opening of the Eastside Trail in 2012, the Atlanta Beltline Arboretum was fully embedded into the corridor's design, and Trees Atlanta had become a full partner in implementation. The organization continues to raise money for trees, provide technical expertise and assistance to the various design teams, perform most of the plantings as a subcontractor during construction, and maintain the trees and meadows through grants and volunteer support. Trees Atlanta's proactive claim to an active role in the implementation of the Atlanta Beltline should serve as a model for other partners.

COMMUNITY STABILIZATION (2011)

The reincarnation of a large warehouse in the Old Fourth Ward as StudioPlex predates the Atlanta Beltline, but it is loosely connected to the

Birth home, Martin Luther King Jr. National Historic Site, Atlanta. (Ryan Gravel, 2014)

economic and cultural opportunities identified by the Cultural Ring. The project began as a defensive move against a proposed re-use of the historic building that would have generated heavy truck traffic. With the idea to support local artists instead, it was converted to artists' studios and housing by Mtamanika Youngblood, a community developer and president of the Historic District Development Corporation (HDDC). Its conversion played a role in the transformation of the Martin Luther King Jr. historic district, which HDDC led throughout the 1990s and 2000s. With an impressive track record of dozens of revitalization projects through historic preservation, non-displacement, and sustainability, the HDDC's work remains a national model. For the Atlanta Beltline specifically, it provides local lessons and proves by example that community stabilization strategies can work.

Models like HDDC go beyond the creation of new affordable housing to also help people who have homes but are at risk of losing them.

They also support things like job creation, commercial redevelopment, crime reduction, and the management of vacant and blighted properties. They are critically important for communities like those in south and west Atlanta, which were centers of mortgage fraud and other reckless lending practices leading into the global Great Recession. Neighborhoods like Pittsburgh were hit especially hard, with brand-new homes sitting empty because their price on paper was multiple times their actual value. While the financial crisis lessened the urgency of gentrification in the near term, it generated all kinds of new problems for families at risk of losing their homes, which is usually the most significant asset with which to build generational wealth.

A 31-acre industrial tract in Pittsburgh presents hope for a large-scale strategy there. It has nearly half a mile of frontage along the Atlanta Beltline and it is owned by the Annie E. Casey Foundation, which plans to meet a high bar for job creation and other community benefits. Another effort in progress is the Atlanta Land Trust Collaborative (ALTC), which was created to protect affordability and diversity in local communities. It functions as an umbrella or incubator for potentially dozens of smaller, resident-controlled trusts, the first of which was developed in Pittsburgh in 2011. While these efforts represent a good start, the broader challenge of community stabilization remains unfinished and increasingly urgent, especially as a revived real estate market turns its interest toward these at-risk, in-town communities.

IT SHOULD BE CLEAR BY NOW THAT all of these layers of ideas for the Atlanta Beltline share a common focus on the lives of people. As the citizens who made it that way, we should feel fully entitled to add more. In addition to elaboration and embellishment of the ideas listed, there's already a nascent idea for a 22-mile food forest where people can pick berries, apples, or herbs along their walk through the city. There have been proposals for networks of bocce ball courts and farmers' markets, citywide plantings for pollinating insects, incentives for green building practices, job training programs, and a business chamber of commerce. While some efforts have been formalized through organizations like the

Atlanta BeltLine Partnership, some are simply the spontaneous actions of people who want to make a contribution.

I'm personally enamored with experiments in Dresden and Paris, where innovators are testing whether freight trams could travel between streetcars to make deliveries to department stores, warehouses, and other businesses. Another dream of mine is to make the back half of every other train open to fresh air, permitting dogs, beer, rowdiness, and an awesome experience of the city. No matter how crazy they seem, these kinds of ideas keep the Atlanta Beltline alive. The ones worth implementing ensure that it will achieve its potential to even further transform our city for the better.

This physical transformation is important because for most people, the project isn't an abstract concept or theory—it's real. It's a big idea, built from an assembly of layers—transit, trails, parks, housing, economic development, art, and a list that continues to grow. Made more iconic by its circular form, the Atlanta Beltline's physicality recalls a sound bite that is attributed to Daniel Burnham, author of Chicago's famous city plan, who challenged us in 1907 to "make no little plans." The full quote is even more illuminating, and relevant to our efforts today.

"Make no little plans. They have no magic to stir men's blood and probably themselves will not be realized. Make big plans; aim high in hope and work, remembering that a noble, logical diagram once recorded will never die, but long after we are gone will be a living thing, asserting itself with ever-growing insistency. Remember that our sons and grandsons are going to do things that would stagger us. Let your watchword be order and your beacon beauty. Think big."[8]

We'll include our daughters and granddaughters, of course, alongside our wives and our sisters. But by advertising its broad program, and by offering itself as a clear, compelling, and simple physical armature that is receptive and ready for even more ideas about our future, the Atlanta Beltline has opened itself up to a much larger impact on our lives.

BREAKING GROUND
ON HOPE

THE GROUNDBREAKINGS START WITH SPEECHES AND end with cheap, gold-painted shovels. I attend them whenever I can—the ribbon cuttings, too. I listen to the leaders lead and dole out their best sound bites for social media. I catch up with a few old friends and then I go back to work. The weight of what we're doing, however, hits me later. Months after the October 2012 opening of the Eastside Trail, for example, I went for a bike ride with my kids. We were traveling south from the future Kanuga Station, and I was taking pictures with my phone, trying not to crash. When we got home, I flipped through the images and was struck by one in particular. It remains my favorite image of the Atlanta Beltline out of the literally thousands of photographs that I have taken over the years.

It captures one of those warm, fragrant, late-spring Atlanta Saturdays that makes you thankful to be alive. But the reason I love it isn't the brilliant blue sky or the bright green leaves fluttering in the wind at the end of every branch. It isn't the mobs of people getting healthy and being social, who are literally smiling because they are so in love with their city again. It's the red-haired lady on the right. She is carrying her groceries, and in the process, she's validating everything we always said the Atlanta Beltline would do.

Atlanta Beltline Eastside Trail, Atlanta. (Ryan Gravel, 2013)

Rendering, Atlanta Beltline, Atlanta. (Perkins+Will, 2013)

Our groundbreaking provided her with the infrastructure for a new way of life, but it was up to her to take advantage of it—and she did. I imagine she watched as the trail was cast in trees and concrete, and when it was finished and she carried her groceries home that day, the red-haired lady became our warm-blooded proof of concept. So when people ask me if the Atlanta Beltline will ever be finished, I say that it already is. "You can use it today," I tell them. "It's already working." It has created a profound physical space for a social and cultural life that we didn't even know we were missing, and its utility has already proved both its value and meaning for our lives.

On other days, my answer to that question is that the Atlanta Beltline will never be finished. I don't mean that in a defeatist sort of way. I mean that we're building a vision for our future that is embedded so deeply in the life of our communities that along with our own personal aspirations, abilities, and relationships, the project will always evolve. This ability to change over time is an essential characteristic of the most captivating, exciting, and vibrant cities in the world—they're never finished.

Of course, the bits and parts and physical things that are required to manifest our vision do have costs and timetables. And already-built elements like parks and trails are working not because of some magical vision, but because literally hundreds of people and dozens of public agencies, nonprofits, local businesses, and consulting firms have been employed over many years to make them work. While my kids notice the pretty trees, fixed-up buildings, and cool new restaurants popping up along the way, I vividly remember the hard work and compromise that was required for that to happen. For well over a decade, our labor was enmeshed in an arduous soap opera of personalities and drama that was often, in spite of itself, the means that got us this far.

When our early grassroots movement began to expand with new partners back in the spring of 2004, that work came together through a loose confederation of organizations in support of common, if not perfectly congruent, goals. When transit studies were under way, for example, MARTA led that discussion, and when the focus shifted to parks, the Trust for Public Land took the lead. By mid-2005, Invest Atlanta was guiding the group toward completion of the Redevelopment Plan and the related effort to secure votes for the TAD. That's also when Cathy Woolard and I agreed to fold Friends of the Belt Line into the newly established Atlanta BeltLine Partnership, which after the successful TAD vote, embarked on a $60 million private fundraising campaign for parks and greenways. The significance of the Partnership's task to tap into the private sector cannot be underestimated, and as the larger movement grew, the Partnership expanded its role to build community awareness for the project and to advance strategic programs that could bring in partners to support other relevant efforts.

Meanwhile, the TAD's approval in the closing days of 2005 had started the clock ticking on a 25-year timetable for completion of the project's physical components. It was a long but reasonable deadline for construction of the transit greenway, all the new parks, housing units, and related ingredients that had been baked into the plan by that time. Invest Atlanta, the Partnership, and others then drafted a plan to spend a projected $427 million over the first five years toward completion of the project's first phase. In addition to physical projects and land acquisitions, it called for the creation of new organizations like Atlanta BeltLine, Inc. (ABI), which would be the project's chief implementing agency, and the TAD Advisory Committee (TADAC), which would provide oversight of ABI on behalf of the Atlanta City Council. Funding for implementation would come to ABI from the TAD bonds and other public sources such as local park bonds and federal allocations for things like transportation and brownfields. Private donations would also be funneled to ABI through the Partnership, providing essential early money for land acquisitions, trail and park construction, and strategic matching funds. ABI's board of directors would be composed of leaders capable of keeping its efforts on track, and as a member of the board, the mayor would help convey a sense of urgency and ensure coordination among the various departments at City Hall.

Fast-forward ten years beyond the Redevelopment Plan and through the economic downturn to see the fruits of our labor. By the end of 2015, the early impacts of construction are undeniable. The most obvious outcome is record-breaking traffic on the modest 2-mile section of the Eastside Trail. Notably, the mobs of smiling people on foot, bike, skates, or skateboard come from every demographic and every part of the region.

If we continue southward from where the image of the red-haired lady was taken, the project's second most obvious impact becomes abundantly clear. The private market is responding strongly to the framework that we established. Ten local master plans have provided guidance for developers in the construction of over 15,000 new housing units and over 700,000 square feet of office and retail space throughout the corridor since 2005. Most of this new growth is concentrated along the Eastside Trail, especially near Ponce City Market. Even though streetcars are still a few years away, the market's new tree-planted bridge connects directly to the future station. Inside, we find crowds of people in search of everything from specialty housewares to climbing gear and handcrafted hats, along with a massive food hall and even amusement rides and a mini–golf course on its roof.

As we continue down the trail, we witness a building boom of apartments, townhouses, restaurants, and other businesses. When we reach ABI's first affordable housing project in Reynoldstown, we find a new wave of development that is beginning to light up Memorial Drive. It includes the renovation of an old school into an arts collective called WonderRoot and several mixed-use projects geared toward a new generation with different ideas about how best to live it up in Atlanta.

We head clockwise and south, crossing over I-20, where for the next several miles we find scattered and smaller new developments. Land speculators here seem to be in a holding pattern, waiting for the next real estate cycle and a more definitive timeline for trail construction. There are even larger tracts of land on this stretch, however, and with ongoing home renovations, modernized schools, new parks, and community gardens, we can see both ample room for an expanding economy and a powerful spirit of civic revitalization.

Along our 22-mile journey, we walk four and a half miles of completed main-line trail and follow three and a half more under construction.

This includes the unprecedented investment of the Westside Trail, which, following a November 2014 groundbreaking, is the first major infrastructure in more than two generations to fulfill its promise for equitable investment on this underserved side of town. On the in-between sections where the trail is not yet built, we're either walking along interim trails on property that the city controls, or along stretches of mostly continuous right-of-way that are finalizing their sale to the city. Only one section of active freight will ultimately remain, and our alignments there will require some unknown future agreement.

We also encounter six new or expanded parks with three more nearing construction, and we sneak a peek at the future largest park in the city, the Westside Park, made out of that old quarry, which has essentially completed its land acquisition. Overall, we see evidence of hundreds of millions of dollars in physical investments and billions in private development. Still, when I point to the abundant land that remains, even along the Eastside Trail, it's worth a reminder that the impact of the Atlanta Beltline has only begun.

As the perfect end to our tour, we find ourselves back on the Eastside Trail. We hike up to a little perch at the top of Three Tree Hill, which is really only half a hilltop that remained after Southern Railway plowed through the other side in 1871. It stands near the spot where, seven years before that, General Sherman watched the burning of Atlanta during the American Civil War, and at the edge of Copenhill, the neighborhood that was razed a hundred years later for the interchange of those unbuilt highways. From our hilltop view, the city's glittering skyline stands tall above the rooftops of Dr. Martin Luther King Jr.'s old stomping grounds, which provide a foreground for our sunset as the echoes of construction finally settle for the night.

The perspective from this vantage point is an obvious milestone on our journey. I find myself there often—sometimes physically, but more often in my thoughts. It has been wild to watch my own life unfold within this larger story. I've become a father of two along the way, and with more than a little heartache, our family moved out of southwest Atlanta into a commercial loft about a mile down the trail from Three Tree Hill. This bittersweet transition, however, has allowed us to more immediately experience the lives we have been working to build.

Every day we see surging bicycle and pedestrian traffic flowing between the trail, Krog Street Market, and other destinations. My simple pleasures in life are much easier here—a pleasant walk, a cup of coffee, or a drink at a bar with a friend. The validation of outcomes that I anticipated, like my own walk home from the grocery, have been supplemented by the unexpected. There's the woman who plays a violin while pulling her dog on the back of a cooler. There's the surprise that biking to many places is not just an option, it's actually faster than driving. And perhaps most gratifying is the infinite joy of watching my children's worldview being shaped by the Atlanta Beltline in the same way that mine was by our perimeter highway.

This last point is real hope for those of us who want a more sustainable, healthy, equitable, and prosperous region. It offers confidence that such an ambitious transformation is possible and that it will be driven by both intuitive and conscious desires to improve our way of life. It also suggests that if we work for it, we can find an abundance of hope about the future of the places we live.

The first hope is the kind I borrowed from Rem Koolhaas. It's about our collective opportunity to leverage our existing conditions into an honest, inclusive, and creative vision for our future. It proposes that we rethink our assumptions about traffic, blight, and sprawl to instead find "as many gains as losses." With creativity and experimentation, we can make them into catalysts capable of satisfying all of our lifestyle goals. This is essentially what the Atlanta Beltline did. It took underutilized assets and used them to reframe a more life-affirming future for the city.

The second hope is personal, and it comes with the construction of those changes. It's about our individual opportunities to take advantage of new conditions like improved mobility, economic activity, or affordable housing. When the red-haired lady chose a new route to the store, she was acting on this kind of hope. She wasn't thinking about the investments that had been made to support that choice. She was simply using them to realize her own goals. Infrastructures of opportunity like the Atlanta Beltline give us hope that we can follow through on our dreams to build a new business, live without a car, or bike to the park after school.

The third and most aspirational kind of hope is that our collective changes in the first hope and our individual actions in the second will add up to something even greater for our world. While this might be a universal hope for humanity, it can also be more specific. I don't know what everyone else wants for the Atlanta Beltline, but my personal hope is that it will redefine urban life in the twenty-first-century South. It seems as if this is happening anyway, especially when I look through my children's eyes. The newness of what I am seeing, however, makes me wonder what it means to be southern anymore, and how the project might make a contribution to an updated southern identity.

When I worked at Perkins+Will on the early design of the corridor, we wanted to make sure that its physical space, its vegetation, and its inanimate objects were appropriate for this place in the world. We proposed shading the trail to keep it cool in the hot Georgia sun. We used the granite from Atlanta's geological foundation for its walls. We amplified the experience of our rolling topography and the other unique features that we found along the route. We chose plants that would not require permanent irrigation, and we accommodated our heavy annual rainfall with sustainable storm-water management. We called for mostly native trees that are suited to our climate, and we employed their form, color, and fragrance to create a series of distinct and meaningful spaces. We expanded our palette of plants with appropriate cultural cultivars like the sweet-smelling Southern Magnolia, which, though not native to this part of Georgia, remains a tangible and generally positive icon of the South.

The physicality of the Atlanta Beltline, however, can do only so much. It is life, after all, not infrastructure, that forms the essence of cultural identity. That life, when it is lived well in the South, yields a casual flavor that is shared across our many divisions. Catching lightning bugs. Sipping whiskey. Eating fried chicken on a plate of collard greens for Sunday supper. College football. Flannery O'Connor. Outkast. The Muscle Shoals Sound. And gospel music flowing from open church windows.

As for the Atlanta Beltline, you can find some local variation of any iconic southern vestige along its route, but as we celebrate the South's virtues, we have to acknowledge that historically, our positive associations have been drowned out by active horror and passive discrimination. Our connection to the policies of separation and inequity, including sprawl, are as real as a hoop skirt or a yard full of rebel flags. It exists. It's part of who we are. And yet, thankfully, in our finer moments that have defined a better South, we have also worked as equals in recording studios, workshops, and kitchens, and we have stood shoulder-to-shoulder as brothers and sisters in protest and solidarity. Few cities in the South have a track record of comparable civic gestures like the hometown of Dr. King. Building from that legacy, these moments of decency, however brief, can be raised as our new model for civic identity.

By bringing people together and building new relationships, we also have perhaps the best chance ever to heal. As we reconcile our past and our future, we can become the South that so many of us want to become, and we can make sure that everyone benefits in our new model for cities of the South. The Atlanta Beltline, considered in this light, can become a circle of hope, a linear meeting ground, a space to be leveraged often and deliberately in ways that can celebrate and cultivate more moments of our southern humanity.

Of course hope by itself is less useful than hope when it is put into action, so it's important that we not lose our momentum. As we continue to break new ground, we'll discover that we're not working alone. We'll find collaborators embracing the best of the South while also building more ideas for our future. And as we construct this new life for ourselves, we have not only the opportunity but also the sober obligation to ensure that the city that brought you Dr. King's dream can remain a place where hope still means action.

CATALYST
INFRASTRUCTURE

AN ELEVATED RAILROAD CROSSED MY PATH NEARLY EV-
ery day during my year abroad in Paris. It had been abandoned, but it was
undergoing a slow restoration of some sort. I walked under it any time I
went to the grocery, boulangerie, or laundromat, but honestly, I didn't
give it much thought. Even though this elegant and rather conspicuous
structure that was over half a mile long and only half a block from my
apartment was about to become the mother of repurposed infrastructure
projects around the world, the only mention I made of it in my journal
that year was a naïve understatement. "There was a viaduct down [Av-
enue] Daumesnil made up of arches. Construction continued the whole
year to make the areas under the arches into stores. They were cool, but
it took so long."

Clearly, I had no idea what they were doing. I guess I was too dazed
by the immensity of Paris to really pay attention. When I went back for
a summer tour in graduate school, the entire brick structure and its more
modern quarter-mile extension had been fully converted into the Viaduc
des Arts. I learned later that these reclaimed spaces were conceived to
generate revenue for the city while providing space for studios, galleries,
shops, and other arts-related businesses. Up top, however, I found an even
more amazing transformation. The 2.8-mile (4.5-km) stretch of railroad

Viaduc des Arts, before. (Ryan Gravel, 1995)

Viaduc des Arts, after. (Ryan Gravel, 2010)

had been reclaimed as a garden walkway called the Promenade Plantée. Large trees and lush plantings enclosed its narrow walkway to form an intimate linear garden that was a striking contrast to the classic Parisian streetscapes nearby.

The Promenade Plantée offers a quiet escape from the bustling city below and an unexpected vantage point on the Parisian cityscape. It has neither the forced grand perspective of Haussmann's boulevards nor the meandering verticality of the city's narrow medieval lanes. Where I lived near its eastern end, the promenade flows easily above the street, uninterrupted by traffic, and lofted in the tree canopy at about the height of third-story windows. I was captivated by the idea that ordinary citizens could occupy such a special space and that it could contribute something to our lives that we didn't even know we were missing.

Following that second trip abroad, my studies in graduate school turned deliberately toward the role that infrastructure plays in enabling a life of both productive and unexpected encounters. This included a

Promenade Plantée. (Ryan Gravel, 2010)

design studio called "Incidental Infrastructure" where I met my future wife. We investigated adaptations to MARTA's train stations—Karen took Garnett, and I had King Memorial. We were among a lucky cohort of students that overlapped with professors Randy Roark, Richard Dagenhart, Doug Allen, and David Green, who pushed a pedagogical model that actively engaged students with the civic life of the metropolis. We worked on projects that could be real, and we connected with actual people in the agencies and organizations who might benefit from our work. We provided an academic laboratory for the generation of ideas that straddled that middle ground of imagination—bold enough to be worthwhile and realistic enough to be accomplished.

Our lab was set at the reasonably dense center of Atlanta's otherwise spread-out landscape, and while I was enamored with Rem Koolhaas, there were also other influences. One came from a reading assignment in the *Journal of Architectural Education*. It was written by Elissa Rosenberg, a professor of landscape architecture at the University of Virginia, and she delivered the challenge to me very simply.

> The relationship between urban functions and the natural environment has become increasingly opaque. . . . The ancient power of water, for example, was understood through its physical presence in many forms; wells and cisterns, street fountains, and aqueducts once occupied a significant place in organizing urban space. Now a vast system of underground pipes make water appear magically at the turn of a faucet. . . . Water has consequently ceased to play a meaningful role in the design of cities.[1]

I was hooked. Rosenberg's article took me back to Paris. "Georges Haussmann's rebuilding of Paris in the 1850s and 1860s perhaps best illustrates the ways in which engineering of the infrastructure became an ordering principle at an urban scale in the modern city."[2]

Words like those are tonic for infrastructure geeks like me, and my obsession with the role of infrastructure in the cultural development of cities has only grown with the success of the Atlanta Beltline. When it is done right, infrastructure can even be sexy. It is seductive—it dares us to go places we might not otherwise go. It is muscular—it shoulders the underlying weight of our social life and economy. It is brilliant—it stimulates us to express ourselves through art and literature, to start a new business, or to invent some new technology. More potently, however, it is sensual—infrastructure forms the physical and sensory space in which we live our lives. In a role similar to that of nature, the public realm made up of infrastructure can have a warmth, breath, scent, and glimmer that combines to create suitable conditions for humans like you and me to catch each other's eye, fall in love, share our first kiss, comfort a friend, or empathize with our neighbors by being present, even anonymously, in the routine of their everyday lives. Infrastructure gets us home in time for dinner, lights our way on a romantic stroll, and draws our bath for a quiet evening at home without the kids.

Of course infrastructure can also turn cold. It can limit our ability to do those things. If we want it to, infrastructure can almost ensure a dull and unproductive condition for living. The reason we so seldom think of infrastructure as sexy today is because we have value-engineered all the sex out of it.

Simply understanding this intimate relationship between infrastructure and our way of life, however, is not enough. If we want to change things, we have to do something, and sometimes we need a catalyst—a kind of urban intervention—to jolt our way of thinking. We need something to show us not only why change is needed, but also that it's possible. Strategic "catalyst infrastructures" like the Promenade Plantée and the Atlanta Beltline are doing exactly that. While they don't solve all our problems, these kinds of projects help move us forward in a way that mere visions or mere actions alone cannot. These are visions that get built, and through demonstration and inertia, they catalyze larger opportunities and make comprehensive change more palatable. In this way, they are preparing us—physically, culturally, and politically—to handle much more daunting change ahead.

In the years since our story in Atlanta began getting attention from other parts of the world, I've had the opportunity to investigate what these kinds of projects mean and why they matter. My research started with the question of how ideas from the Atlanta Beltline might translate to other places. I was also looking for similarly transformational projects in other cities. I toured everything from the Los Angeles River to the Rail Corridor in Singapore to the Harahan Bridge in Memphis and in most cases, I connected with local advocates working the ground game in their cities to learn more from their experience. From this field research, I have developed a catalog of dozens of projects and begun to extrapolate their lessons.

The motley collection of infrastructure that provides the content for this catalog is coming organically from every corner of the world and, without a doubt, these experiments do mean something. Frustrated with the status quo, citizen activists and progressive leaders are reinventing underutilized assets in hopes of creating a better life for themselves. Together, their efforts are capturing the zeitgeist of our time, and their progress has convinced me that a new kind of city is emerging.

At first I imagined this kind of catalyst infrastructure as a project type. For example, given any obsolete infrastructure like an old railroad, canal, or roadway, we simply need to identify an appropriate combination of new program elements like transit, trail, and wildlife habitat and impose them on the corridor. These variables, compounded by variations in scale, context, and rates of progress from conceptual to complete, do produce a truly awesome, if slightly impossible, matrix of results. It's also way too simplistic. What I've learned is that this kind of infrastructure really represents a way of thinking. It reflects a more intuitive and organic understanding of how to build cities for actual people instead of abstract census numbers. It also teaches us to reconsider all the infrastructure in our lives, no matter whether it's an elevated urban freeway or a simple rural greenway. Eight lessons have emerged from my research that I hope will point us in that direction.

1. THINK BIG.

Ambition is one of the primary attributes that differentiates catalyst infrastructure from ordinary public works projects. It brings to the

The High Line, New York City. (Ryan Gravel, 2013)

investment an intention to enrich our lives in multiple ways. It offers a breadth of program that maximizes the utility of infrastructure and, in doing so, attracts a wider set of constituencies for political and financial support. Ambition also generates a kind of attractiveness and urgency for infrastructure that compels us to believe in projects and to fight for their implementation. The very best big ideas find ways to strike that delicate balance between being bold enough to be worth our efforts and realistic enough to be accomplished.

Some of the most powerful big ideas come in small packages. Built in the 1930s to lift freight trains off city streets, the High Line is a remnant of the formerly industrial West Side of Manhattan. It was built as an elevated freight railroad running 1.5 miles (2.4 km) through the now-fashionable Meatpacking District, West Chelsea, and Hell's Kitchen. In 1999, two curious neighbors left a community meeting about the fate of the structure, which was targeted for demolition. They decided to save it if they could and started a grassroots movement of ideas that would change the High Line's fate forever. Their first big victory came before they even had control of it—an international competition in the summer of 2003 that branded it as a venue for big ideas.

Joshua David and Robert Hammond formed Friends of the High Line around the basic impulse to save this dark and mysterious structure as a new kind of park in the sky. Robert described their intentions to uncover its latent potential. "The competition would be just for ideas—and the ideas didn't have to be realistic, or fundable, or buildable. The competition would free people up to think about the High Line in different ways."[3] The Friends got an astonishing response with over 700 submissions from 36 countries. Ideas ranged from the expected rooftop urban gardens and social spaces to a less conventional variation stacked five stories high. There was one that proposed prison cells built into the High Line's structure. There was a waterfall pouring off of its length, a "crawling" black market that made the structure move, and a roller coaster built over the otherwise-untouched weeds that had occupied the line for more than two decades.

Participants depicted their ideas with everything from cartoon diagrams to photo-realistic renderings and they were mounted to standard-sized boards. All of them were then showcased at a fundraising event in Grand Central Station. The *New York Times* described the submissions: "They ranged from pure whimsy—several contemplated turning the High Line into a cow pasture and one of the winners imagined it as a 7,920-foot-long swimming pool—to visions as starkly provocative as the structure itself, which can be seen as a romantic industrial relic or as a dangerous blight."[4] The exhibit of bigger-than-life ideas captured the public's imagination and got the attention of City Hall. The *Times* quoted the Department of City Planning's Manhattan office director saying, "no matter what the design of the High Line ultimately is, something great will occur." He continued, "It's obvious from this competition that the conceptual is going to get us to the real."[5] It did. Along with virtually everyone else, the city bought into an ambitious vision that would ultimately transform much more than the High Line itself.

As that vision was implemented over the next decade, the project's ambition to elevate the role of public space also began to spread. New York City alone has been amassing quite an impressive collection of similarly big ideas that are inspired by the High Line's success. Neighborhoods across the region have been scouring their back alleys and forgotten corners to find any obsolete infrastructure or otherwise abandoned space that might be repurposed for transformative effect. There's the 3.5-mile (5.6-km) QueensWay in Queens that proposes a multiuse trail and greenway. There's the Harsimus Stem Embankment across the Hudson River in Jersey City, which envisions a six-block-long nature walk and wildlife habitat. One of the most experimental ideas is the Lowline on the Lower East Side, where visionaries have invented "remote skylights" to draw sufficient natural sunlight into an abandoned subway terminal to permit photosynthesis in plants and transform the space into the world's first underground park.

The High Line's influence now spreads far beyond New York to other cities that are also striving for new life. It inspired support for the 606 in Chicago, which includes a multiuse trail. In St. Louis, similar ideas have been referenced for the Iron Horse Trestle, which one day may offer views of downtown and the Mississippi River while also providing a valuable crossing over I-70. In Rotterdam, proposals for de Hofbogen would reinvent a reinforced concrete viaduct that was declared a national monument. As each project adds its own twist to program and context, this expanding collection of repurposed railroads offers multiple models for what residents might one day envision along Vancouver's 6.8-mile (11-km) Arbutus Corridor, Singapore's 14.9-mile (24-km) Rail Corridor, or Buffalo's 15.0-mile (24.1-km) Belt Line.

In what seems like a strange sort of infrastructural frenzy, it is important to note that Joshua David and Robert Hammond not only grabbed hold of an incomparable relic of history at exactly the perfect time, they also had the personal traits and chutzpah to bring their vision to life. Other projects that are similarly innovative and successful seem to also begin with people who see what others cannot, and you can feel the latent power of their proposals when you talk to them. They spend less time talking about plannerly topics like moving people from point to point or the percentage of greenspace in their city. Instead, they seem fixated on how the project will improve their lives and the lives of their friends and neighbors.

The Rail Corridor, Singapore. (Ryan Gravel, 2015)

I met such a visionary working on a promising proposal for an old railroad in downtown Philadelphia. Paul vanMeter of VIADUCT-greene, a group once organized in support of what is now called the Rail Park, told me about their vision for a 3-mile greenway made out of two old branch-line railroads, and he offered to give me a tour if I was ever in town. So when I was there in 2012, I set aside an extra half day to meet up with him. A professional landscape gardener, horticultural-ist, amateur historian, artist, and railroad enthusiast, vanMeter gave tours of the project quite often, and on that spectacularly beautiful fall day, he led me and a handful of other new friends on an amazing hike along the corridor.

We started along the City Branch of the former Philadelphia and Reading Railroad, which runs one mile through a magnificent tunnel below Pennsylvania Avenue. It continues along a second mile that is open to the sky but still below street level. The project's third mile is made from the handsome 9th Street Branch or Reading Viaduct, which had tragically just had its rails removed. The viaduct turns north from downtown, lifting up over the neighborhood and offering spectacular views of the city skyline. This stunning three-part sequence of linear spaces creates an astonishing variety of physical experiences and also makes valuable connections between several museums, schools, redevelopment areas, and the convention center.

Paul vanMeter passed away in 2014. I shared with him a sort of stubborn partiality for a vision, and vanMeter had no shortage of big ideas for the viaduct. He knew Robert Hammond and he understood the value of a strong and compelling story. He imagined the railroad transformed into "a garden of intersecting culture and wildness along the soaring and submersive landscape infrastructures that are the Philadelphia and Reading Railroad 9th Street and City Branches."[6] He described it as a "garden-park" that includes space for walking, biking, and other people-powered travel, but his emphasis was consistently on the experience and landscape of the space—"a greenway defined by its varied neighborhoods; its historic industrial character; and its exciting, existing spontaneous vegetation, carefully curated and managed with limited interventions."[7]

Philly's project continues forward with Friends of the Rail Park, and like all of these projects, its vision will necessarily evolve. The point that I want to make here is that a clear and compelling vision is critical for this kind of catalyst infrastructure. Big ideas inspire people, build momentum, and protect accountability. Some initiatives become even bigger by taking on expanded programs and tackling larger geographies. Projects like the Atlanta Beltline and the Underline in Miami are not only much longer, they include other core elements like transit and a deliberate focus on health and community development. Others, like the East River Blueway in New York, take on even more daunting tasks like addressing climate resiliency.

A mother lode of big ideas, however, has had me smitten from the start. The Los Angeles River is spectacular. It is sublime in the best sense of the word. Even in its existing condition, the river is magical because its potential for transforming not only Los Angeles but our national policy about the built environment is both immense and likely.

I got to experience the river firsthand back in the summer of 2011 when Leigh Christy, a former colleague at Perkins+Will's office there, introduced me to some of the primary players. She knew them well because she had managed a collaborative pro bono effort the previous year to reimagine the Piggyback Yard, a 200-acre (81-ha) rail yard and intermodal transfer facility just opposite the river from downtown. I was mesmerized by what they were doing.

Like the railroads in Atlanta, the Los Angeles River gave the city its original reason for being and nourished its early cultural life and economy, but many people today don't even know Los Angeles has a river. It was once a wild waterway with tributaries flowing south from the San Gabriel Mountains, sustaining life like steelhead trout, grizzly bears, and sycamore as its outlet to the sea moved back and forth across a geological timeframe between somewhere near Santa Monica and today's port at Long Beach. In the twentieth century, that wildness became a threat to the great city that was prospering along its banks. Raging floods

The Los Angeles River, Los Angeles. (Ryan Gravel, 2011)

devastated the downtown area in 1914, 1934, and 1938. In response, the Army Corps of Engineers began to channelize the entire 51-mile (82.1-km) river for flood control in the late 1930s. From the suburbs of the San Fernando Valley to its harbor on the bay, literally 80 percent of the riverbed was paved with concrete by the project's completion. Lewis Mac-Adams, one of the cofounders of Friends of the Los Angeles River, told me that the last day they saw steelhead trout in the river was the day they finished channelization.

MacAdams's big idea to get the steelhead back and restore the flood-control channel into a viable urban waterway started as a grassroots initiative in the 1980s. The group grew steadily as master plans were completed by the county and later by the city of Los Angeles. Other partners joined, building momentum for their cause over time, and to-day, the river's revitalization is under way with new projects "to protect and restore the natural and historic heritage of the Los Angeles River and its riparian habitat through inclusive planning, education and wise stewardship."[8] These efforts will transform what is now a linear concrete backdrop for every post-apocalyptic film coming out of Hollywood into a reclaimed civic corridor. It will restore an invaluable natural resource for both humans and wildlife, connect critical parts of the region, and reinvigorate communities along its route. Specific components of the project include flood detention, storm-water filtration, water quality, water re-use, greenways, parks, multiuse trails, economic development, fishing, and boating.

When I first visited the river and asked people about the revitaliza-tion effort, most looked at me as if I didn't know what I was talking about. Today, things are different. Mayors are kayaking in its waters and federal agencies are lining up to help. The river has become a collective story about how sacred resources defiled by previous generations now of-fer us a chance to make amends. It's a big idea and it's going to take a while, but as the river's new story unfolds, its ambition to reframe not only its banks but the entire future of Los Angeles is an undeniable asset in its chances of being accomplished.

2. INCLUDE EVERYONE.

When you're truly thinking big, you're already including others because the project is inherently too complex to achieve all by yourself. If we really want everyone to participate in the development of a vision and the delivery of an infrastructure that can be supported by the full diversity of our community, however, then the set of physical projects that makes up our inclusive vision must also be designed to serve everyone. When we look at the catalyst infrastructures that are driving this movement, we consistently see projects organized around transportation and its related public space, flood control and other water systems, and urban ecology, or what we used to simply call "nature." Maintaining a focus on people, then, our quest for inclusion looks at the range of users that we find along this set of adapted infrastructures.

The High Line and the Promenade Plantée can only be enjoyed by foot, stroller, or wheelchair. Dogs are not allowed, and neither are bicycles, skates, or skateboards. Most of the more recent projects like the newly opened 606 in Chicago, the proposed Rail Park in Philadelphia, and the coming Rail Corridor in Singapore take on these other people-powered modes of transportation. The proposed Green Line in Toronto would be fashioned out of a high-power transmission line, not a railroad, but it envisions a similar set of users. But even bikes do not work for everyone at every time of day or in every season. Winter cold, summer humidity, pouring rain, driving snow, the dark of night, visual impairment, physical disability, physical injury, chronic pain, heavy or cumbersome loads, travel time, and long distances are all good reasons to offer transit service where it's needed and where it's possible. It helps ensure that everyone can benefit.

The vision for the Atlanta Beltline began with transit at its core, but in the early days of our movement we were hard-pressed to find examples of what our old freight railroad would look like after being transformed by dual modes of transportation. The most relevant case study that we could point to was a lucky coincidence of sorts in Minneapolis. The Midtown Greenway began as a basic rails-to-trails project with a small group of neighbors in the early 1990s. They imagined a bike trail along this section of the "Milwaukee Road" railroad even before the freight trains stopped running. They got their wish, but because the railroad by that time was owned by the transit agency, they were required to preserve an alignment for future transit. By doing so, they created an inspired, if accidental, infrastructural innovation.

The Midtown Greenway trail was built in phases starting in August 2000 and has generated measurable economic development. It forms a 5.6-mile (9-km) segment within the Twin Cities' extraordinary regional network. It connects trails from the western suburbs and around the Chain of Lakes to several bus routes and the Mississippi River in the east, where for a short section it also shares its corridor with infrequent freight rail. Though yet unbuilt, transit continues to gain momentum, and its guideway remains protected. Alongside the trail, it cuts a near-perfect line across several neighborhoods just south of downtown Minneapolis, crossing below nearly 40 city streets and creating a lovely rhythm of overhead bridges and earthen embankments.

The Midtown Greenway, Minneapolis. (Ryan Gravel, 2015)

The Blue Line LRT and Hiawatha Trail, Minneapolis. (Ryan Gravel, 2004)

When I attended a conference put on by the Rails-to-Trails Conservancy in 2005, I joined 100 other cyclists on a ride along that route. We took the greenway and then turned south along the Hiawatha Trail, which follows closely alongside a light rail line. When the train passed by, I got the proof that we were looking for—transit and trail could comfortably coexist. We used that image everywhere.

Big surprise, I guess, that the Twin Cities, a prosperous region that consistently ranks at the top of lifestyle lists and that invests continuously in the expansion of both trails and transit, would come together to support such a project. But this movement of catalyst infrastructure is emerging in less obvious places, too. The Dequindre Cut Greenway is a similar project made from an abandoned section of the Grand Trunk Western Railroad in Detroit. Like the Midtown Greenway, it includes a multiuse trail and space for a future transit line. It is sunk below street level and runs for 1.3 miles (2.1 km) along the eastern edge of downtown from a point just north of Gratiot Avenue to the Detroit River. It offers valuable connectivity as it glides effortlessly below street grade, providing a traffic-free link for bicycles and pedestrians between the Detroit Riverfront, Eastern Market, and several neighborhoods.

It's tough to find examples of this type of converted railroad that includes transit already in service. The first one I found that also has a trail is the Orange Line in Los Angeles. It's made out of the old Burbank Branch Line of the Southern Pacific Railroad. It runs the length of the San Fernando Valley, and in 2005 it opened as an 18-mile (29-km) linear greenway with a wildly popular rapid bus service and a wide trail along its route. Almost a decade later, an example with rail transit began operation as the S-Line in Salt Lake City. At a much shorter 2-mile (3.2-km) length, this project opened in 2014 along a branch line of the old Denver and Rio Grande Western Railroad. Several other transit lines across the country, like the Blue Line that I saw in Minneapolis or the first phase of a different Blue Line in Charlotte, have casually incorporated segments of trails along their routes. Like the S-Line, however, a slew of new projects are very deliberately adding higher-quality branded trails to existing transit corridors, including the northward extension of Charlotte's Blue Line light rail and trail. Two others are the extraordinary Underline in Miami, which will soon follow for 10 miles (16.1 km) along the linear shadow of Metrorail's elevated south line, and the still-conceptual East Bay Greenway in Oakland, which would similarly follow BART.

The Los Angeles River takes a similarly inclusive approach for all of its layered networks. It optimistically includes naturalists, fishers, and kayakers among the more common user groups of runners, cyclists, and skateboarders, and it targets both commuters and recreational users. It also makes the conceptual connection between catalyst projects oriented primarily around railroads with those focused primarily on the revitalization of obsolete, degraded, reengineered, or otherwise modified urban waterways.

A hybrid example is the Lafitte Greenway in New Orleans. Once an important portage route between the Mississippi River and Bayou St. John, which leads north to Lake Pontchartrain, the line was converted in the late 1700s into the Carondelet Canal and became a productive and celebrated service route into the French Quarter for well over a hundred years. In 1938, the canal was filled in for the construction of a railroad, and soon after that it was abandoned altogether. Today, the corridor's 3.1-mile (5-km) route connecting Louis Armstrong Park to Canal Boulevard in Lakeview is finding another new role—this time as a greenway trail that also supports neighborhood stabilization and investment. Looking ahead, future plans include an expanded "blueway" concept that would replenish the corridor's historic connection to water. A new naturalized canal would support groundwater recharge, wildlife habitat, additional recreation, and improved flood control.

By welcoming automobile infrastructure into our catalog of catalyst visions, we see potential for a much larger impact and opportunity for an even broader set of constituencies. One of the best early examples is the clever adaptation of underperforming traffic lanes on overly wide arterial streets in downtown Indianapolis. Completed in 2013, the Cultural Trail is an 8-mile (12.9-km) system throughout the city's central business district that connects schools, shopping, and various cultural assets. It claims the newfound space of streets to create a high-quality, branded pedestrian and bicycle loop and link that integrates seamlessly with the city's bikeshare and carshare networks.

Few projects, however, are as inclusive of the car as the still-conceptual East River Blueway. Its proposed warm embrace of the elevated FDR highway in Manhattan stands in contrast to my knee-jerk desire to just knock it down. I understood the idea better, however, after speaking to Claire Weisz of WXY Architecture + Urban Design about the accommodation of cars into a more life-affirming condition. The Blueway is a broad community-based planning initiative that follows the East River waterfront for nearly 4 miles (6.4 km) below the FDR from the Brooklyn Bridge north to 38th Street. Weisz framed the proposal for me in this way: "Throughout the design process, we had the idea that the relationship between the FDR and the park just can't be a negative one. Of course we know that when you remove a freeway that everything gets better. At the same time, in dense urban environments like New York, there's a certain advantage of having conduits like the

FDR, and so I think the Blueway Plan is a way to look for smart relationships there."[9] The proposals certainly do that.

While the East River Blueway remains on the drawing boards, roadway redesign does have a remarkable built example. The reconstruction of the M-30 motorway in Madrid has created a 20-mile (32.5-km) multimodal corridor that circles the city's historic center. Begun originally in the 1960s as a typical highway, the project was not completed until the 1990s. By then, its negative impacts on the life of the city had already convinced leaders to reroute major sections of the highway into tunnels. The enormously expensive task of reconstruction was completed in 2007 and has both increased vehicular capacity of the highway and improved surface traffic by reworking the network of streets that connect it to the city. More importantly, the land reclaimed from the formerly at-grade highway reopened in 2011 as an expansive, 300-acre (120-ha) esplanade along the nearly forgotten Manzanares River. The remaining two-thirds of the loop also includes new parks, greenways, multiuse trails, and housing. In the end, the transformation of the M-30 not only has reconnected the river to the life of its people but has prepared the city for a more promising future.

That future requires more than infrastructure, of course, and our life as humans is further enriched by the life of other beings. When we start talking about the re-use of old infrastructure, therefore, and about the utility of parks and greenways, we can't ignore the role of nature. She has a tendency to reclaim forgotten things.

I swear I didn't realize that there is an amazing loop of largely dormant railroads circling Paris until nearly a decade after my year abroad. And it wasn't until I made a trip back to Paris with Karen in 2010 to celebrate our tenth wedding anniversary that I was finally able to see the Petite Ceinture for myself. This is the belt line of Paris. Its 20-mile (32-km) circumference is nearly the same as Atlanta's, and it encloses almost every recognizable place in the city. From the Eiffel Tower to Montmartre to the Bastille to Montparnasse, the "Little Belt" encircles all the museums and monuments and all the older quarters of the city. It was built during Haussmann's renovation of Paris in the 1850s and 1860s as a loop route to transfer freight and people between the major train terminals that were being built by different railroad companies on the outskirts of the old city. It also helped to service operations along the Thiers Wall, the last defensive structure built around the ancient center of Paris. Passenger service was discontinued in 1934 because ridership was shifting to the Métro, the city's modern new subway system as it burrowed under the grand boulevards beginning in 1900. Freight service continued on some parts of the loop until about 1993. Today the Petite Ceinture sits just inboard of the Périphérique, the city's perimeter highway, which was completed in the 1970s in the space created by the demolition of the Thiers Wall.

Conceptually, the Petite Ceinture's original proposal for adaptation was similar to that for Atlanta's Beltline, but various circumstances prevented that vision from being realized. For example, heavy-rail transit (RER C) already occupies the loop's western front. In the east, deep tunnels and trenches create challenges like access, security, and ventilation for people who are not on trains. Still, a larger vision moves forward with practical adaptations. Along its southern crescent, the 9-mile (14.5-km) first phase of the T-3 tramway opened for service in 2006 along the parallel Boulevard des Maréchaux, which was excessively wide and only half a block away. This required the reconstruction of the entire boulevard, which was transformed with a beautiful grass-track guideway for a high-visibility transit line, space for street parking, bicycles, wider sidewalks, and public space. Extension of the tram continues in both directions, roughly parallel to the Petite Ceinture.

As for the railroad loop itself, debate continues about running transit in its narrow corridor. Despite this, three short segments with a very different vision were opened to the public in 2013. They unveil a sharp contrast to the highly urbanized cityscape along the Boulevard des Maréchaux. With a deliberate focus on biodiversity and ecology, humans are restricted to narrow, soft-surface trails along these segments. Nature has taken priority along the abandoned tracks, continuing her decades-old reclamation. The idea is that over time this will create a *véritable corridor écologique* partly encircling the heart of Paris and offering homes for over 200 species of plants and animals. In these segments,

The Boulevard des Maréchaux with T3 line, Paris. (Ryan Gravel, 2010)

An undeveloped section of the Petite Ceinture, Paris. (Ryan Gravel, 2010)

stewardship practices like reseeding, reforestation, limited lighting, and the reintroduction of lost species help maintain the corridor for its growing population of birds, butterflies, beetles, microorganisms, fungi, and wood-boring insects, as well as the largest colony of bats in Île-de-France.

3. PROMOTE AUTHENTICITY.

Complementing an ethic of inclusion is consideration for the history and conditions of a place and the people who live there, if any. When we're engaging old infrastructure, chances are that it exists for a reason. It may be a railroad that expanded the industrial base of the city or a bridge that connects over the river. In sharp contrast to car-dependent sprawl, which has an uncanny ability to make every place look the same, these big ideas can leverage the authentic character and value of a place. Done well, catalyst infrastructures support our human desire for uniqueness, identity, and meaning in the places where we live and work.

The most compelling proposals leverage historic or natural assets like bridges, railroads, or rivers as central elements in a community's revitalization and offer a new way of life that is characterized by a reflection of that place. By making cities special, the design of infrastructure can make them more competitive. We have already discussed several examples, including the High Line and the at-grade railroad that preceded it, which first supported the growth of an industrial district on the West Side of Manhattan. Likewise, the Los Angeles River has played a similar role on a regional scale.

Another extraordinary effort can be found in Houston, where critical drainage features are connecting people to each other in new ways that don't rely on cars. I had read about Buffalo Bayou, but only after seeing it firsthand and connecting with some of the project leaders through an old colleague did I really understand the magnitude of the transformation under way. This city was born on the bayou—a lucky confluence of water, land, and two determined brothers. The terrain is very flat, and its soils do not absorb rainwater, which withdraws slowly, making even a short thunderstorm an urgent and sometimes dangerous celebration of storm-drainage design. The last and largest components in this infra-structure system are the bayous that carry all that water slowly out to sea.

Buffalo Bayou flows from the western suburbs through the heart of downtown and eastward to one of the busiest ports in the world. Buf-falo Bayou Park follows the bayou for about 3.5 miles (5.6 km) along its downtown stretch and has become a signature public meeting ground for Houston's social and cultural life. Renovations began with modest improvements in the 1980s and continued more recently through the complete reconstruction of what has become the bayou's namesake park today. Future extensions are planned for the stretches to the east and west. In addition to new parks, trails, public art, and wildlife habitats, ongoing improvements call for substantial additional investments in flood control, recreational amenities, entertainment facilities, and private-market ser-vices like cafés, bikeshare, and boat rentals.

This bayou is more than a playground, however. It is the very rea-son the city exists. Houston was founded in 1836 at the confluence of

Buffalo Bayou Park, Houston. (Ryan Gravel, 2012)

Buffalo and White Oak Bayous, and natural flooding of these bayous is an integral part of the city's history, including decisions about its physical infrastructure. Floods raged in 1915, 1919, 1923, and 1929. In 1935, a particularly devastating hurricane provided the most damaging deluge to date and became the impetus for establishing the Harris County Flood Control District, which took advantage of federal dollars to channelize most of the bayous in the region. "Politically, the timing of the hurricane was perfect. Federal works projects, particularly huge water infrastructure programs, were being created all over the country during the 1930s. In 1936, the US Army Corps of Engineers stepped in to begin planning a limited flood-control program that would move high water away from Buffalo Bayou."[10] As the city expanded in the twentieth century, most of the bayous were straightened and streamlined into sterile, lifeless versions of their slow, meandering, biologically rich natural condition. Simultaneously, the region exploded with car-dependent growth, sprawling relentlessly across the floodplain and lifting a powerful economy that made Houston the fourth-largest city in the nation.

With that last impression in mind, my experience during several visits to Houston has been something of a surprise. It wasn't what I expected. I stayed in a hotel downtown with access to new light rail lines in every direction. I saw fresh new parks and pockets of a more vibrant life emerging all over the city. And on one particularly enjoyable evening, I took a bike from the city's bikeshare and rode out along Buffalo Bayou Park to the west of downtown. People of all stripes were out on foot and bike, enjoying this new public greenspace in the city even before construction was complete. I saw the swell of storm water rushing along the bayou from a light rain earlier that day, and then just before sunset, I watched 200,000 Mexican free-tailed bats emerge out over the bayou from their home underneath the bridge at Waugh Drive. It was breathtaking.

This experience—including the delightful ballet of thunderstorms and swelling bayous that most locals seem to take for granted—demonstrates how the physical adaptation of a city's basic infrastructure, Houston's bayous in this case, can change the way we think about the places where we live.

Like much of the nation, Houston has invested heavily over the years in a civic brand of car dependency. But today, by directing some funding into a more life-affirming infrastructure, the city is rebranding itself—perhaps unwittingly—with a new civic identity that is tied to its unique place in the world. The value of this opportunity to reposition the city for the future is enormous, and it calls into question other capital investment proposals that would expand yet another freeway to support yet another mall. If it can continue to build instead on its authentic appeal, Houston will be better prepared for a future that doesn't care so much about malls.

4. COMPEL CHANGE.

When we're working on infrastructure, it's easy to forget that the physical design of our waterfront, transit line, or sewer is not our only objective. Our primary goal is more basic—to create opportunities for people to lead the kind of lives that they want. In many communities, this requires change, so when infrastructure is done well, it compels others—hundreds, possibly millions of people—to create a better life for themselves. It provides them with the incentive and opportunity to build an apartment building, start a new business, host a picnic, perform a dance, or tip their hat each morning when we see them at the market. That's the change I'm talking about. While new infrastructures might also create beautiful landscapes or make convenient connections, their central purpose is to compel people to bring their city to life.

When we consider infrastructure in this way, we can start mobilizing ourselves to action. We can compel change at an individual level and effect a greater transformation in the process. Given the construction of a new trail, for example, I may decide to ride my bike to work one day because I want to give it a try. On the second day, I do it again because it's cheaper and surprisingly faster than driving. On my way, I pass by the woman with the red hair walking with her groceries, which compels me the next day to stop on my way home for some fresh milk and bread. As dozens of others also start buying groceries in this manner, the store improves its access to the trail, compelling more change at a community level. We also find ourselves getting healthier, making new friends, and empathizing with our neighbors as a direct result of not going everywhere sealed up inside a car. Suddenly, an entirely new way of life seems possible in a way that it didn't before.

The ability to compel social and cultural change is especially powerful and important in car-dominated places like Houston, Los Angeles, and Atlanta, and it is striking that these cities are hosts for some of the largest and most compelling catalyst infrastructures. Buffalo Bayou, for example, has become a venue for regional cultural events like the city's Fourth of July fireworks, the Buffalo Bayou Regatta (which is the largest canoe race in Texas), the Dragon Boat Festival, the Anything That Floats contest, and the decades-old Art Car Parade, which follows annually alongside the bayou on Allen Parkway. The open greenspace, miles of trails, skate park, dog park, bat colony, boat rides, and public art collection have all contributed to the appeal of what is essentially a drainage ditch. Its new desirability, however, has not only sprouted new life and development in adjacent communities. In 2012 it compelled voters to support a regional referendum for the Bayou Greenways Initiative, which will invest $100 million into an overall $480 million plan to similarly transform all ten bayous across the metropolitan area.

As our physical investments begin to inspire new cultural expectations about the way we live, they also compel similar change in our politics. For example, early resistance from the Georgia Department of Transportation, which historically had little involvement with transit or public-realm projects, has shifted to active support for the Atlanta Beltline. The agency has put reasonable price tags on the two segments of railroad it owns, committed to an aggressive schedule to ensure federal money for trails, and also traded lanes of cars for new connecting bike lanes along thoroughfares like Ponce de Leon Avenue. Similarly, in Los Angeles and Houston, project momentum has helped compel changes to outdated policies on flood control. Infrastructure proposals with real benefits for people's lives were being held up by storm-water management practices that actually have negative consequences for the region. As a sign of our changing times, however, agencies like the Harris County

Flood Control District and the Army Corps of Engineers have agreed to—and in some cases are leading the way on—restoration projects and critical changes in policy. They may not yet have gone far enough, but then again, our movement has only just begun.

5. INSPIRE LIFE.

Design makes everything better. It offers much more than mere aesthetic—good design makes infrastructure work. And like the Brooklyn Bridge, truly great design transforms our encounter with public works beyond mere utility and makes it a life-affirming experience. It imparts into the physical presence of infrastructure the kind of beauty and respect for nature and humanity that would make anyone fall in love with their city.

In late 2003, inspired by the success of their ideas competition, I cold-called Friends of the High Line, asking for help, and spoke to Joshua David. We were modeling Friends of the Belt Line (FBL) on their efforts, and we had similar aspirations. They were following a parallel but faster path toward implementation, and even with significant differences between the two projects, I found a kind of camaraderie between our efforts. Not only were we both reinventing old railroads through organized grassroots campaigns; we were both up against impossible odds. Their success was encouraging to me, especially in the way they insisted on high-quality design.

The following summer, I wrote in our newsletter about Friends of the High Line's design team. As a designer myself, I wanted to stress the importance of their selection of landscape architect James Corner Field Operations with architects Diller, Scofidio & Renfro and planting designer Piet Oudolf for the project. I wanted the people who supported our effort to understand that the way in which our project in Atlanta was implemented would be almost as important as if it happened at all. I quoted the *New York Times:*

> The preliminary design succeeds in preserving the High Line's tough
> industrial character without sentimentalizing it. Instead, it creates a

seamless blend of new and old, one rooted in the themes of decay and renewal that have long captivated the imagination of urban thinkers. Perhaps more important, the design confirms that even in a real estate climate dominated by big development teams and celebrity architects, thoughtful, creative planning ideas—initiated at the grass-roots level—can lead to startlingly original results.[11]

Friends of the High Line was able to maintain those high standards, and the project has been acclaimed around the world largely because of their attention to design. It's hard to imagine that a more conventional outcome would have compelled enough people to climb up onto the High Line and make it the top tourist destination in New York City.

By drawing the public into a civic dialog through its ideas competition, Friends of the High Line embedded expectations for high-quality design into the very essence of the project, and this strategy has produced staggering results. With support from this extraordinary client, the design team was then able to create a truly unique, internationally recognizable, and incredibly popular social space. With a planting palette and walking surface inspired by the rhythm of the railroad broken by the wild beauty that characterized its abandoned years, they curated an extraordinary physical, visual, and in every other way sensual experience through a sequence of both open and compressed civic spaces.

At a cost of over $150 million for its first mile, however, the High Line may seem like an anomaly. Great design doesn't require that kind of budget. What it does require is a creative sensibility and an inventive way of thinking from everyone involved, especially project leaders. In the case of the Rail Park in Philadelphia, the vision that Paul vanMeter described to me certainly has this potential, and I am hopeful that the new project leaders will capture it because his perspective was uniquely inventive.

Of particular design interest to me is vanMeter's notion of "spontaneous vegetation" and "limited interventions," which reveals a persuasive devotion to the horticulture of reclaimed landscapes. All along our tour of what cannot be overstated as a stunning urban dreamscape, he rattled off the names of native and invasive plants alike, with expressive descriptions

The future Rail Park, Philadelphia. (Ryan Gravel, 2012)

of their colors, shapes, and smells in every season. He seamlessly intertwined this narrative with the story of Philadelphia's industrial heritage, explaining why these old railroads and these extraordinary plants had a reason for being there and how their combined story was an essential part of their undeniable beauty and their contribution to city life.

A few months after I met him, vanMeter gave the same tour to Piet Oudolf, who, along with his direct experience on the High Line, brings an appropriately fresh view to the redesign of old railroads that is very much in line with vanMeter's vision. "Like many former industrial sites, their poor and sometimes polluted substrate, which hardly earns the name of 'soil,' is actually very good for encouraging a wide range of plants; it is a counter-intuitive fact of ecology that stressful environments often support more species diversity than fertile ones."[12]

VanMeter took that notion to another level, proposing essentially that the real opportunity for Philadelphia lies in the inherent stress and complexity found not only in the railroad's soil, but also in the richness of relationships between that soil and the city's physical, cultural, and historical context. This surprisingly fertile condition, vanMeter knew, could similarly spark unexpected innovation in the social and cultural adaptation of these two branch-line railroads to improve people's lives. That was the genius of vanMeter's vision.

This integration of purpose and place in design is similar to what I wanted in Atlanta, and vanMeter and I commiserated as project advocates on the difficulties of achieving such a vision. For the design of the Atlanta Beltline corridor, our team was led by Perkins+Will and included James Corner Field Operations. We were determined not to end up with the same idea smeared around 22 miles, but simultaneously, we wanted the Atlanta Beltline to be recognizable from one side of town to the other. We saw that, unlike the main-line railroads that ride the ridges into the heart of downtown where the city was first founded, the belt lines slice across its rolling topography. This creates a sequence of very different physical spaces like wide-open vistas and closed narrow channels. In the preliminary designs, we then amplified that variation though planting strategies,

The Atlanta Beltline Eastside Trail, before condition. (Ryan Gravel, 2010)

lighting, and art to celebrate the diversity of the experience. Then, just like the few basic elements that make a railroad a railroad—its rails, ties, spikes, and such—we designed a restrained palette of things that would allow the new program to function. This includes the trail's material and dimension, the stations, bridges, signage, stairs, ramps, walls, railings, and all of the other elements the project needs to operate within what is otherwise an expressive sequence of spaces.

Without a partner like Friends of the High Line fighting for design quality, we'll have to wait and see how well those ideas are implemented. In any case, it's important to remember that the aesthetic of design should always support and prioritize its function. Non-designer advocates need to be aware that as much as design can help make a project more successful for people, it can also fail in this regard. Bad design can even prevent you from accomplishing project goals.

Beyond aesthetics and this kind of basic functionality, if we let it, the design of infrastructure can also push us further. Inventive designers can help expand its utility by tackling larger challenges like public health or social justice. The East River Blueway on Manhattan's east waterfront is still largely conceptual, but with the likelihood of another Hurricane Sandy, the design team claimed a role for the project in climate adaptation and resiliency. As it was described to me, the Blueway integrates relevant strategies for storms and sea-level rise as it stitches existing parks and trails into a more cohesive public waterfront. For example, in addition to improved connectivity for evacuation and emergency response, it includes various flood-control mechanisms and the addition of marshes and rock outcroppings to slow water along its banks. Public art and education programs would further support a dialog that is timely and uniquely provocative within this growing global portfolio of infrastructure redesign.

6. STAY FOCUSED.

I don't want to suggest that the details of how to implement these expanded expectations for infrastructure don't matter—they do—but if we shape our vision around only what seems possible today, we surrender our opportunity to structure a really great life for ourselves. Big changes and compelling visions require some leaps of faith. Sometimes we have to trust what we don't understand and believe in things we can't see. So as we navigate the complexity of implementing big ideas, it is essential that as much as possible, we keep the resolution of details in service to our overall vision.

To do this, it is important that our broad collection of advocates at least get on the same page about the most fundamental objectives of their pursuit. This is particularly true in the face of powerful real estate development forces, where less-well-funded public interests can easily get lost in the mix. The Embankment in Jersey City, for example, was almost demolished to make way for private development. Similarly, landowners nearly killed the High Line with their initial desire to tear it down. In Atlanta, a developer proposed a 3-mile string of narrow towers that would have destroyed the very thing that was supposed to change the market and bring about our community revitalization. He was going to kill the goose that was about to lay billions of golden eggs.

Real estate development is not the only challenge for these catalyst projects. General agreement on the overall scope of program for the project is critical, especially in early development. This challenge can be seen in the controversy over a proposed highway in Dallas. It would follow the Trinity River Corridor Project, which is a big idea to transform the river's wide flood zone into a new signature park with lakes, trails, and improved flood control. The river project will also spur economic development, increase people-powered transportation and recreational opportunities, and support environmental restoration. It will connect other regional projects like the expansion of the 6,000-acre Great Trinity Forest and similar investments as far as Fort Worth. It anticipates development along its downtown frontage, including dense, transit-oriented housing, office, retail, restaurants, and galleries.

The thorny part of its pitch, however, is the proposed Trinity River Parkway, a six- to eight-lane roadway that would be built within the flood zone to channel commuters past downtown. Opponents rightly argue that the highway would not only further divide downtown from its river and take away valuable parkland but also undermine decades' worth of investment in light rail transit, parks, and redevelopment. It would destroy the very goals they were working toward and would reinforce a downtown environment dominated by cars instead of people.

Whether the parkway is built or not, its story underscores the inherent challenges of developing a big, inclusive vision. Some ideas are mutually exclusive. While some proposals provoke healthy dialog and compromise is sometimes necessary, there are times when certain aspects of the project start to undermine the very essence of our vision.

Other controversies endanger more than just vision. They put the entire project in jeopardy. Projects built on old railroads seem to be especially vulnerable because of land-ownership issues, their typically narrow dimensions, and their utility for regional transit. I joined a tour of the QueensWay in 2013 and was introduced to its unique set of possibilities. At that time Friends of the QueensWay was a reasonably new start-up with a vision for a linear park and "cultural greenway" for 3.5 miles (5.6 km) along an unused railroad through central and south Queens. Abandoned for over fifty years, the railroad today is mostly an overgrown earthen embankment with bridges that disengage it from the life of city streets. It bisects a large park at its middle, and its southern end, like the Promenade Plantée but in a somewhat less elegant way, runs for half a mile atop a viaduct occupied by shops and businesses below.

As envisioned by its Friends, a new greenway and trail will replace the tracks, connecting several parks in Queens and spurring economic, job, and cultural development while also supporting small community businesses, promoting healthier lifestyles, and generally improving environmental conditions in the communities along the way. This vision has endured vocal challenges from a few small groups. One has argued to preserve the line in order to reactivate rail transit to Rockaway Beach, a service that was discontinued by the Long Island Railroad in the early 1960s and that the transit agency has no current plans to revive. Other groups are concerned about new noise levels along the long-dormant corridor.

Disputes like this are not uncommon—the Atlanta Beltline withstood early questions about its utility as a bypass for freight around downtown. Also, solutions are not always mutually exclusive—in Paris, the debate about transit versus nature along the Petite Ceinture continues. A group called L'Association Sauvegarde Petite Ceinture that has been advocating for its adaptation for transit is also trying to foster a dialog around creative solutions that can build consensus and accomplish *la mixité des usages* for the corridor as much as possible.

My point is that the need to negotiate the politics of urban planning is common with these linear infrastructure projects. On the one hand, the residents of adjacent communities should be able to determine their own fate. This is especially true where the obsolete corridor in question has been a primary contributor to physical separation, pollution, blight, and economically depressed conditions, and conversely, where its adaptation as a more life-affirming infrastructure holds the best opportunity for community transformation. On the other hand, infrastructure corridors like railroads, roadways, power lines, or waterways often serve a much larger regional purpose and once they are transformed for local uses, their utility in that regard can become far more difficult to restore. Project visionaries and advocates for change cannot ignore the pragmatic realities of these corridors for regional infrastructure networks, and sometimes they may even need to adapt their visions in order to survive.

7. EMPHASIZE PEOPLE.

Big, transformative infrastructure projects are not built by grassroots coalitions alone, but the most successful ones do find ways to capture and leverage the energy of the people who made them possible in the first place. Beyond that initial effort, citizens and advocacy organizations can remain critical partners in planning, design, and construction. Throughout the process, when we make people our priority and when people know we are implementing their vision, they will fortify our efforts with ideas, fundraising, data collection, and political support.

The most fascinating catalyst projects are often driven by people with a naïve understanding of the effort that success will require. "Our lack of experience was a key to the High Line's success," recalls Robert Hammond in a remarkably familiar sounding memoir he and Joshua David published years later. "We were so naively optimistic: we thought we could just get the ball rolling and it would happen."[13] It did happen, of course, but it took a Herculean effort. A decade passed by the time the first half-mile section opened and became the climax of their much-celebrated story. By the end, two ordinary citizens had created a powerful grassroots organization that was fueled by a generous and celebrity-studded fundraising effort and a smart campaign of political and technical support.

Friends of the High Line was able to maintain a direct and vital role in the implementation of the physical project. In Atlanta, we had been eager to learn from them, the Midtown Greenway Coalition, and other likeminded efforts. This new generation of people-focused infrastructure, it seemed, was also being delivered by a new kind of coalition of advocates. Other groups emerging at the same time included the Friends of the Bloomingdale Trail in Chicago. Now renamed the 606, early advocates there also envisioned a renewed conduit for community revitalization and have been able to remain a partner in the project's implementation.

Friends of the Belt Line did not survive fully intact as we had hoped, and I sometimes see where the role of organized community advocacy is missing in our progress. My last trip to Salt Lake City, however, inspired me to consider its resurrection. While I was there, I took some time to see the S-Line, which is a physically shorter but otherwise similar project to ours. Implementation had been led primarily by the transit authority and they had recently begun transit operations. It was the first time I could experience what it will one day feel like to ride the train past my neighbors on their bikes, or to experience the Atlanta Beltline's trail while a streetcar is passing.

It was a real thrill, but the real inspiration from that trip was Friends of the S-Line, a fledgling organization that has grown in response to the project's construction. A grassroots effort was born after the fact to ensure that the community is able to take full advantage of the project's potential

The S-Line, Salt Lake City. (Ryan Gravel, 2014)

by supporting appropriate development, improving connectivity, expanding the arts, and working on related initiatives. It's early yet to see their impact, but I was nonetheless impressed that people there were organizing in response to new infrastructure. I hadn't seen that before, and it made me hopeful that we might reclaim such a role in the future.

From my research, I'm more convinced than ever that project-based, organized, funded, nonprofit community advocates bring a lot of value to the implementation of catalyst projects. They push for critical concepts and unheard voices, and while they don't always bring funding, technical expertise, or political connections to the table, they do bring an intense understanding of local conditions, persistent political motivation, lots of noise, and exuberant celebration. They also have the ability and willingness to say things that government agencies cannot. Their demonstration of a diverse and enthusiastic base helps support the broad goals of philanthropy. Their commitment to principles other than the bottom line allows businesses to focus on theirs. And they provide a deep well of citizen advocates who can be relied on to support the ongoing and long-term needs of the agencies that will implement and operate these projects. Certainly there are occasions when their passion gets in the way. On the whole, however, organized groups of citizen advocates that remain accountable to project momentum are essential partners in any effort that claims the improved lives of people as its primary goal.

If we are committed to such a vision, we must remember to build our advocacy efforts around everyone, and this is especially important for people at risk of displacement. In many cases the infrastructural assets in question are located at least partly in low-income communities. The social and economic challenges and the land assets found there are also often the things that make the larger effort possible by attracting both public and philanthropic funding alongside private development interests. The Atlanta Beltline's tax allocation district, for example, was feasible only because we could make assumptions about improvement to the "blighted land" in the communities of south and west Atlanta. People there became involved in our movement and supportive of that funding because the project offers the kinds of solutions and opportunities they need. And because they have been such a critical part of our effort from the beginning, our definition of success is also measured by metrics that include them.

In New Orleans, disaster-related funding has uniquely flowed to the Lafitte Greenway in the wake of Hurricane Katrina. Envisioned as a catalyst for community revitalization in adjacent neighborhoods like Tremé, this money has allowed for a reasonably quick implementation of the physical greenway itself. Bart Everson, co-founder of Friends of the Lafitte Corridor, described to me how in the aftermath of the storm, people were being forced to talk to one another. He said it brought together "a diverse collection of people who cared, or people who now knew that they should."[14] As their effort matured, this new dialog proved valuable for the greenway. It built trust that allowed advocates to discuss their proposal with people who were different from them.

Together, they envisioned a highly programmed greenway and multi-use trail that connects neighborhoods, new parks, and economic development projects, while also promoting public health and environmental sustainability. Thankfully, the effort at least began with an inclusive dialog that has paid earnest attention to existing residents, many of whom still fear economic and cultural displacement. This includes a parallel effort focused on the revitalization of adjacent public housing, job training, and other community stabilization initiatives. It operates in partnership with the Sojourner Truth Neighborhood Center, which is located physically in the Lafitte Greenway.

It's too early to say how efforts to emphasize people throughout project execution will play out in Atlanta and New Orleans. Both projects remain organic and evolving conversations that are far from perfect. For now, however, we can at least say for sure that they have become willing venues for an important dialog, and that they are beginning to help us articulate certain needs for community voice and engagement in the implementation of this new kind of infrastructure.

8. BAND TOGETHER.

Not all catalyst infrastructure projects begin as grassroots initiatives, but their complex nature always brings multiple agencies and organizations to the table. Ideally, these groups band together as a strategic alliance to hash out compromise, improve project logistics, and explore funding opportunities together. They create partnerships and, where necessary, they cross political boundaries. They find accountability and endurance for the long haul to completion, and where advocates on certain issues may be missing altogether, catalyst projects can even help to establish and nurture new partners.

Because of its sheer size, the Los Angeles River Revitalization has a uniquely organic and multifaceted coalition. My former colleague Leigh Christy described it this way: "The City of Los Angeles is focused on a broad vision, but only three-fifths of the river is within the city limits. Agencies that have jurisdiction and interest over its full length are focused only on certain aspects of the vision. The Army Corps of Engineers, for example, works mainly on flood control and habitat restoration. Absent any one entity being 'in charge' of the entire river or its entire vision, a two-part strategy has taken hold organically."[15] The first strategy provides a proof of concept through the gradual execution of discrete projects like new parks, trails, or other things like business incubators. The second strategy shapes larger policy by embedding the project in the processes of various governments, including small-area plans, storm-water-management practices, and long-term assumptions about the use of publicly owned land. Both are supported through public, private, and nonprofit efforts.

The most visible partners are the Friends of the Los Angeles River, the Los Angeles River Revitalization Corporation, and LARiverWorks, the coordinator of river efforts at City Hall. Along with other advocacy organizations, partners in other jurisdictions both upstream and down-stream, and government agencies at every level, Los Angeles has formed a messy but essential alliance around an exceptionally complex and nation-ally significant vision.

The diversity of their coalition illustrates how a big vision can get people working toward common goals. By banding together around a physical project, organizations and agencies build trust and relationships that not only deliver that specific set of tasks, but also achieve more com-prehensive change over time. Ideally, however, not every good idea would require the 30 years it took advocates in Los Angeles to establish a grass-roots movement, build partnerships, and together, eventually achieve such an unexpected and monumental success.

As an alternate approach, the bayou in Houston stands out. Rather than emerging from a grassroots effort, early ideas for Buffalo Bayou were led incrementally by the downtown business association and later accel-erated by the Buffalo Bayou Partnership. The Partnership laid out an ambitious vision in 2002 and then essentially willed it into being over a remarkably short time frame through determined leadership, strategic partners, and deep-pocketed donors.

Projects with this "grasstops" approach can miss out on community needs and other opportunities for transformation. Their political stabil-ity and funding are also often dependent on the leadership of a headline organization, which is more vulnerable to personalities and politics. To overcome these challenges, advocates working this way need to be particularly proactive in seeking community input and establishing partnerships to address needs that they themselves are unable to undertake. A greenway project, for example, may need to seek partners for transit integration or affordable housing to make sure they are built in a robust and equitable manner.

In concert with the more technical implementation focus of Atlanta BeltLine Inc., the Atlanta BeltLine Partnership plays a strategic role in this way. It facilitates support in funding, education, and volunteer efforts through a wide range of partners like the PATH Foundation, Trust for Public Land, Trees Atlanta, Park Pride, Hands on Atlanta, and many others. Where there is need but no partner, it has also helped to establish and cultivate new ones, including the Atlanta Land Trust Collaborative and Atlanta BeltLine Health Advisory Group. The idea is to incubate partners where they are needed, but ultimately to hand them the reigns.

CONSIDER THESE EIGHT LESSONS a loose first draft on an open-ended proposal for shaping a more life-affirming infrastructure. There are no surefire answers yet, but by the time there are, our movement will be over anyway.

To see what I mean, look back 70 years or so when people were similarly experimenting with ideas for a better future. In a competitive spirit of trials and testing, they developed new and unexpected infrastructure. Alongside advances in automobiles, roadway innovations contributed to a visionary era that was emerging at the close of World War II. The concept of a limited-access interstate highway, for example, did not develop overnight. It evolved in fits and starts with innovators checking in on the progress of others and then building on that success with breakthroughs of their own. Standardization came over time as the kinks were worked out. Along the way, new organizations and agencies at every level of government were molded to support and implement what became a national effort. Businesses in every sector reorganized themselves to cater to changing expectations from consumers. Only decades later were freeways as ubiquitous as they are today, having already catalyzed a dramatically different way of life by that time.

In other places, or in other eras, similar experimentation led to similarly dramatic changes—America's transcontinental railroad, the subways of London, or the aqueducts of ancient Rome. These examples further illustrate how technology is either enabled or limited by the advancement of infrastructure. Conversely, they show how infrastructure's utility is either maximized or left underutilized by technological exploration. Sometimes the technology *is* the infrastructure, but in any case, together they push the limits through constant experimentation.

This tension between technology and infrastructure forms the space where we live our lives, and it matters to our health, wealth, and the way we spend our time. When the planning of infrastructure thoughtfully considers our lives as human beings, things get better instantly. When that infrastructure is designed for more than just our basic needs like moving around, drinking safe water, or turning on a light, it becomes a powerful tool for shaping our way of life. When we deliberately leverage the tools we have to accomplish our hopes and dreams, like economic prosperity, professional fulfillment, and a sense of belonging and community, we become innovators in this much larger movement of cultural experimentation.

We may not know where this new era is leading us, but the experiments outlined in this chapter suggest that change is ahead. To prepare, we need to recognize that the decisions we make about infrastructure matter to the way we live, and because we have limited public resources to spend on roads, sewers, parks, and transit, we should make sure that the outcomes of our decisions meet the goals that we have for our lives.

As we begin to articulate those outcomes, we may see the role of infrastructure become more overtly political. We will no doubt engage in those politics, and we should. We can't be afraid to look our neighbors in the eye, across party lines and other divisions, and do the hard work of developing a common vision for our future.

If we do, we'll see that in a collaborative, messy, grassroots, democratic kind of way, these experiments are reinserting the civic role of infrastructure back into our thinking and challenging us to make better decisions about the places where we live. The real power of these projects, however, comes if we acknowledge their potential as catalysts and then leverage them to achieve a much larger set of improved physical, cultural, and political conditions for everyone. The momentum of our time is already working in our favor. All we need to do is grab hold of it and engage more fully in the politics of change.

AN INFRASTRUCTURE FOR HEALTH AND WELL-BEING

I FOUND MYSELF WALKING DOWN THAT STRETCH OF Santa Monica Boulevard through Hollywood and East Hollywood that feels like a continuously peeling veneer of brokenness, parking lots, fences, and mini-marts. At exactly the same time, I was thinking about those very words as the opening line of this chapter, and I had to laugh because it sounds so ridiculous. It's hardly the kind of street that people walk along if they have a choice—especially at one o'clock in the morning. And yet there I was because when I travel, often the only time I have to explore the city is at night. In Los Angeles, I especially love a long *dérive* around the winding roads and sparkling vistas of the Hollywood Hills. On this particularly epic walk, I had made my way down from the Hills and was heading five miles east for the similarly dynamic but more eclectic streets of Silver Lake.

As I left the vibrant nightlife of West Hollywood behind, I observed that this lonelier stretch of historic Route 66 has all of the same ingredients. Storefront buildings frame short urban blocks to create a street that is neither too wide nor too fast. Buses pass by periodically, and although far from perfect, its assembly of sidewalks, streetlights, occasional trees, and other accoutrements creates a perfectly adequate public realm. I started thinking about health because after a long flight and a full day of meetings, it felt really good to take a long walk. Yet despite having all the basic physical elements of a healthy environment that we planners pine for, the corridor was no poster child for health. The public realm was working fine, but that clearly was not enough.

As I experienced the street at a pedestrian speed, it became evident that this stretch of Santa Monica Boulevard is a perfect example of the "before" condition for a powerful revolution that is already under way all across the United States. It will have radical implications for our way of life, and its changes will be most dramatic along streets just like this. They will become magnets for redevelopment because they offer competitive land values, built-in walkability, and suitability for transit. Health will be both a leading agent and a beneficiary of this change. In fact, health will create the policy framework through which revitalization of communities like East Hollywood are advanced.

This change will be led by visionary health practitioners who see their job as providing more than just the cure for disease. Their collaborators will be city planners, designers, vocal citizens, and politicians who will increasingly hold them accountable to this expanded definition. Even if only out of legal obligation, they will become more and more engaged in the development of solutions for our declining national health. In addition to related health programs, and alongside many other partners, their jobs will begin to include the spatial and economic reorganization of the places where we live.

This argument is based in a holistic view of health, which the World Health Organization defines as "a state of complete physical, mental, and social well-being and not merely the absence of disease or infirmity."[1] If we are to apply this goal to the places we live, then we must make sure that their physical arrangement, design, and program promote healthy behaviors and support all aspects of individual and community health. Among other things, this includes general walkability, transit service, and access to jobs and fresh food. To do that, however, and to achieve a sufficiently broad political momentum that can carry out the long-term, sustained, expensive, and impactful physical changes needed to make most American cities healthy, our approach must also be considered an integrated part of a much larger movement that includes complementary economic, social, and cultural levers for change.

THE WESTERN STRETCH of Santa Monica Boulevard that runs through West Hollywood toward Beverly Hills has already been successfully transformed by those levers. It was even named one of America's "Great Streets" for its "festive atmosphere" by the American Planning Association in 2011.[2] Along the boulevard's eastern end, however, where I found myself walking that night, I recognized a less desirable set of descriptors including personal insecurity, homelessness, and blight. Drifts of smashed soda bottles and cigarette butts heightened the ambiguity of health along the boulevard. As I laughed about the chapter's opening sentence, I wondered how we might better communicate its underperforming opportunity to support public health.

Although it has at least the bones of best practices in urban planning, from a health perspective, Santa Monica Boulevard is a microcosm of so much that is wrong with our expectations for public health in contemporary America. Once-proud streets just like it across the country, from Gratiot Avenue in Detroit to Memorial Drive in Atlanta, have become sad physical reminders of our collective stated preference for car dependency. This preference has left us socially impoverished, physically disconnected, politically polarized, and highly dependent on an expensive and energy-intensive built environment. It has also created new and very real barriers to good health. All across our metropolitan regions, long stretches of perfectly respectable urban fabric like Santa Monica Boulevard remain unable to realize their latent potential for supporting "a state of complete physical, mental, and social well-being." Tragically, collectively, and largely through our own doing, we are now dealing with new challenges like chronic diseases, escalating health-care costs, depression, isolation, and eroded social capital.

All of this is about to change and, not surprisingly, one of the most powerful drivers will be our legal obligation to public health. In the

United States, the same 1920s-era ideas about how to best protect the "health, safety, and welfare" of the American public that drove us to car dependency also solved—if heavy-handedly—many urban health problems. That's why I didn't see a single child working the late shift on my walk that night in Hollywood, and why I wasn't traipsing through raw sewage along the way. It's why our cities are no longer hotbeds of infectious disease or overly burdened with industrial pollution. And it's why any fair observation today of Santa Monica Boulevard's physical condition will describe a corridor not only devoid of those problems but well poised to help resolve many of our new health challenges.

The attributes that support this argument include the boulevard's relative compactness, its options for mobility, and its diversity of social and economic opportunities. A survey of any city will find similar corridors as appealing counterpoints to disconnected sprawl. As we begin to articulate their built-in potential to mix land uses, encourage transit, promote walking, and generally bring people together, we can begin to make a big difference. Planners and health practitioners can translate this potential into action, leveraging urban corridors as powerful prescriptions to combat the negative health consequences of sprawl. This role reversal for cities—from root of most evils to near silver bullet—suggests that the United States is due for a new legal interpretation of what policies and regulations can best protect public health.

The near-term prospect for such a new day in court may seem unlikely, but when it eventually happens, the long-term implications will be huge. Like the infamous *Euclid v. Ambler* case of 1926, which is the foundation for American land-use controls, a new legal interpretation of how laws should support public health will become the hook on which dramatic changes to our built environment become not only possible, but required. Even if we are not licensed health practitioners, you and I can help create a political environment that is able to support that legal challenge by openly discussing the now obvious relationships between those policies and our health today.

If inspiration is necessary, consider cigarette smoke as a relatively recent precedent for such a collective undertaking. While its dangers had been well known for some time, laws against smoking in restaurants, bars, and public buildings were only really made possible by a shift in public opinion. Rising awareness and public concern about the negative health consequences of secondhand smoke provided the political cover and impetus for new regulations. Over a short span of ten years or so, our lives were dramatically changed.

As we take similar steps to develop a new legal interpretation for health and the built environment, we'll face a far more daunting problem. By reframing the legal basis on which decisions about policies like zoning or transportation are made, we will see massive adjustments in land value. The inefficiency and inflexibility of communities built by sprawl, for example, will make them unbearably expensive to fix in any comprehensive way, and many areas will flounder in political turmoil. The seismic shift in our economy that follows such inaction will accelerate current growth trends toward areas that are able to adapt. In addition to economic, social, and cultural improvements, most cities and town centers will see positive outcomes for public health. This is not the problem.

The problem is what we leave behind. As America finally grapples with the true costs of sprawl, the challenges here will be suffocating. People with resources and choice will gravitate toward places with alternatives, and the ultimate burden of sprawl will fall disproportionately on the poor, who will have little choice but to move there. Geographically isolated and stuck in traffic, many areas will experience decline. With diminished local buying power, retail and other services will decay, making the distance between things even greater. Combine this with the rising costs of car ownership and no real hope of effective transit service, and it's hard not to paint a bleak scenario for the future of many outlying areas. In some ways it will look like urban blight in the twentieth century, but this will be compounded by the isolated nature of sprawl. If we do nothing, the negative consequences for these communities, including public health, will almost certainly be even more devastating.

Catalyst infrastructure projects can be conceived as prescriptions to combat these health inequities. Their advantages are obvious, especially for physical activity. Dr. Richard Jackson lived in Atlanta while he was the director of the National Center for Environmental Health at the Centers for Disease Control and Prevention. He's now a professor and chair of Environmental Health Sciences at UCLA and is one of our nation's leading voices on these topics. In a 2012 documentary called *Designing Healthy Communities,* he said prophetically, "I can write all the prescriptions in the world for high blood pressure and weight loss and I'd never do as much good as the Beltline has done or can do for Atlanta."[3]

Catalyst infrastructure projects also support other health outcomes like restored social capital and improved access to nature, retail, and other services. When they deliberately include additional levers for change, they become even more potent. When they help build a stronger economy, for example, they support the important health benefits for families associated with secure employment, stable school attendance, and better nutrition. In communities facing decline, these projects can open linkages with economically stronger areas, connecting markets for new local businesses. In communities facing growth, they protect greenspace and affordability, and they support healthy travel choices for people who would otherwise be stuck in traffic. In fact, the scope and range of their benefits are limited only by our willingness to build them.

Much more valuable than any direct health benefit, however, is our broadening expectation for the role of health practitioners like Dr. Jackson. Their research provides the technical basis of our new legal interpretation of public health, and their articulation of this basis helps create the political space for action. They empower the rest of us with knowledge.

As that knowledge changes our preferences, practices, policies, and law, the intentional reorganization of the places we live based on principles of public health will come easily to urban corridors like Santa Monica Boulevard. In sprawl, however, it will require dramatic and expensive physical changes. Perhaps the best precedent for health in this role is Haussmann's renovation of Paris. By draining low-lying land and bringing sunlight into formerly dark spaces, the grand boulevards catalyzed a whole new way of life for its residents that, alongside other economic, social, and cultural improvements, has had profoundly positive impacts on health.

Of course, Paris is only one example. In the eighteenth and nineteenth centuries, the shortcomings of sewage and sanitation systems in every pre-industrial city were amplified by new health concerns during industrialization. Around the world, challenges like population growth and pollution led to a range of new city plans. Whether through thoughtful ordinances in Stockholm, or pragmatic local slum clearings in London, the renovation of existing cities reflected a new global standard of progress at a time when public health was indistinguishable from urban planning.

In the context of our democracy today, this kind of urban renovation is more difficult. The need to engage and educate the public regarding these challenges is compounded by the fact that we have somehow managed to separate those two disciplines. One role for catalyst projects, therefore, is to reintegrate these discussions so that health becomes standard for every investment and every conversation we have about the places we live.

Of course, global resiliency is our ultimate challenge for health, and everything we do to shape our cities should also serve the health of our planet. In most cases, the actions or policies needed to counter climate change or adapt us to its anticipated realities also inherently support local health. This is certainly true for policies like curbing sprawl or investments like the restoration of coastal wetlands, but other less-obvious actions can also support health at both scales. For example, our ability to accommodate more frequent and violent natural disasters and the flood of refugees that often accompany them requires a robust, responsive, and integrated transportation network. We must be able to evacuate large populations in any direction and deploy emergency response teams, supplies, and services. Viewed locally, these events are simply more spectacular versions of what happens every day at rush hour, and we have already established the vital link between transportation and our health. If our communities are planned well, they can deliver positive outcomes both locally and globally.

I have no doubt we can do that. We can unleash the hidden potential of cities to set a new global standard for health in our built environment.

If we are serious about action, and about making a lasting transformation, and if we appreciate the gravity of the health challenges we face today, then we will advance this reorganization by utilizing all of our levers for change, including our moral and legal obligations to public health. Only then can we even begin to achieve "a state of physical, mental, and social well-being."

AN INFRASTRUCTURE FOR ECONOMIC PROSPERITY

EVERY VISIT TO THE HIGH LINE IS SHOCKING. FROM THE Whitney Museum and other designer buildings to hot local restaurants and celebrity sightings, there is always something new. Every corner of New York seems to be booming, but between Gansevoort and West 34th Streets, where the High Line connects block to block through the air, the construction intensity has a uniquely provocative vibe. More than any waterfront park or public square in the city, the High Line emanates a kind of good-looking lifestyle that, so far, seems to be timeless.

Even if that novelty fades, however, and as locals grow more and more tired of its torrent of tourists, overhyped eateries, and exorbitant rents, there's no question that the project itself has delivered, with great care in design, maintenance, and programming, a lovely and soul-lifting idea taken to a beautifully logical extreme. The urgent pressures of gentrification notwithstanding, the High Line has maintained a valuable integrity to its place in the world and has created a built memory of time that otherwise would not exist. By almost any account, its only shortcoming is that people just love it too much. With its hordes of doting fans, looming tower cranes, and new landmark neighbors, it's hard not to recognize the High Line as a new infrastructure of economic prosperity.

Whether that brand of prosperity can translate to other cities, or even to other parts of New York, remains to be seen. For anyone trying, it's important to understand that the High Line's success has come within a historical context. It may be alluring, but much more than that is required to achieve such an economic transformation. Earlier investments and revitalization efforts like the West Side Highway Replacement Project, Hudson River Park, Bryant Park, and Times Square all pre-date the High Line by decades. As improved public spaces, each with their own great story, they helped to create suitable conditions for growth in New York City, and they built a social and political context that made the High Line's conversion believable, at least to that first handful of people. Even those conditions, however, were enabled by the work of a previous generation that, beginning in the 1970s, turned around the city's notorious reputation for crime, population loss, and general decay. With just a trickle of gentrification by the mid-1980s, they led the city and the nation into a new era of urban growth by the end of the century. Since then, and with increasingly deliberate intensity, our growing national cultural interest in urban life along with effective local political leadership have made New York City a revitalized American powerhouse and a magnet for the 1 percent.

In addition to this historical context, the High Line's success has also been supported by other more modest, but equally impactful innovations. Concurrent projects that simply reclaim the space of the street for people instead of cars are making a difference across the entire city. Broadway, as noted earlier, has been closed to vehicles as it passes through Times Square and Herald Square, reallocating the public way to pedestrians and bikes by means of inexpensive measures including asphalt paint, bollards, and planters. In the shadow of the High Line, there are similar spots along Gansevoort Street that create adaptable space for crowds to spill out over the curb. The city's other park improvements, transit enhancements, bikeshare program, cycle tracks, and waterfront greenways all play similar roles. They create welcoming systems and spaces for residents, workers, and visitors alike by making a simple distinction in the priority of people over cars.

This subtle shift is no affront to the people who are inside the cars. In fact, these changes often improve vehicular flow. It's just a smarter approach to focus first on the needs of people. When we do, we find that, increasingly, they prefer to do things other than driving. They'd rather spend their time and money in neighborhood restaurants, stores, galleries, and hotels. In the process of doing so, they activate the city's sidewalks and squares, and this vibrancy and retail vitality then attract a talented and sought-after workforce to live in the area, creating a magnet for the businesses that need them.

Meanwhile, as every downtown across the country scrounges for some similar scrap of old infrastructure to infuse with a similarly good-looking new lifestyle, the question of whether the High Line's economic success is replicable remains largely unanswered. Any project can make physical improvements to a community, and if advocates have resources, they can hire hot designers to deliver beautiful and memorable spaces. As is true of the High Line, however, the economic success of those efforts will also depend on a combination of other investments, policies, and market demands.

The story is similar in Atlanta. The dramatic east-side improvements that are so visible today are built on investments and changes that began long before the Atlanta Beltline's Eastside Trail came to life. Most of the adjacent neighborhoods started to turn around back in the 1970s, but two decades passed before they saw any significant growth. By the mid-1990s, several loft conversions, reclaimed parks, and extraordinary efforts by parents to turn around district schools all helped build a blossoming cycle of improving conditions that stimulated a growing economy. This was the energy that actually lifted the Atlanta Beltline to life in the first place as a strategy to manage that same growth. Like the High Line, the Eastside Trail became an organizer, amplifier, and accelerator for change, making big investments like Ponce City Market possible within our lifetime.

This ability to amplify infrastructure as a driver for economic growth often brings with it a new set of challenges. The skyrocketing land values and densities near the High Line, for example, point to one of the dangers of economic success. A 2005 rezoning of West Chelsea allowed the people who owned land below the structure to sell their right to develop it to nearby properties, increasing the height of those buildings. This transfer of value was exchanged for preservation of the structure itself. The High Line's stunning conversion to a park in the sky might not have been possible otherwise, but the result has been taller neighbors than were previously allowed. Now a shadow-heavy density has forever altered the open vistas from the track level and the serendipity of neighboring small buildings that described its prior condition. An article in the *New Yorker* aptly sums up the dilemma: "As a catalyst of neighborhood change, the High Line has been to usual gentrification what a bomb is to bottle rockets. Giant new apartment buildings and swanky renovations cuddle up to its flanks, having routed tenants and businesses of middling means. But I see no virtue, let alone a remedy, in refusing to enjoy a place that is free and open to all, and terrific."[1]

The High Line itself is not the problem. The problem is how we manage change, especially when it happens quickly. New density was probably coming to West Chelsea anyway, driven by the broader context of growth in New York. For our experience of the High Line, the difference between tall and taller neighbors might be debatable, but for adjacent residents and businesses, the challenges of rising costs are very real.

Surely, however, the solution for the resulting threat of displacement cannot be to *not* create beautiful spaces, or to *not* invest in the local economy. The problems are primarily financial, and they require financial solutions. Our ability to find, create, and utilize these tools will depend on the same context of cultural and political conditions that made the physical investment possible in the first place. In New York City specifically, such an understanding might suggest the taming of an overzealous accommodation for development and the political will to capture its market value in such a way that it can actually underwrite the protection of scale, identity, affordability, and in essence, the very life of the city.

In Los Angeles, advocates for the river have a long way to go before reaching such urgency, but they have already set their sights on the challenges of change at this scale. A chapter titled "Create Value" in the Los Angeles River Revitalization Master Plan notes the need to ensure that economic benefits are "carefully evaluated, planned, and organized to maximize and fairly distribute the gains."[2] It does this by underscoring challenges like the potential for displacement, insufficient affordable housing, and the loss of industrial jobs. While it does not spell out specific mitigation strategies in any detail, it at least assigns responsibility to the Los Angeles River Revitalization Corporation, an organization created in 2008 as an outcome of the master plan. Channeling a growing anxiety about these challenges and the river's potential, especially in Elysian Valley communities like Frogtown, Mayor Eric Garcetti told the *Los Angeles Times,* "That's always a balance—everyone wants the good of gentrification and not the bad."[3]

The complex dynamics of equity in the construction of a new economy are frustrating—often paralyzing—and, unfortunately, we don't have to look far to see the results of inaction. When the first highways were built, they were also an innovative new infrastructure of economic prosperity, and they worked exactly as they were intended to. Nearly every new stretch of asphalt was as celebrated locally as the High Line is today. National planners drew a web of connections between major cities, and where highway off-ramps intersected small towns and once-rural roads along the way, they offered those places a ticket to the national economy. For its target population, this created a sought-after, transformative, and profitable suburban frontier. For everyone else, growth came at a cost that was manifest in displacement and decay far more devastating than anything we're doing today.

Largely uninterested, or maybe just dazed by the immensity of change we saw coming, America continued to mythologize the new suburbs, knowing instinctively that they could only flourish with continued capital investments. We made those investments, but even as our efforts drained the life out of every major city and spilled it into neighboring counties, we also began to see how, just like the High Line and Atlanta Beltline today, the most successful places were supported by a powerful context of other market differentiators. These differences began to distinguish between Houston and Detroit, and beginning in the 1950s, along fresh ribbons of asphalt, the country's economy began a slow national migration to the American South and West.

The urbanizing regions of the American Sunbelt became the eager beneficiaries of this national growth because they provided conducive conditions for change and reinforced a vision of the future that a lot of people aspired to achieve. The Sunbelt took advantage of these new lifestyle demands by offering much more than just a fresh set of highways. Technological advances in air-conditioning, for example, made southern heat and humidity tolerable as a permanent escape from northern winters, and a largely undeveloped landscape was made wide open for cheap housing to support America's burgeoning middle class. With a relaxed business environment, a lower-wage and non-unionized labor force, a lower cost of living, lower taxes, and fewer regulations, the Sunbelt made it possible to build a new kind of city unencumbered by the old ways of doing things. More powerfully than any northern suburb, the Sunbelt as a whole leveraged its new infrastructure and good-looking new lifestyle as a convincing context for economic success.

This argument is further supported by a nuanced view of the Sunbelt itself. Looking closely, you can see that the most explosive new growth was not found in the older port cities. Of course development came to the suburbs of Savannah, Charleston, Mobile, and New Orleans just as it came to Detroit, but the national story was written along the freeways of upstart regions with far fewer barriers to growth. It flourished in metropolitan boomtowns like Atlanta, Houston, Phoenix, and Los Angeles, which offered both physical and political openness. Consequently, they dominated American growth for the better part of six decades.

What became clear in this change is that the most successful places in the American Sunbelt offered the market exactly what it wanted. These regions built a vast and unprecedented new landscape for cars that incentivized the construction of a nearly endless vista of office parks, strip malls, and subdivisions. They further supported that growth with relaxed policies and open politics on a scale that older, more established, or more socially divided communities could not offer.

And by organizing themselves in this way, they appealed directly and intentionally to the older white male executives who were driving our economy at that time.

Not only did those market drivers ignore any question of equity, today they are increasingly inverted and, therefore, the physical places they constructed are proportionately less relevant. It is now more often the lifestyle desired by top talent, not executive leadership, that is driving regional and national growth. This more diverse workforce is moving back into central cities all across the country, but just as we saw in the Sunbelt during the last century, these young, educated, well-traveled cohorts are looking for cities that offer them the lifestyle they want.

By no means does this collective momentum away from car dependency suggest that we are going back to a pre-automobile way of life. It just means things are changing again. The mobility of cars is still desirable, but our dependence on driving has become a discernible burden in a way that it never was before. It's a pain, and our acknowledgment of this fact is creating a powerful new context for change. It can be seen in technological advances that encourage car sharing and will soon automate our cars to the point that we won't even need to drive them. It is becoming evident in a backdrop of alternative public works projects, including the reallocation of space on Broadway and other accommodations for bicycles, pedestrians, and transit that are under way in almost every city. And as this broad context continues to develop and drive physical, cultural, and political change, the most competitive communities—as always—will be those that invest in the people who are driving their economy.

For many cities, this target population is composed of what urban thinker Richard Florida calls the "creative class," a broad group "spanning science and technology, arts, media, and culture, traditional knowledge workers, and the professions."[4] Other places may need to define their targets differently. Some cities, for example, might more successfully steer their efforts toward students, seniors, or immigrants if that is their best opportunity for growth. Interestingly, and in any case, there seems to be increasing consensus among these groups for more urban and car-free lifestyles.

Urban areas have clear advantages, therefore, but even in places like New York that have been investing in these populations for decades, projects like the High Line are still needed. They are able to catalyze new economic, cultural, and social conditions that generate unexpected outcomes. By doing so, such projects call attention to public investment priorities and they help catalyze a public dialog about who benefits from the decisions we make and the direction we set with our infrastructure. While our first generation of prototype projects may not be perfect in this regard, they do begin to suggest both methods and urgency for addressing the challenges of change.

This experimentation is essential because people have always leveraged their infrastructure to create better conditions for economic growth, and despite its real challenges, growth is still a principal goal for most communities. So as we look ahead and prepare for change, we simply need to support those investments with all the tools at our disposal, including everything from zoning regulations to schools, in order to ensure that our growth is both sustainable and equitable. This is our most strategic course of action—to align the hopes and dreams we have for our lives with key investments and policies so that our communities can meet the changing demands of economic prosperity.

AN INFRASTRUCTURE
FOR EQUITY

I FOUND MYSELF SLINGING OLD TIRES UP ONTO A DES-
olate street called Estes Drive that had been nearly sliced away from
civilization by the construction of an adjacent highway. Along with
a handful of neighbors, I was standing on top of a pile of steel-belted
rubber that had been dumped down a low slope of trash. A million angry
mosquitos fought in vain to protect their habitat, and the murky water
that splashed on our clothes combined with summer morning sweat to
produce a hard-earned testament to our work. Working side by side, a
motley group of do-gooders—black and white, young and old, college
degrees and GEDs—we hit several dumping hot spots that day and made
a meaningful contribution to our community. Just about the time we
finished, however, we looked up to see a rusty truck rumbling around
the corner toward us. Its bed was stacked high with worn old tires like
the ones we had just picked up. And although its license plate was from
Rockdale County, over twenty miles away, nobody had to ask why they
had come so far just to dump their tires. We already knew the answer.

Our presence scared them off, but no doubt they came back at another time. On any other morning, the only potential witnesses for these
dumping grounds would be the hundreds of motorists hurtling by just a
few feet away, their gaze face-forward and their music blaring. It was in

heart-sinking moments like these over the course of many years that I caught a small glimpse of my new community's long struggle. I had chosen to move here and to get involved with the lives of my neighbors. But I really had no idea where I was or where this new journey would take me.

Karen and I ended up in that particular neighborhood mostly because it was what we could afford. By the time I finished graduate school at Georgia Tech at the end of 1999, I was well educated on both the broad geography and street-by-street subtlety of Atlanta's in-town housing market. With gentrification running rampant all up and down the east side of downtown, I had become increasingly nervous about the city's rapidly shrinking number of affordable prewar neighborhoods. In the year after graduation, I suddenly realized that I was naïvely renting half a basement in a Grant Park fixer-upper for a little less than my landlord's entire mortgage payment. But when I looked at current prices for houses on my street, I was shocked to discover how out of range this newly desirable neighborhood was for a couple of young architects.

Frustrated with the cost of buying a home within the limited geography of Atlanta that could pass as a thriving urban environment, Karen and I talked about moving to another city—to a *real* city like Chicago or New Orleans. Things were looking up for the central city, but there were really only three compelling reasons to stay. First, there was something about Atlanta's youthfulness and energy that for me was somehow able to transform its emptiness and other shortcomings into more of an opportunity than an insult. Second, all that fresh energy was becoming manifest in new in-town housing, office, and retail development, which was injecting new life into formerly abandoned landscapes and providing a lot of interesting work for young architects.

The third reason was a direct result of that growth. For those of us professionally engaged in urban planning, policy, and design, Atlanta provided a career opportunity that few other cities could match. It gave us the chance to live real time through a potentially dramatic regional transformation and to help redefine what a twenty-first-century city might become. Physically and conceptually there was space here for the development of bold solutions to nagging issues like regional traffic, pollution, blight, and sprawl. Atlanta truly was "a wide-open place," and it seemed possible to transform the city into the kind of community where we wanted to live.

So, in 2001, Karen and I began the process of looking for a place that we could afford. The housing bubble had not yet burst and the anxiety created by in-town land speculation was exceptionally high. Like most of our city-loving, upwardly mobile cohorts, we quickly faced a decision between a small condo in Midtown, a fixer-upper in red-hot East Atlanta, or a fine brick home in a less thriving part of town. But what really sounded the alarm on the urgency for homeownership was an article in *Atlanta Magazine* by an Atlanta writer, flight attendant, and local legend named Hollis Gillespie that I happened to read while I waited dutifully for my newlywed bride to finish Christmas shopping at Lenox Square Mall. Like me, Gillespie had "a moderate income and a festering jones for a home of [her] own."[1] But time was wasting.

> I finally reconciled myself to the fact that the only neighborhoods I could afford classified as close-in but uncool "fringe" communities, but that took some time. While I was reaching that conclusion, Kirkwood, Reynoldstown, Cabbagetown and especially East Atlanta slipped out of my price range like greased wieners. So I turned my eyes to Capitol View in the West End, just about the only community left in Atlanta where you could buy a house for hardly more than the price of the crack peddled to you through your car window by the neighborhood dealers.[2]

Seizing the same opportunity, and hastened by the frenzy of a housing market unknowingly on the brink of a slump, we settled on a little piggy-looking house in adjacent Sylvan Hills literally one month later. And while Gillespie eventually left the neighborhood, as chronicled in her seminal text, *Bleachy-Haired Honky Bitch: Tales from a Bad Neighborhood*, the deluge of "creative poor people . . . with their body-piercings and cargo pants, their retro furniture and upscale burrito breath, snatching up houses like pigeons attacking an abandoned picnic" continued into Capitol View and surrounding communities.[3] It was during this time that

I met Cathy Woolard and the Atlanta Beltline's vision caught fire among in-town neighborhoods including my own. Three years later we moved to nearby Capitol View Manor for a larger house within a couple blocks of its route.

My time in this community offered a twelve-year window into the lives of urban communities of color struggling first through a booming economy and later through a tragic recession. It was an essential part of my evolving perspective on both the potential and challenges ahead for the Atlanta Beltline. Through neighborhood meetings, cleanups, debates over rezoning and code compliance, and battles over recycling plants and cell phone towers, the cultural complexity of the city's historic demographic shifts and barriers became very real. New relationships and experiences offered a more nuanced insight into the long-term consequences of issues like white flight, redlining, and mortgage discrimination, along with the more current shades of gray that color seemingly unanswerable questions of gentrification. In this way, I found myself treading very consciously into the politics of difference.

Outside the rhetoric of a couple of political leaders who survived only by amplifying that difference, however, my experience in southwest Atlanta was overall incredibly positive. People of all stripes were simply trying to make their communities better, and for the existing residents I came to know, the wave of "creative poor people" into the community was only the latest change in four decades of shifting demographics. If anything, the young, educated, and not exclusively white new residents were bringing fresh energy and professional expertise to subjects like zoning and transportation that were increasingly needed. And when a new resident's arrogance about the abandoned buildings and lots down Metropolitan Parkway made the rest of us cringe, someone would gently pull that person aside and fill them in on the success that those lots represented. After decades of fighting the strip clubs and seedy motels, the community was winning, and in fact, our presence as newcomers was evidence that the community was improving. We wouldn't have moved there otherwise.

Others may tell contradictory stories, but for me personally, this sentiment was consistent with my general experience for many years in our larger grassroots organizing efforts all over the city in support of the Atlanta Beltline. In stark contrast to historic racial polarization, the reaction among Atlanta's in-town communities was overwhelmingly collaborative and positive. Of course physical, economic, and racial tensions exist at varying degrees throughout the center city and across the region. But in the civic dialog among in-town communities about whether or not we should connect ourselves along these old railroads, there was remarkably little differentiation between "us" and "them."

That point is astonishing, really, considering the range of difference around the loop, Atlanta's history, and the pace of change at that time. As in the other large revitalizing center cities across the country, newcomers like me were rapidly changing the demographics of in-town Atlanta. Traffic in the suburbs was combining with a growing desire for urban living to fuel a speculative wave of gentrification throughout most of the downtown neighborhoods. Many of us were living in communities like Capitol View, and because we were active participants there, slinging old tires alongside a diverse band of neighbors, the potential displacement of residents—real people we knew—was an important concern from the early days of our work. It helped to define the Atlanta Beltline as a neighborhood-oriented grassroots movement. As a result, the project was evaluated on the merits of its vision, even by those at most risk from the downside of gentrification. They loved it too; they just wanted to be around to enjoy it.

The neighborhoods of south and west Atlanta may have looked rough around the edges, but their potential was obvious to anyone who was paying attention. When the tax allocation district was approved at the end of 2005, even our naysayers knew that some version of the Atlanta Beltline would be built, and there is little doubt that our new confidence stoked the fire of gentrification in neighborhoods where change might otherwise have come more slowly. Despite the threat of displacement, however, people seemed to understand intuitively that the answer was not to deny communities better access to transit and trails, or to not improve district schools, or to not attract grocery stores. There had to be a better way to address displacement than to hold these neighborhoods down.

The problem was not the Atlanta Beltline. It was and remains the basic market reality that in a growing economy with increasing desirability of neighborhoods, there is usually a corresponding rise in land values, taxes, and rents. This additional cost of living then threatens to displace existing residents and make the community unaffordable for others who might like to live there.

Absent a larger political dialog or action on these issues, however, it became clear that these challenges were more likely to be addressed if the people already working to solve them became a part of the project's vision rather than organizing against it. Those of us working the front lines of our movement insisted earnestly that this was the case, and the organizations that represented key issues like housing affordability and labor were already participating in the organic, headless coalition that was cobbling the Atlanta Beltline together at that time. Georgia Stand Up, for example, was demanding community benefits agreements before most people, including myself, even knew that such a legal contract was possible. The larger coalition provided a table at which they could voice ideas about the Atlanta Beltline's implementation, and they did.

As a result, at least some of their message became embedded in the project's public vision, providing an honest sense of accountability on these issues. For example, with support from housing advocates, the stated commitment to lower-income residents compelled the tax district's inclusion of housing subsidies and formation of the Beltline Affordable Housing Advisory Board. The Atlanta BeltLine Partnership also worked with students at Morehouse College to compile a resource manual of existing tools like tax exemptions, mortgage assistance, access to home equity, home-repair programs, and other low-hanging fruit that can help people stay in their homes if they want to. Over the next couple of years, a few additional tools were put in place to support existing families on low or fixed incomes, including the Atlanta Land Trust Collaborative, which wouldn't exist otherwise. These efforts will not be enough, but they're a start.

As we continue working on that, it is important that we also keep looking ahead. The most obvious application for lessons about a more equitable infrastructure may be similar urban revitalization projects, but if we are paying attention, it's not hard to see an equally urgent and much more perplexing set of challenges. These can be found primarily in sprawl on both the regional and national stage, where our culturally entrenched political discord seems poised to disenfranchise almost everyone in some way. Like the flight of wealth out of central cities in the twentieth century, these challenges will be especially hard on families who cannot afford the luxury of choice when it comes to where they live.

For people living in Capitol View and most of the neighborhoods around the Atlanta Beltline today, the economic challenge is gentrification—*Will people with low or even moderate incomes be able to afford to live in these communities in twenty years or even sooner?* The term "gentrification" for this broader discussion, however, is really too specific because it is associated with affordability and displacement from local economies that are growing. We need, instead, a bigger and more nuanced dialog that includes the related issues of equity and access, which can also apply to economies in decline—*Are investments in our economy like roadways, parks, or business incentives being made equitably to support all populations? Do people in these communities have the same access to jobs, health care, and fresh produce?*

These questions go beyond affordability to highlight the challenges of geography in an equitable approach to infrastructure. They acknowledge that because distance naturally limits access, the geographic allocation of projects not only matters, it reflects our regional priority for equity. For example, we often see the need for traffic relief in well-performing areas prioritized over the need for a similarly robust economy in others. By putting our money consistently toward reducing congestion rather than investing in growth in other areas, we reinforce those places of privilege. Predictably, our investments generate even more growth and congestion, and the inertia of inequity continues.

As we rethink this strategy, we need to also develop an expanded public dialog and policy framework on issues like affordable housing and income diversity relative to our investments. This is critical, because even with equitable distribution of infrastructure, if we don't have appropriate policies to support our goals, we will only be reshuffling community divisions. People with choice will migrate to the desirable areas while people without choice will end up in the places left behind.

Historically, our understanding and dialog around equity and access for people with less choice has been focused on the fate of declining urban communities. But today, with rampant gentrification in many center cities and skyrocketing poverty in outlying areas, our conversation is expanding geographically into the suburbs. In this new environment, equity and access are finding an entirely new set of challenges inherent in the physical structure of car dependency. We have already discussed the difficulties of distance between day care, schools, jobs, and home, which complicates productivity, family time, and the delivery of social and human services. In a doomsday scenario, the people with the least choice due to economic disparity will be stuck in traffic or at the end of a cul-de-sac, invisible to the rest of the world.

As we try to avoid that scenario and invent a more equitable approach, it's important to remember that the suburbs are not what they used to be. The "open road" has been exposed as a mirage propped up by continuous expansion. And while the population in the suburbs continues to diversify, the physical structure of sprawl will remain essentially rigid. So if we want these new residents to prosper, we need to find ways to recondition that old way of life. We need to do something different and, to accomplish it, we're going to need to engage and empower people there to build a new vision for their future.

Perhaps no place better illustrates this need than Gwinnett, the next county outbound from my childhood home in Chamblee. In 1970 it had a population of roughly 73,000, and it exploded with growth in the following decades to over 842,000 by 2012. Growth in those first three decades was almost exclusively white, but since 2000, Gwinnett has lost over 40,000 white residents. Still, the county has managed to grow through increased racial and ethnic diversity, achieving a net population increase of over 35,000 in that same time frame. These newcomers have made Gwinnett the most diverse county in Georgia, and its many minority groups, primarily with ties to Latin America and Asia, have together become its majority.

Gwinnett is officially embracing this reality and is looking for ways to redefine an economy around its truly impressive diversity. A senior vice president for economic development at the chamber of commerce highlights that the county's "dramatic shift was fed by a rapid influx of foreign-born residents, who represent more than 120 countries and account for more than a quarter of the total population." He further advertises this new diversity in businesses, schools, and cultural offerings as "a soft landing point for international companies and executives transitioning into the U.S. Market."[4]

While it is smart to leverage these changes as an economic opportunity, it is not yet clear how the county's now-congested roadway network will provide a still-growing population with the same economic lift to prosperity that it did for the original white settlers. Because growth in Gwinnett has been so spread out and because voters have historically opted out of regional rail transit even for the county's most concentrated areas, its quality of life is completely dependent on reasonably free-flowing roadways. They are the lifeblood of the county's economy, but they are increasingly jammed. Upgrades can help, but they will be expensive and limited, and no matter what happens locally, traffic from beyond the county's borders will only continue to overwhelm its roadways.

This is not only a problem for Gwinnett. Regionally and nationally, in the exact same way, we are all finding ourselves stuck by the shortcomings of our infrastructure. As we move forward, our ability to reorganize around a more inclusive system will vary, but our common need is a more robust approach to infrastructure that makes equity, not traffic-congestion relief, its top priority.

In traditional downtowns or along strategic suburban corridors, the goal of equitable infrastructure can be achieved by simply organizing growth around existing assets and in places where redevelopment potential can justify the cost of new systems. Physical investments here should be paired with appropriate policies and incentives to ensure equitable outcomes. Where transit makes sense, improved service can reduce the cost of living. For residents in areas that are likely to remain dependent on driving but that are still well positioned and strong, strategic sites like old malls can be rebuilt with new streets, community gathering places, and dense mixed-use development in order to generate economic value, accommodate more lifestyle options and incomes, and eventually attract transit expansion.

In historically underperforming urban neighborhoods like Capitol View or East Hollywood that are shifting from decline toward growth, the goal of equitable infrastructure is similarly straightforward. Their primary needs are things like improved transit service and revived economic conditions, along with financial solutions for affordability and displacement. Where these do not exist, catalyst projects, strategic investments, engaged grassroots, and forward-thinking leaders can provide attention and momentum for new answers.

In the outlying expanse of sprawl, however, a more realistic goal is simply economic stability. Significant growth here would only create more roadway congestion, and meaningful new street connectivity will be cost prohibitive for most places. Communities will have to rely instead on methods that contain sprawl like growth boundaries, comprehensive buyouts, or other experiments. Strategies for improved economic access might include the loosening of regulatory controls to unlock innovation or the introduction of policies to support things like basement apartments, intergenerational families, and new models for co-housing. Technology will play an enormous role here by protecting productivity through greater reliance on home offices, real-time integration of transportation networks, and vehicle automation.

No matter which part of the region we focus on, however, if affordability is not protected at a scale commensurate with our need, people who require low-cost housing will do what they have always done to survive. They will seek communities they can afford, often those defined by economic stagnation or decline. Priced out of urban centers and other desirable corridors, they will reluctantly move to the forgotten edges of the region. If failing urban economies and schools defined challenges for equity and access in poor urban communities in the twentieth century, the social and physical isolation of sprawl will multiply those challenges exponentially.

I HAD A GUT FEELING that Gwinnett County's 2014 State of the County luncheon would be worth the hundred bucks it cost me to get a seat, and it was. Charlotte Nash, the county commission's unassuming chairwoman offered a keynote address that, except for her unique southern drawl, sounded surprisingly familiar. It carried me back ten years or more to those dinnertime community meetings and weekend workshops in southwest Atlanta where along with our diverse band of neighbors, we visualized a new future for ourselves. Nash wasn't exactly calling for a Saturday morning tire cleanup, but she was asking an increasingly motley crew of do-gooders to work hard and make meaningful contributions to their community. With the weight of the county's next hundred years as her aim, she charged the crowd to "get involved and be ready to work with us."[5]

Nash's attention to notions like "revitalization," "optimism," and "pulling together" was not only familiar. It was notable for a county that during the formative years of my youth had topped national growth charts with little concern for the communities left in its wake. Her language that afternoon reminded me of how much things have changed, and it helps me to re-conceptualize sprawl as changed—because it has. It's less white and more poor, and as we determine what we should do next in the region, Gwinnett illustrates a more nuanced view of who we are, both locally and nationally.

No matter what we do, any equitable outcome will require us to set aside our preconceptions and include everyone in our discussion—not only because we care but because everything we care about depends on it. And while it's too early to know where exactly that new dialog will lead us, what I do know for sure, after standing both physically and metaphorically on that pile of dumped tires and watching a new load come rumbling around the corner, is that our futures are inextricably linked. No matter what our divisions, we must all see ourselves as part of the same future and then work together to make a difference.

AN INFRASTRUCTURE
FOR CIVIC IDENTITY

THE AUTOMOBILE INDUSTRY POWERED DETROIT THROUGH nearly a century of innovation and expansion. It built what was once the fourth largest city in the nation, a global industrial powerhouse, and an icon of American ingenuity. The city become a symbol of the Motor Age not only because it raised industry giants like General Motors, Ford, and Chrysler; Detroit also built an amazing network of roadway infrastructure to accommodate its modern lifestyle. Streetcars and sidewalks gave way to wide arterial streets and miles upon miles of freeways. Elegant old buildings were demolished for parking lots, and downtown façades were skinned over with fresh metal panels and brightly colored graphics in order to compete with the future that was growing at the edge of town. Of course a similar story could be told of most American cities, but somehow the fact that Detroit actually fabricated the technology of the future seems to have emphasized its need for a new infrastructure with which to celebrate our newfound freedom and mobility.

To support Detroit's signature industry, local governments led a national effort to innovate and invest in roadway redesign. For example, because the speed and reliability of automobiles were limited as much by infrastructure as they were by technology, the city was among the first to pave a section of its principal street, laying a mile of concrete down Woodward Avenue as early as 1909.[1]

> The experiment was a success. Road engineers from around the country flocked to Detroit to assess the innovation, and returned home as converts, setting the stage for the rapid expansion of the nation's roadway system. . . . The new roadways also made it easier to build houses in outlying areas of Detroit, sowing the seeds of suburbanization and sprawl that eventually would empty the city core. And it bears noting that without government-funded road projects, the market for the new auto industry likely would have been severely curtailed. The entrepreneurs innovated, but it was government help that launched the industry.[2]

With the wind at its back, Detroit paved its way to an enviable new civic identity, harnessing the muscle, grit, and pride of its people to build an original industry now synonymous with the city's name. If only for a moment, the Motor City's investments made it a model city of the future.

Ultimately, however, America's enthusiasm for the automobile was too closely associated with its cultural desire to get away from the city— away from the sooty, crowded neighborhoods with their noise, crime, and social unrest, and out to the countryside where it could invent a fresh and less troubled lifestyle. The new highways not only enabled and encouraged that exodus, they served a devastating blow to Detroit's center. They severed existing communities with crosstown highways, eroded neighborhood economies and social capital, and ensured what seems like the city's near-abandonment today. Waves of middle-class whites moved outward along its highways, and in later decades, empowered by advancing civil rights, many blacks and others followed them well beyond the city limits.

Detroit's 1950s peak population of nearly 2 million plummeted by over half during the next sixty years while the metropolitan statistical area gained 2 million in the same time period. This subsidized shift to the suburbs left behind a city once called "the Paris of the West," with its baroque-inspired street plan of radiating grand boulevards that pre-dates Haussmann's Paris by over half a century. Detroit had harnessed the future, but the city itself was laid bare by the process. Catastrophic job losses due to offshoring and mechanization, along with the physical abandonment of blocks of buildings and nearly entire neighborhoods by the suburbanizing middle class, led to failing schools, closing businesses, and struggling institutions. The city found itself in a cycle of decline that seemed unstoppable, generating a new national cultural expectation for its fate and sealing its late twentieth-century image as a symbol of urban decay. It was still the Motor City, but instead of the future, its identity became symbolic of what the future left behind.

Fortunately, the world has changed, and so has Detroit, and the real-ity is that the city was never truly abandoned. It was redefined. And its new physical, social, economic, and cultural conditions have made it into much more than a spectacle of decay. They have permitted unexpected innovation and opened the door to an emerging new identity—another model for the rest of the world.

Today, despite Detroit's historic bankruptcy and the cheap shots from the blogosphere, things are stabilizing. The city's dirt-cheap real estate, weighty remaining architecture, and iconic spirit are attracting a new brand of innovators in the arts, in agriculture, and in business networks built around human relationships with corporate citizens and anchor institutions. Like other forgotten urban districts across the na-tion, but necessarily on a grander scale, Detroit is proving the point that when you're at the bottom, you have to be creative to get anything done. This kind of scrappiness and openness to experimentation are the seeds and fertile soil for transformative cultural change. You can do things in Detroit that you simply can't do anywhere else. Figuratively, it's a wide-open place.

LITERALLY, ALSO. During a visit to Detroit on a winter day in 2011, some feathery roadkill caught my attention sufficiently that I slammed on the brakes of my rental car. Even though it was midday on what seemed like a fairly major thoroughfare, the open road was so open that I was

Temple Street at 16th Street, Detroit. (Ryan Gravel, 2011)

absolutely alone. I parked my car in the middle of the street and got out to take a look. Lying there on a smooth blanket of asphalt was a beautiful ringed-necked pheasant. I had never seen one so close. When I looked up, I saw its pastoral habitat, which, if not for the remaining streetlights, fire hydrants, sidewalks, and manholes, could easily have been mistaken for a Michigan prairie not dissimilar to those trodden by the French over 300 years ago. What might have been farmhouses that dotted the landscape were actually lonely reminders of the thousands of buildings that once stood there cheek by jowl to support Detroit's roaring economy.

The bird's casualty was either a symbol of nature truly reclaiming this city or of urban farming gone awry. Either way, it got me thinking about the generators of city identity. Automobiles were the defining mobile devices of yesterday. Today, the constant flow of information and communication from the devices in our pockets is producing seismic shifts in the way we think about and construct the world around us. Once again, businesses are positioning themselves to take advantage of new ideas, and forward-looking governments are laying the groundwork to support that innovation. Together, they are reinforcing our changing cultural expectations about how we live, altering the real estate dynamics of the places we consider most desirable. As our auto-oriented culture did nearly a century ago, this new way of life is going to require a new kind of thinking and, ultimately, a new kind of city.

The good news is that we don't have to create the infrastructure for this new city from whole cloth like we did for sprawl. In fact, the best examples today leverage existing assets that, exactly like those pheasant fields in the middle of Detroit, are lying fallow everywhere in plain sight. By reinventing existing developed places, upcycling their strategic assets and infrastructure for a new and better purpose, we can discover all kinds of opportunities that we could otherwise never afford to build from scratch.

It was this kind of intuitive understanding of value that made people in Savannah and beautiful cities everywhere put up a fight for their preservation through the dark days of car dependency. It also explains why so many people in creative industries are enamored of Detroit, and how recent reinvestments there reflect a deep yearning for distinctiveness in the places where we live. Contrasting with thin-layered sprawl, the appeal of older places includes their social and cultural networks, physical compactness, walkable scale, architectural heft, and obsolete infrastructure networks that, as we have seen, now beg for creative adaptations.

On previous visits to Detroit, before my encounter with that pheasant, I had been shuttled by taxi from the airport. On that trip I rented a car, and with my hands on the steering wheel, the city took on a discernible feeling. My 2011 Ford Focus might as well have been a classic American muscle car, fueled by the streets of Detroit that were so consciously designed for driving. The experience was extraordinary. The wide lanes, huge turning radiuses, and vast neighborhood grids of one-way streets are designed to handle more cars than I could imagine, yet this incredible network of infrastructure is now significantly underutilized in a way not too different from Atlanta's belt railroads or the river in Los Angeles. The nine lanes of asphalt that are dedicated to cars along thoroughfares like

Gratiot Avenue, for example, create a great space for drag racing or for postapocalyptic competitions of any sort, but they're not the kind of place where you would prefer to raise your family.

Conceived as emptiness, the roadways are unsettling at best; at worst, they are a burden for taxpayers and a clear barrier to redevelopment. Interpreted as spaciousness, however, the city's empty streets take on the aura of untapped opportunity. This same network of infrastructure, combined with an appropriately open-minded political atmosphere and just a nudge or two of vision, could be repurposed in such a way that it not only transforms the physical realm of the city, but inspires us to rethink what this city can become. The reinvention of its roadway infrastructure could change the paradigm of Detroit, helping to accommodate its smaller population and smaller tax base in a way that actually elevates quality of life for its residents rather than simply reducing the infrastructure they are obligated to maintain. Perhaps no other city offers a more provocative and poetic opportunity to do this. Rather than simply abandoning entire sections of town, as is often proposed, more subtle adjustments to the design of its street grid can reposition this forgotten asset as the signature element of a more sustainable city future.

The beauty of this kind of idea is that it builds on the city's most authentic and valuable infrastructure through physical and cultural adaptation rather than simply erasing it and inventing a new identity entirely. It can remain the same Motor City that raised the auto industry and nurtured the musical legends of Motown, but with innovation and action, in the span of the next generation, its name can evoke yet another meaning and become a powerful driver for a more sustainable and modern identity.

That's why, for me, any talk about abandoning wide swaths of central Detroit is alarming. In the economy of the future, these streets frame the most desirable and viable parts of the region. Just like Manhattan's famous grid, they provide a physical structure that is flexible enough to accommodate any of many possible futures. The unsustainable parts of Detroit, as is true for most American cities, are out at the edge, where car-dependent populations are stuck in a disconnected composition of cul-de-sacs and outparcels that are virtually impossible to meaningfully adapt over time, and where the interconnected network of infrastructure found in central Detroit would be impossibly expensive to replicate.

Beyond the physical asset of these streets, it's also important not to separate the people of Detroit from their story. These communities survived the thrill and tragedy of the twentieth century, if barely, hanging on with muscle and determination when everyone else let go. They have earned the dignity of leading their city's revitalization, and in fact, if empowered to do so, they will be the fuel and essence of its successful transformation. Their passion and energy is desperately needed because there are still many barriers ahead. It is also increasingly clear that if they want to jump-start that thriving future, they are going to need a catalyst that can break through the region's auto mind-set and fuel the city's transition from a place that is built for cars back into a place built for people. While other cities go scrounging for such catalysts, however, Detroit is flush with opportunities—that's what makes it so seductive.

Because of this, my research on catalyst infrastructure has always drawn me to Detroit. So I was especially intrigued to learn about the adaptation of a 30-mile (48.3 km) loop of old railroads circling the downtown area. On my next visit I went down to City Hall to meet one of the project visionaries in the Department of Public Works. Then I took to the open road to explore the proposed Inner Circle Greenway. The transit component remains largely conceptual, but pieces of its trail are already built or under way. Like other loops in Paris and Atlanta, it's a big idea geographically, so the journey to see it took me well beyond the limits of my previous visits. And as I ventured out into the far-flung neighborhoods, the physical scale of the city's challenges became sublime. The place is beautiful and full of opportunity; it has truly amazing assets everywhere. But I was in awe of the sheer dimension of its sadness.

The scale of Detroit's decline has fixed the eyes of the world on the next chapter of its story, and anybody with a conscience is rooting for its success. Urgently, and because culturally we are all somehow collaborators in its decline, I believe we also have an obligation to help. Obvious conduits for support are policies and funding to help protect its communities, infrastructure networks, architecture, and cultural institutions so that future generations will still have those assets to build on. With time, these remaining resources can offer substantial value in the reconstruction of civic identity and a competitive advantage in the solicitation of a future economy.

With that said, like many of her Rustbelt sisters, Detroit is already pioneering much more aggressive solutions than most of us are aware of. With the fight and fans of the underdog, and born from the grit of necessity, the city is finding its way. A remarkable new place is emerging here, one where much of the country will soon again come looking for answers. In this way, the city of Detroit presents one of the world's most valuable laboratories for the invention of the future city. You might think we could never afford the cost of creating such a perfect condition for urban experimentation, but in fact, the people of Detroit have already paid that price.

If the scale of the city's overhaul, however, makes it a long-term proposition, we can look to formerly distressed areas in other cities for ideas about its future. Their smaller geographies and faster-growing economies permit bite-sized prototypes for what we might one day see unleashed more spectacularly in Detroit. While differences certainly exist that are often exploited by both the media and blogosphere, the similarities are also undeniable. In fact, when I stumbled into Slows Bar B Q on Michigan Avenue, which stands just outside the shadow of the long-abandoned Michigan Central Station, I had the sense that I had just walked into Brooklyn.

IT DIDN'T HAVE TO BE Brooklyn that came to mind when I walked into Slows. The Corktown neighborhood where it resides could have been any number of urban neighborhoods in transition—Silver Lake in Los Angeles or Bucktown in Chicago. But I had just visited my cousin in Brooklyn's Williamsburg, a district most recently synonymous with highly successful artisan-maker industries and other forms of cultural capitalism. Jon runs a "creative collective" there, and alongside dozens of restaurants that rival Slows, an array of craft breweries and specialty shops of handmade wares, local food products, and bespoke clothing, his performance dance and public art workshop called the Windmill Factory fits into an eclectic but beautiful juxtaposition of old and new. Ideas comingle on the sidewalks, and community is formed within a physical space that has many layers of stories to tell. It represents exactly the kind of urban reinvention that so many Americans are craving and trying to replicate in their own hometowns. And while questions of equity, access, affordability, and diversity are increasingly urgent here, it seems hard to argue that this kind of reoccupation is worse than just watching the city fall apart.

It's also important to remember that Williamsburg's bearded, hand-crafted, fixed-gear story is only the latest yarn in Brooklyn's cultural tapestry, and the hipster aesthetic found here or in Corktown is not a required ingredient for urban innovation. Notwithstanding its skyrocketing rents and new waterfront towers down by the East River, Williamsburg's disposition for local businesses, products, people, and stories translates beyond style and reflects a fitting model for the forlorn downtowns and industrial districts of any small town or city. These efforts leverage existing assets like dilapidated old buildings along with emerging technologies to support a way of life that, unlike historic urban renewal initiatives, is fundamentally sustainable and economically positive. Their attention to small industry, the arts, and local food and business embraces city life in a powerful way, and while the intensity here helps to illustrate the opportunities and challenges for revitalization on a large scale, more modest variations can also be found in cities as diverse as Albuquerque and Chattanooga. Because of this, we should not underestimate what creative people are doing here. They are helping to reshape our cultural expectations for living, and they are defining a positive urban identity for America, which is good for a lot of reasons.

We can see through these examples that the accumulated assets of older urban districts across the country are increasingly enlisted by our cultural momentum to the front lines of innovation. This includes underutilized infrastructure, which, because it is so embedded in the identity of place, can help differentiate that otherwise familiar aesthetic found in Corktown, Williamsburg, and Silver Lake. In any case, it's apparent that whether we are talking about the sublime street grid of Detroit, Atlanta's adventurous railroads, or the unruly Los Angeles River, the low-hanging fruits of opportunity are in the places that can most easily meet our changing market demands.

Unlike the thinness of sprawl, the draw of these places is that they are already built upon layers of shared infrastructure networks. Their history, geography, topography, and climate have already resulted in unique collections of physical spaces. They have already been occupied by people in both expected and unexpected ways, both successfully and unsuccessfully over time. They already have an adaptable public realm, economy, culture, and social life to build on, and more than that, all of these attributes add up to places with their own special identity.

This identity is important because it is what we are all yearning for today. Tired of placelessness, people want to live and work in communities that matter. That's Detroit's strong suit—it matters. And as we have watched its identity be redefined over the last century from a model city of the future to economic disaster and decline to a more recent reputation for innovation and renewal, we can begin to learn from its example. We can begin to see more clearly the opportunity for a conscious approach to civic identity, and we can see the role of infrastructure in that effort. We may not know exactly what it means for the juxtaposition of cultural creatives and waterfront towers, which can also be found in Detroit, but we can certainly see that it matters, and we can identify ways to engage.

Regionally and nationally, as our access to technology and our desire for authenticity drive changing expectations for our lives, we will be developing a new brand of ingenuity in the design and creation of place. If we do it well, we'll not only leverage existing infrastructure, architecture, and city plans, we'll unleash the human capital of the places we live—in Detroit, Brooklyn, sprawl, and everywhere—and we'll engage them more assertively in the construction of our physical world.

UP
AHEAD

WHEN I THINK ABOUT THE ORIGINAL PROPOSAL FOR adapting Atlanta's belt line railroads for a new purpose, I like to imagine some gentlemen city planners dressed in suits and standing in the street near my old house on Manford Road in southwest Atlanta. It's 1952, and they're leaning against the hood of a convertible Buick Roadmaster while they discuss and assess the conditions of the changing world around them. They smartly anticipate that the industries along the belt lines will shift their freight from trains to trucks. They predict with precision the negative impacts those trucks will have on neighborhoods throughout the city. They foresee with clarity that many industries will eventually leave the city, seduced by the easy flow of the ever-expanding highways that they themselves are planning. They grasp at straws for what to do, developing an idea that in retrospect seems both visionary and naïve.

Their concept will never be built, but over the next ten years, as their predictions about this ring of industry are realized, I imagine they still think about what might have happened if it had. I bet they continue to meet from time to time, perhaps at Manuel's Tavern, which opens just a couple of years later and becomes a place for people who care about the city's future. They stand there, beers in hand, staring with their eyes wide open, yet essentially powerless to do anything about the tsunami of change that is headed their way. Nostalgia and good intentions, it seems, are no defense against the tremendous cultural momentum of the twentieth century.

My anecdote may be fiction, but the predictions and proposal were real. The idea was called the Inner Belt Highway and it was part of the Up Ahead regional plan of 1952. It proposed that the four belt lines, almost in their entirety, be remade as a new loop route for trucks circling downtown. It would connect the struggling old ring of industries to the new network of highways that were being plowed through the central city.[1] As awful as this would have been for the communities along the way, the idea seems to have been the only attempt by city planners at the time to protect the viability of in-town industrial land. Against a backdrop that might be characterized retrospectively by neglect and even hostility for the center city, the loop highway seems almost refreshing.

Far more visionary, perhaps, is that the Inner Belt Highway proposal was paired with another new loop called the Outer Belt Highway to be located several miles outside of town.[2] With the intention of creating a much larger regional industrial belt, traffic on the outer loop was also planned primarily for trucks, and it included a parallel belt railroad. Together they would connect the spokes of new highways and existing mainline railroads coming out of downtown in every direction.[3] Remarkably, these prophetic planners also called for the outer loop to serve as a sort of growth boundary for the region.[4]

That last point might have been a minor suggestion on their part, but take a minute to imagine if that had happened. It's genius. Metropolitan Atlanta would be a very different place if those gentlemen planners had had their way. But when a version of the Outer Belt Highway was actually implemented a decade later as I-285, access was not limited to trucks; its companion belt railroad was never built; and most critically, the policies required to support the growth boundary were never put in place.

Standing on Manford Road today, it's not hard to feel like one of those planners looking wide-eyed at the changing world around us. Instead of a few white men around the hood of a convertible, however, a much more diverse coalition is connected by smartphones to an even larger assembly of citizen-planners and thought leaders around the world. We can see very clearly that a similar tsunami of change is coming directly toward us. Like the wave that resulted in sprawl, it is the confluence of many forces and it will be nearly impossible for us to resist. Looking ahead, with our eyes wide open at the repercussions that these changes will have on the metropolis sprawled before us, it seems as if we are powerless to do anything about them, but we're not.

SIX DECADES OF BUILDING a physical environment organized primarily around cars instead of people has profoundly changed us. The serious and intransigent problems facing our country today are just now beginning to sink in. While they may yet go unnoticed in Congress or in state legislatures, they are increasingly evident in corporate conference rooms and around family dinner tables.

In the five decades since Jane Jacobs wrote her landmark book, *The Death and Life of Great American Cities,* the physical growth of our metropolitan areas has been defined primarily by the forces she was fighting against. She was our preeminent citizen-planner and community activist. She fought with pragmatism, not nostalgia, in defense of the essential inner workings of public life that make our cities worth living in. The places she wrote about were still coherent communities that were only just beginning to unravel under the devastating acts of highway construction, displacement, and urban renewal. Her world and her counsel were sensible, but unfortunately, we did not heed her advice. Instead, we built a world that is transformed by those practices, now spread across a vast landscape and embedded soundly in our cultural expectations. It is not likely that we will ever quite make it back.

During that time of truly revolutionary change, there have been generations of people, including myself, who grew up with the shopping mall as the highest standard for how we should live. Office parks, big-box retail, and superblocks pervaded our formative years. Most of us never went shopping in a vibrant downtown district, rode transit on a regular basis, or enjoyed the "sidewalk ballet" that Jacobs so eloquently described in 1961.[5] Sure, she and thousands of lesser-known heroes understood what was at stake and fought valiantly to improve urban conditions rather than abandon them, but ultimately, as it was for those gentlemen planners, the cultural weight of the century was too much for them to bear.

Even so, and with ironic clarity, we can recognize the story of sprawl that followed as an insightful roadmap for our future. After all, what happened last century was not some grand conspiracy. It emerged incrementally as a decades-long cultural and political momentum—a logical response to a vexing set of physical and social conditions. The regions that we live in today are the result of both the good and the bad consequences of millions of individual decisions. So it is strategic for us to recognize that while there was plenty of supporting ideology being brandished about at the time, the real momentum behind sprawl was changing consumer demands.

Changing cultural conditions led to changes in public policy, which led to dramatic physical changes in the way we built our cities, which reinforced further cultural change. Today, in the exact same way, we have the opportunity to harness a similar cycle of change and create the kind of cities that we have been looking for. But before we jump headlong into polarized, partisan political debates about exactly what those changes should be, it will be helpful if we first answer two essential questions. We should ask ourselves, *What kind of place do we want to live in?* and with the assumption that there is more than one right answer, *How can we start to build that vision?*

We need honest answers and we need them urgently, because as I look wide-eyed at the future, holding my own beer at Manuel's Tavern, which is about to become engulfed in a new mixed-use development, it would be hard to miss the change that is coming in our direction. Acknowledging that, and with the presumption that we'd all like to harness its energy to accomplish our goals for our lives, I suggest we start working in earnest. We don't need to know exactly where we're going, and we don't even need to make a conscious decision. Like the people of Atlanta who fell in love with a vision that then compelled them to action, we simply need to start moving.

With a sort of subconscious strategy, and in response to desire more than logic, hundreds of people thrust the Atlanta Beltline to the forefront of local policy and investment initiatives through a collective intuition—an unspoken, unchoreographed, and unbranded sense of common purpose. They didn't buy into an ideology about urban planning or catalyst infrastructure. They simply recognized the many ways that this particular proposal could improve their lives. They claimed ownership of making it happen, piling on some more ideas of their own. And with every expansion of its vision, the project not only accommodated new goals, it reinforced our changing consumer demands.

In a similar way, we can't sit back and expect someone else to shape the world on our behalf. We have to look out for ourselves and, in the face of dramatic regional and cultural change, build communities that we actually want to live in. To start this process, all we have to do is look ahead, step forward, define what we want, and then start working together.

If we want our actions to achieve the most thoughtful and prosperous outcome, we need to forget our tired old arguments about traffic, pollution, blight, and sprawl, and instead decide that those conditions are now assets for the transformation of our communities into something far more interesting than anything we've seen so far. We need to accept the mistakes of our past—mourn, memorialize, and mitigate them if necessary—but then claim the opportunity that they offer to improve our lives before we get drowned by change. Let's acknowledge the terrifying tsunami that is inevitably coming toward us and then decide to leverage its energy to reorganize our way of life.

A thoughtful reorganization will only be possible if we can articulate a future that, along with the visions of our friends and neighbors, is worth our collective effort. We can probably agree on places described as resilient, connected, mobile, healthy, sustainable, economically thriving, and diverse. But these adjectives are just a starting place. They're talking points, not solutions. If we want a vision that is strong enough to compel action, we need to get specific, deliver some proposals, describe some common ground, and be willing to engage consciously with the politics of change. Here are four positions that might kick-start this new dialog.

1. We need to experiment with ideas. We can start small by trying easier, faster, and even temporary projects, including guerilla gardening and food trucks. We can go big with other forms of catalyst infrastructure, like connecting the ends of cul-de-sacs to break people free from isolation and traffic. We can unlock private-sector innovation with ideas that emerge from open data and loosened land-use regulations. Whatever kind of experiments we engage in, we need to get comfortable with not knowing all the answers and be willing to test ideas that don't seem possible.

2. We need to develop a political structure for change. This is critical because, otherwise, some of the best ideas never see the light of day. We need to find reliable ways to get them to the table, vet their eligibility for our vision, organize efforts to support them, integrate them with other ideas, and protect their integrity over time. Technology and social media can be a starting place, but we'll need to develop more formalized models. Whatever these look like, we need to invite everyone to participate, and we need to make sure that a nonpartisan structure is an integrated part of our vision from the start.

3. We need to stop sprawl. This is essential no matter where we live, but for communities already defined by it, this is the only way to effectively ensure their long-term quality of life. Stopping new sprawl will protect the value of existing sprawl by keeping the roadways on which its life and economy depend relatively free-flowing. It will require a variety of code reforms, new business models, and changes in capital investments, but if we don't stop it, any measure to make roadways more efficient, such as streamlined intersections, managed lanes, or vehicle automation, will only create more sprawl, more congestion, and, therefore, a declining standard of living.

4. We need to redirect growth. Future growth should be organized into more suitable places, both regionally and nationally. We can do this through better infrastructure, policy, and incentives. As

our changes incrementally reframe the parameters of the free market to reflect the high public cost of sprawl, the built-in value of existing places will be revealed. We'll instinctively shift our investments there, revitalizing urban neighborhoods and historic downtowns, and refashioning the vast commercial strips of outlying areas into vibrant transit-centered corridors.

These four ideas are far from mutually exclusive. In fact, together they begin to describe a vision that includes a reasonably positive outcome for everyone. Accomplishing them will be difficult, of course, and will require a cultural and political momentum. For now, they're simply meant to start a conversation. If, however, we are willing to take action and engage with the politics of change, I believe they can shape a new and better direction. They can help us develop a vision that is bold enough to match the overwhelming scale of both our challenges and our opportunities.

With all of this in mind, the plausible, if politically daunting, course of action that I am proposing is that by experimenting with new ideas, cultivating a political structure for change, stopping sprawl, and shifting to more sustainable growth strategies, we can generate significant and positive change. We can create a wide-open place where anything is possible. We can interpret the scars of the twentieth century as an opportunity, not a burden, and we can leverage the change we see coming to catalyze a better life for ourselves.

Whatever shape that takes, and whatever road we take to get there, we'll have to build broad support around an aspirational view of our future. This will require us to dream, think, and plan, but we will also need to take action—voting with our feet and at the polls, building coalitions, changing rules, modifying budgets, and investing in new infrastructures that support health, economic prosperity, equity, and a more sustainable civic identity. While there will be plenty of time for consultants and naysayers to pick at the technical details, we will also need to demand that those efforts come in service to the realization of our vision, not the other way around. Only in this way will we break through the red tape of our collective conscience and see our big, bold vision as real. If it is real, then we can believe in it. And if it is doable, then we should do it.

We have to trust ourselves that we can do this. We have to look each other in the eye. And while our journey will be difficult, our only chance for making change is if we work together. This will not require an act of Congress. In fact, for now, Congress should largely stay out of it. All it requires is for you and me to decide, perhaps naïvely, that we can actually make a difference.

NOTES

CHAPTER 1: AS MANY GAINS AS LOSSES

1. Guy Debord, "Introduction to a Critique of Urban Geography," in *Theory of the Dérive and Other Situationist Writings on the City,* ed. Libero Andreotti and Xavier Costa (Barcelona: Museu d'Art Contemporani de Barcelona, ACTAR, 1996), 20.
2. Ibid., 18.
3. Ibid.
4. Libero Andreotti, "Introduction," in *Theory of the Dérive and Other Situationist Writings on the City,* 8.
5. Ibid., 7.
6. Guy Debord, "Towards a Situationist International," in *Participation,* ed. Claire Bishop (Cambridge, MA: MIT Press, 2006), 100.
7. Ryan Gravel, *Belt Line—Atlanta: Design of Infrastructure as a Reflection of Public Policy* (Atlanta: Georgia Institute of Technology, 1999), 1.
8. Rem Koolhaas, "Toward the Contemporary City," *Design Book Review* 17 (Winter 1989): 15, 16.
9. Gravel, 1.

CHAPTER 2: "INFRA-CULTURE"

1. Thomas D. Wilson, *The Oglethorpe Plan: Enlightenment Design in Savannah and Beyond* (Charlottesville: University of Virginia Press, 2012), 1.
2. Ibid., 52.
3. Ibid., 21.

CHAPTER 3: CYCLES OF CHANGE

1. Chris Webb, "Hemphill's Heyday Ended with Westward Campus Growth," *The Technique,* March 14, 2003, accessed June 27, 2015, http://technique .library.gatech.edu/issues/spring2003/2003-03-14/14.html.
2. Paul Crater, *Baseball in Atlanta* (Charleston, SC: Arcadia Publishing, 2007), 39.
3. Ibid., 49.

4. "Sweet Auburn Endangered," GPB News, June 6, 2012, accessed June 27, 2015, http://www.gpb.org/news/2012/06/06/sweet-auburn-endangered.

5. Atlanta Region Metropolitan Planning Commission, *Atlanta Region Comprehensive Plan: Rapid Transit* (Atlanta, 1961), 2.

6. Atlanta Region Metropolitan Planning Commission, *Now . . . For Tomorrow, a Master Planning Program for the DeKalb-Fulton Metropolitan Area* (Atlanta, 1954), 56.

7. Ibid.

8. Atlanta Region Metropolitan Planning Commission, *Up Ahead, A Regional Land Use Plan for Metropolitan Atlanta* (Atlanta, 1952), 31.

9. *Now . . . For Tomorrow,* 56.

10. *Up Ahead,* 33.

11. *Now . . . For Tomorrow,* 26.

12. *Up Ahead,* 31.

13. H. W. Lochner & Company and De Leuw, Cather & Company, State Highway Department of Georgia and Public Roads Administration, Federal Works Agency, *Highway and Transportation Plan for Atlanta, Georgia* (Chicago, 1946), xiii.

14. Robin Toner, "Atlanta 'City of Future,' Meets Its Past," *New York Times,* February 7, 1987, accessed June 27, 2015, http://www.nytimes.com/1987/02/07/us/atlanta-city-of-future-meets-its-past.html.

15. *Up Ahead,* 11.

CHAPTER 4: THERE'S NOTHING WRONG WITH SPRAWL

1. Gerry Morris, Family history, November 21, 2013.

2. Federal Highway Administration Office of Highway Policy Information, *Most Traveled Highway Sections,* Table, July 27, 2010, accessed June 27, 2015, http://www.fhwa.dot.gov/policyinformation/tables/02.cfm.

3. Howard Frumkin, Lawrence Frank, and Richard Jackson, *Urban Sprawl and Public Health: Designing, Planning, and Building for Healthy Communities* (Washington, DC: Island Press, 2004), 146.

CHAPTER 5: TOUGH LOVE

1. Nick Paumgarten, "There and Back Again," *The New Yorker,* April 16, 2007, accessed June 26, 2015, http://www.newyorker.com/magazine/2007/04/16/there-and-back-again.

2. Howard Frumkin, Lawrence Frank, and Richard Jackson, *Urban Sprawl and Public Health: Designing, Planning, and Building for Healthy Communities* (Washington, DC: Island Press, 2004), 142.

3. Ibid., 94

4. Ibid., 97.

5. Ibid.

6. Ibid., 82.

7. David Goldberg, "Protect, Don't Prosecute, Pedestrians," *Washington Post,* August 4, 2011, accessed June 26, 2015, http://www.washingtonpost.com/opinions/protect-dont-prosecute-pedestrians/2011/07/28/gIQAny45uI_story.html.

8. Radley Balko, "Grieving Mother Faces 36 Months in Jail for Jaywalking after Son Is Killed by Hit-and-Run Driver," *Huffington Post,* September 20, 2011, accessed June 26, 2015, http://www.huffingtonpost.com/radley-balko/raquel-nelson-jail-for-jaywalking_b_905925.html.
9. Frederick Law Olmsted and James Croes, New York City Board of the Department of Public Parks, *Preliminary Report of the Landscape Architect and the Civil and Topographical Engineer Upon the Laying Out of the Twenty-Third and Twenty-Fourth Wards* (Document No. 72. December 20, 1876), accessed June 26, 2015, http://www.library.cornell.edu/Reps/DOCS/olmst_76.htm.
10. Ibid.

CHAPTER 6: AN IDEA WITH AMBITION

1. Randy Roark, telephone conversation, September 27, 2013.
2. City of Atlanta Department of Planning and Development Bureau of Planning, Department of Parks and Recreation Bureau of Cultural Affairs, Mayor's Green Ribbon Committee, *Atlanta Parks, Open Space and Greenways Plan* (Atlanta, 1993), 16.
3. Ibid., 63.
4. Ibid., 64–65.
5. David A. Crane, "Toward a Legacy of Economic Growth & Transformation" (working paper developed in 1993), 2.
6. Master Planning Technical Advisory Committee, *The Atlanta Cultural Ring Economic Development Initiative* (Georgia Institute of Technology College of Architecture, March 16, 1995), 4.
7. Ibid.
8. Ibid., 8.
9. Ibid.
10. Selznick International Pictures, *Gone with the Wind,* dir. Victor Fleming, quote perf. Vivien Leigh, US release January 17, 1940.
11. Letter to Mr. Frank Jones, Esq., Chairman, Great Park Authority, from James B. Grant PE, December 15, 1980.
12. Ryan Gravel, *Belt Line—Atlanta: Design of Infrastructure as a Reflection of Public Policy* (Atlanta: Georgia Institute of Technology, 1999), 32.

CHAPTER 7: A WIDE-OPEN PLACE

1. City of Atlanta Department of Planning, Development, and Neighborhood Conservation, *District 2 Rail Corridor Inventory and Assessment,* Bureau of Planning (Atlanta, February, 2001), 18.
2. Ibid., 15.
3. Letter to Cathy Woolard, from Ryan Gravel, Sarah Edgens, Mark Arnold, with attachment *Design of Cities—Design of Infrastructure,* July 30, 2001, 3.
4. VanDerKloot Film Studio, *Atlanta Belt Line,* dir. William VanDerKloot, quote perf. Cathy Woolard, release September 10, 2003.
5. Ibid.
6. Rebecca Burns, "Can Atlanta Go All In on the BeltLine?" *The Atlantic's CityLab,* May 6, 2014, accessed June 27, 2015, http://www.citylab.com/work/2014/05/can-atlanta-go-all-beltline/9036/.

7. Office of Atlanta City Council President Cathy Woolard, email, May 23, 2003.

8. Office of Atlanta City Council President Cathy Woolard, memorandum, *Statistics—School Enrollment,* March 29, 2004.

9. Friends of the Belt Line, Inc., Newsletter 1, April 26, 2004.

10. Clarence N. Stone, *Regime Politics: Governing Atlanta, 1946–1988* (Lawrence: University Press of Kansas, 1989), 162–163.

CHAPTER 8: AN EXPANDABLE VISION

1. Letter to Cathy Woolard, from Ryan Gravel, Sarah Edgens, Mark Arnold, with attachment *Design of Cities—Design of Infrastructure,* July 30, 2001, 3.

2. Atlanta Region Metropolitan Planning Commission, *Atlanta Region Comprehensive Plan: Rapid Transit* (Atlanta, 1961), 7.

3. Atlanta BeltLine, Inc., *Annual Report 2014* (Atlanta, 2014), 9.

4. Randy Southerland, "The HITS Keep on Coming," *GeorgiaTrend,* November 2013, accessed June 27, 2015, http://www.georgiatrend.com/November-2013/The-Hits-Keep-On-Coming/.

5. Alexander Garvin, James Schroder, David Haskell, Alex Garvin & Associates, Trust for Public Land, Community Housing Resource Center, *The Beltline Emerald Necklace: Atlanta's New Public Realm* (Atlanta: Trust for Public Land, 2004), 2.

6. Ibid., 51.

7. Catherine L. Ross and Harry West, Center for Quality Growth and Regional Development, Georgia Institute of Technology, *Atlanta BeltLine Health Impact Assessment* (Atlanta, 2007), 11–16.

8. Charles Moore, *Daniel H. Burnham, Architect, Planner of Cities,* vol. 2 (Boston: Houghton Mifflin Company, 1921), 147.

CHAPTER 10: CATALYST INFRASTRUCTURE

1. Elissa Rosenberg, "Public Works and Public Space," *Journal of Architectural Education* 50, 2 (November 1996): 89.

2. Ibid., 90.

3. Joshua David and Robert Hammond, *High Line: The Inside Story of New York City's Park in the Sky* (New York: Farrar, Straus and Giroux, 2011), 53.

4. David Dunlap, "Many Proposals for Rusty Rail Line on the West Side," *New York Times,* June 1, 2003, accessed June 26, 2015, http://www.nytimes.com/2003/06/01/nyregion/01HIGH.html.

5. Ibid.

6. Paul vanMeter, "What to Do with the City Branch: Make It Part of a 3 Mile Linear Park and Non-Motorized Transitway," *Hidden City Philadelphia,* June 8, 2012, accessed June 27, 2015, http://hiddencityphila.org/2012/06/what-to-do-with-the-city-branch-make-it-part-of-a-3-mile-linear-park-and-non-mo torized-transitway/.

7. Paul vanMeter and Leah Murphy, "Placemaking 101," *Philadelphia Social Innovations,* not dated, accessed June 27, 2015, http://philasocialinnovations.org/journal/articles/search-by-theme/57-perspectives-and-predictions/429-placemaking-101?showall=1&limitstart.

8. Friends of the Los Angeles River, brochure, not dated.

9. Claire Weisz, telephone conversation, December 23, 2012.

10. Barrie Scardino, "H$_2$Ouston," in *Ephemeral City:* Cite *Looks at Houston,* ed. Barrie Scardino, William F. Stern, and Bruce C. Webb (Austin: University of Texas Press, 2003), 30.

11. Nicolai Ouroussoff, "An Appraisal; Gardens in the Air Where the Rail Once Ran," *New York Times,* August 30, 2004, accessed June 26, 2015, http://www .nytimes.com/2004/08/12/arts/an-appraisal-gardens-in-the-air-where-the -rail-once-ran.html.

12. Piet Oudolf and Noël Kingsbury, *Planting: A New Perspective* (London: Timber Press, 2013), 19.

13. David and Hammond, vii, 11.

14. Bart Everson, telephone conversation, July 24, 2014.

15. Leigh Christy, telephone conversation, May 18, 2011.

CHAPTER 11: AN INFRASTRUCTURE
FOR HEALTH AND WELL-BEING

1. International Health Conference, *Preamble to the Constitution of the World Health Organization* (Official Records of the World Health Organization, no. 2, April 7, 1948), 100.

2. "Great Places in America: Streets, 2011," *American Planning Association,* accessed June 26, 2015, https://www.planning.org/greatplaces/streets/2011/.

3. Media Policy Center, *Designing Healthy Communities,* dirs. Harry Wiland and Dale Bell, quote perf. Dr. Richard Jackson, release January 2012.

CHAPTER 12: AN INFRASTRUCTURE
FOR ECONOMIC PROSPERITY

1. Peter Schjeldahl, "High Line Rhapsody," *New Yorker,* October 7, 2014, accessed June 26, 2015, http://www.newyorker.com/culture/cultural-comment /high-line-rhapsody.

2. City of Los Angeles, Department of Public Works, Bureau of Engineering, *Los Angeles River Revitalization Master Plan* (Los Angeles, 2007), 7/3.

3. Louis Sahagun and Catherine Saillant, "Big Plans, and Concerns, Surround L.A. River's Revitalization," *LA Times,* May 24, 2014, accessed June 26, 2015, http://www.latimes.com/local/la-me-lariver-development-20140524-story .html#page=1.

4. Richard Florida, *The Rise of the Creative Class* (New York: Basic Books, 2011), vii.

CHAPTER 13: AN INFRASTRUCTURE FOR EQUITY

1. Hollis Gillespie, "Little House in the Fringe Hood; Diary of an Urban Pioneer," *Atlanta Magazine,* December 2000, 88.

2. Ibid.

3. Ibid., 90.

4. Nick Masino, "Gwinnett County: Diverse Community, International Destination," *Global Atlanta,* June 5, 2013, accessed June 27, 2015, http://www

.globalatlanta.com/article/26339/gwinnett-county-diverse-community-inter national-destination/.

5. Charlotte Nash, transcription of speech, January 16, 2014.

CHAPTER 14: AN INFRASTRUCTURE FOR CIVIC IDENTITY

1. Scott Martelle, *Detroit: A Biography* (Chicago: Chicago Review Press, 2012), 72.
2. Ibid., 72–73.

CHAPTER 15: UP AHEAD

1. Atlanta Region Metropolitan Planning Commission, *Up Ahead, A Regional Land Use Plan for Metropolitan Atlanta* (Atlanta, 1952), 65, 72.
2. Ibid., 65, 72.
3. Ibid., 65, 72, 75.
4. Ibid., 65, 74.
5. Jane Jacobs, *The Death and Life of Great American Cities* (New York: Random House, 1961), 50.

INDEX

*Page numbers in italics refer to
photographs and maps.*

Alexandria, Louisiana, 42–3, *43*
Allen, Doug, 14, 140
American Civil War, 10, 25–7, 29–30,
    132
American dream, 52, 61
Annie E. Casey Foundation, 125
Army Corps of Engineers, 149, 160,
    163, 174
Arnold, Mark, 91–3
Athenahealth, 115
Atlanta belt line railroads, 28–40
    Atlanta & West Point Belt Line,
        29–31, *31,* 36
    Louisville & Nashville Belt Railroad,
        30, 32, 36
    Seaboard Air Line Belt Railway, 25,
        29, 36
    Southern Railway, 28, 32, 36, *37,* 79,
        84, 86, 90, 102, 132
Atlanta Beltline, 56–7, 73
    Arboretum, 123
    Lantern Parade, 120
Atlanta BeltLine, Inc. (ABI), 130–1
    Atlanta BeltLine Partnership, 101,
        126, 130, 176, 200
    Atlanta Beltline Street Framework
        Plan, 119
    BeltLine Affordable Housing
        Advisory Board, 200
    and brownfields, 118, 122, 130
    and community stabilization, 123–5

Eastside Trail, *115,* 123, 127, *128,*
    166, 189
    and economic development, 113–15,
        189, 191–2
    and equity, 195–205
    Friends of the Belt Line, 100–101,
        117, 130, 163, 171
    future adaptations of, 217–19
    greenways and trails, 93, 109–11,
        115–17, 130
    groundbreaking, 127–30
    and hope, 133–5
    and housing, 118–19, 195–201, 204
    loop formation, xii, 78–80, 85–6,
        106, 109–10, 113, 199, 213, 218
    and neighborhood conservation,
        111–12
    and new parks, 115–17
    and PATH Foundation, 95, 109–10,
        115–16, 123, 176
    and political support, 102–7
    and preservation and restoration, 120
    and public art and cultural facilities,
        120–2
    and public health, 122, 183–4
    and public realm, 119
    and public support, 96–102
    and quality of life, 90, 91, 101, 126
    Redevelopment Plan, 102, 114, 118,
        130
TAD Advisory Committee
    (TADAC), 130
tax allocation district (TAD), 114,
    118–20, 130

thesis origins, xii, 11–12, 77–80, 85–8, 89–95, 99, 115
and transit as protection of quality of life, 112–13
and Trust for Public Land, 116–17, 123, 129, 176
Westside Park, 117, 132
and zoning, 56, 80, 90–1, 97, 111, 198
Atlanta Development Authority, 114. *See also* Invest Atlanta (formerly Atlanta Development Authority)
Atlanta history and development
African American community, 31–2, 36, 81, 103–5, 208
as capital of the South, 104
Civil War and Reconstruction era, 25–8
Corporation for Olympic Development in Atlanta, 83–4, 120
Cultural Ring, 83–4, 86–7, 120, 124
Cultural Ring proposal, 83–4, 86–7, 120, 124
Great Park proposal, 81–3, 86
Jim Crow era, 32
and Motor Age, 33–5, 38–40
Neighborhood Planning Unit X (NPU-X), 55–6, 96
Neighborhood Planning Units (NPUs), 55–7, 96–7, 103, 105, 107, 111
politics, 32, 38–9, 78, 80–1, 87–8, 91–3, 96–107, 114, 130
quality-of-life zoning district, 91
railroads' role in development, 25–6, 27, 27–32
Atlanta Land Trust Collaborative (ALTC), 125, 176, 200
Atlanta neighborhoods, areas, and streets
Atlanta Trailer City, 55–6, 73
Buckhead, 38, 39, 90, 116
Cabbagetown, 36, 78, 197
Capitol View, 56, 197, 199, 201, 204
Capitol View Manor, 31, 33, 56, 198
Copenhill, 99, 102–3, 132
Downtown, 39, 44, 52, 59, 79–84, 113, 196, 199, 218, 219
Druid Hills, 81, 94
Grant Park, 102, 196
Hemphill Avenue, 23–4, 38, 99
Inman Park, 31, 33, 56–7, 91–2, 99
Lightning, 38, 99
Manford Road, 217–19
Midtown, 24, 92, 197
Perimeter Center, 39, 59–61
Pittsburgh, 31–2, 125
Ponce de Leon Avenue, 29, 39, 79, 103, 162
Poncey-Highland, 94, 98–9, 102–3
Reynoldstown, 36, 81, 97, 131, 197
Stewart Avenue (Metropolitan Parkway), 31, 55–8, 61, 73–4, 192
Sweet Auburn Historic District, 32
Sylvan Hills, 56, 197
Virginia-Highland, 57, 72, 92, 94
Washington Park, 32, 36
Atlanta parks, sites, and destinations
Atlanta Botanical Garden, 116
birth home of Martin Luther King, Jr., 32, *124*, 124, 132
Centennial Olympic Park, 82
Freedom Parkway, 82, 99, 103
Jimmy Carter Presidential Library, 99, 116
King Plow Arts Center, 116
Krog Street Market, 133
Manuel's Tavern, 100, 102–3, 217, 220
Perimeter Mall, 45, 59
Piedmont Park, 24, 25, 29, 83, 86, 90, 92, 95, 102, 103, 110, 117
Ponce City Market, 29, 114–15, 131, 189
Sears and Roebuck (Ponce City Market), 29, 39, 79, 114
Zoo Atlanta, 116
Atlanta Regional Commission, 98, 106
Atlanta transit and transportation
I-285, 44–6, 48–9, 218
automobile traffic, 33–5, 38–40
Hartsfield-Jackson Atlanta International Airport, 56, 58, 94, 104
MARTA, 26, 80, 86–7, 93–4, 98, 101, 104–6, 110, 112, 129, 140
Outer Belt Highway, 218

passenger rail service, 33–4
and quality of life, 112–13
streetcar system, 10, 31–3, 56, 72, 79
trackless trolleys, 33
truck traffic, 34–5
See also Atlanta belt line railroads

baseball, 29, 38–9, 79
Atlanta Crackers (minor league), 28, 38–9, 79
Black Crackers (Negro League), 29, 39
Battle of Ezra Church, 30
Baudelaire, Charles, 6
Bellwood Quarry, 117
Betz, Reid, 89–90, 99
bikeshare programs, 5, 154, 159, 160, 188
Boston, Massachusetts, 16, 18, 68
Buffalo, New York: Belt Line, 145
Burnham, Daniel, 126

Caillebotte, Gustave, 5
Center for Quality Growth and Regional Development, 122
Centers for Disease Control and Prevention (CDC), 122, 184
Chamblee, Georgia, 34, 43, 47, 51, 59, 74–5, 82, 202
Chamblee Plaza, 44, 63, 74, *75*
Huntley Hills, 43–6, 52, 64
Charleston, South Carolina, 16, 192
Charlotte, North Caroline: Blue Line, 153
Chattahoochee River, 25, 116
Chicago, Illinois: Bloomingdale Trail (renamed the 606), 171
Christy, Leigh, 148, 174
citizen-planners, 219
city planners, 7–8, 10, 34, 50, 79–81, 117, 144, 180, 218–20
Civil Rights Act of 1964, 23
civil rights movement, 52, 98, 103, 104
Civil War, 10, 25–7, 29–30, 132
CODA. *See* Corporation for Olympic Development in Atlanta (CODA)
Corporation for Olympic Development in Atlanta (CODA), 83–4, 120
Cultural Ring, 83–4, 86–7, 120, 124

Croes, J. James, 67

Dagenhart, Richard, 80, 140
Dallas, Texas: Trinity River Corridor Project, 168–9
Dannenberg, Andrew, 122
David, Joshua, 144, 145, 163, 171
Davis, Jefferson, 28
Debord, Guy, 8
dérive (unplanned journey), 1–3, 6, 8–10, 179
Detroit, Michigan, 192
and civic identity, 207–16
Dequindre Cut Greenway, 152–3
Gratiot Avenue, 152, 181, 211–12
Inner Circle Greenway, 213
Temple Street, *210*

economic development, 78, 83–4, 109, 151, 168
and Atlanta Beltline, 109, 113–15
and infrastructure, 187–94
Edgens, Sarah, 91–3
Environmental Protection Agency (EPA), 118
Environmental Protection Division (EPD), 118
Euclid v. Ambler, 60, 182
Everson, Bart, 173

flâneur (conscious actor in a city), 6–10
Florida, Richard, 193
Foote, Anna, 102–4
Fortner, Aaron, 91
Franklin, Shirley, 98, 114
Friends of the Belt Line (FBL), 100–101, 117, 130, 163, 171
Friends of the High Line (New York), 144, 163–4, 167, 171
Friends of the Lafitte Corridor (New Orleans), 173
Friends of the Los Angeles River (FoLAR), 149, 175
Friends of the QueensWay (New York), 169
Friends of the Rail Park (Philadelphia), 147
Friends of the S-Line (Salt Lake City), 171–2

Garcetti, Eric, 191
Garvin, Alexander, 117
Georgia
    admission to Union, 28
    capital of Atlanta, 28
    Department of Transportation, 98,
        162
    founding of, 13
    and passenger rail, 33
    Redevelopment Powers Law, 118
Georgia Institute of Technology
    (Georgia Tech), 14, 23–4, 38–9,
        81–2, 90, 96, 105, 199, 122, 196
Georgia Stand Up, 200
Goldberg, David, 66
Gone With the Wind, 26–7, 39, 84,
    103
Grant, James, 86
Great Recession, 114, 125
Green, David, 119, 140
greenways and greenway trails, 84, 142,
    145–55, 176, 188, 213
    and Atlanta Beltline, 93, 109–11,
        115–17, 130
    Atlanta Parks, Open Space and
        Greenways Plan, 82–4, 91
    Bayou Greenways Initiative
        (Houston), 162
    and Cultural Ring proposal, 83–4,
        86–7, 120, 124
    Dequindre Cut Greenway (Detroit),
        152–3
    Inner Circle Greenway, 213
    Lafitte Greenway (New Orleans),
        153–4, 173–4
    Midtown Greenway (Minneapolis),
        150–2, 171
    and Orange Line (Los Angeles), 153
    PATH400 trail, 116
    QueensWay (New York), 145, 169
    Rail Park (Philadelphia), 146, 147,
        150, 164–5
Gwinnett County, Georgia, *51*, 202–3,
    205

Hammond, Robert, 144, 145, 147, 171
Hanson Motor Car Company, *121*, 121
Harris County Flood Control District,
    160, 162–3

Hartsfield-Jackson Atlanta International
    Airport, 56
Haussmann, Baron Georges-Eugène,
    3–4, 6–7, 9, 139–40, 155, 184,
    209
health. *See* public health
Hicks, Matt, 98
Historic District Development
    Corporation, 124
Houston, Texas: Buffalo Bayou Park,
    157–9, *159*, 160, 162, 175
Hunziker, Walter, 79, 86

Indianapolis, Indiana: Cultural Trail,
    154
infrastructure, 138–42, 176–8
    and authenticity, 158–61
    and big thinking, 142–9
    and change, 161–3
    and civic identity, 207–16
    and economic prosperity, 187–94
    and equity, 195–205
    and focus, 167–70
    and inclusivity, 150–7
    and partnerships, 174–76
    and people, 167–74
    and public health, 179–86
    and quality of life, 163–7, 179–86
Invest Atlanta (formerly Atlanta
    Development Authority), 98, 101,
    111, 114, 129–30

Jackson, Maynard, 81, 96, 104–5
Jackson, Richard, 183–4
Jacobs, Jane, 8–9, 219–20
jaywalking, 66–7. *See also* walking
Jones, Frank, 86

King, Martin Luther, Jr., 32, 124, 132
Koolhaas, Rem, 11–12, 133, 140

Langford, Jim, 116–17
Lantern Parade, 120
Las Vegas Strip, 61–3
Levine, Greg, 123
Lewis, John, 98
Lincoln, Abraham, 26
Los Angeles, California
    Friends of the Los Angeles River,

149, 175
  Los Angeles River, *20,* 20, 35, 142,
    147–8, *148,* 149, 153, 158, 174–5,
    216
  Los Angeles River Revitalization
    Corporation, 174–5, 191
  Orange Line, 153
  Piggyback Yard, 148
  See also Santa Monica Boulevard
    (California)
Lumpkin, Wilson, 26

MacAdams, Lewis, 149
Maddox, Lester, 23–4
Madrid, Spain: M-30, 155
MARTA. *See* Metropolitan Atlanta
    Rapid Transit Authority
    (MARTA)
McBrayer, Ed, 82, 109–10
Metropolitan Atlanta Rapid Transit
    Authority (MARTA), 26, 80,
    86–7, 93–4, 98, 101, 104–6, 110,
    112, 129, 140
Miami, Florida: Underline, 147, 153
Miller, Panke, 104–5
Minneapolis, Minnesota
  Blue Line, *152,* 153
  Midtown Greenway, 150–1, *151,* 152,
    171
Moses, Robert, 8

Napoleon III, 3–5, 9, 16
Nash, Charlotte, 205
Negro League, 29, 39
Neighborhood Planning Units (NPUs),
    55–7, 96–7, 103, 105, 107, 111
  Neighborhood Planning Unit X
    (NPU-X), 55–6, 96
neighborhoods. *See* Atlanta
    neighborhoods, areas, and streets
Nelson, Arthur C., 80
Nelson, Raquel, 66–7
New Orleans, Louisiana, 192, 196
  Friends of the Lafitte Corridor,
    173
  and Hurricane Katrina, 173
  Lafitte Greenway, 153–4, 173–4
  Sojourner Truth Neighborhood
    Center, 174

New York City
  Empire State Building, 68
  Friends of the High Line, 144,
    163–4, 167, 171
  High Line, *143,* 143–5, 150, 158,
    163–5, 167–8, 171, 187–91, 194
  Lowline, 145
  Manhattan grid design, 67–9
  postwar urban design, 7–9
  West Chelsea, 143, 190
  Williamsburg (Brooklyn), 214–15

Oglethorpe, James, 13–14, 16, 18, 85,
    119
Olmsted, Frederick Law, 67–8
Olympic Games, 82–5, 106, 110
Oudolf, Piet, 163, 165

Paris, France, 1–3
  Boulevard des Maréchaux, 156, *157*
  Boulevard Haussmann, 3, *4*
  boulevards, 2–6, 16, 139, 156, *157,*
    184, 209
  Champ de Mars, 2, 47
  as City of Light, 2, 5
  Eiffel Tower, 2
  and Impressionism, 5
  L'Association Sauvegarde Petite
    Ceinture, 170
  Métro, 1, 3, 5, 47–8, 156
  Périphérique, 156
  Petite Ceinture, 155–6, *157,* 170
  Place de la Bastille, 3
  Place de la République, 5
  Place du Trocadéro, 1–3, 9
  plane trees, 2, 3
  Promenade Plantée, *139,* 141, 150,
    169
  River Seine, 2, 3, 8, 10, 18
  Rue de Lyon, 3, *7*
  Rue Traversière, 5–6, *6*
  Thiers Wall, 156
  Trocadéro, 1
  Viaduc des Arts, 137, *138*
parks. *See* Atlanta parks, sites, and
    destinations
PATH Foundation, 82–3, 95, 98, 101,
    109–10, 115–16, 123, 176
Perkins+Will, 134, 148, 166

Philadelphia, Pennsylvania: Rail Park, 146–7, 150, 164, *165,* 165–6
Philadelphia and Reading Railroad, 146–7
Piedmont, 28, 39
public health
  and Atlanta Beltline, 122, 183–4
  and infrastructure, 179–86
  and sprawl, 65–6, 182–3, 185
public transportation. *See* Atlanta transit and transportation

Rails-to-Trails Conservancy, 82, 152
Roark, Randy, 79–81, 83, 140
Robinson, Helen, 98
Roney, Danielle, 120
Rosenberg, Elissa, 140
Ross, Catherine, 122

St. Louis, Missouri: Iron Horse Trestle, 145
Salt Lake City, Utah, 153, 171–2, *172*
Santa Monica Boulevard (California), 179–84
Savannah, Georgia, 13–16, *17,* 17–19, 25–6, 33, 68, 119–20, 192, 211
Sherman, William Tecumseh, 26, 132
Singapore: Rail Corridor, 142, 145, *146,* 150
Situationist International, 1–2, 7–9
sprawl, 12, 15, 42–54, 70–4, 219–23
  advantages of, 50–1
  and Atlanta, 39, 55–9, 73–4, 79–80, 100
  and car-dependency, 61–7, 79, 158 219–20
  and Chamblee, Georgia, 43–6, 74
  and commuting, 42, 51
  and Detroit, 208
  as distinct from suburbs, 42
  and equity, 135, 197, 201–2, 204–5
  and inflexibility to change, 67–70
  influence on modern culture, 52
  and isolation, 49–51, 60, 135, 183, 204
  origin of the term, 59
  and public health, 65–6, 182–3, 185

and public realm, 68, 72–3
and segregated low density, 59–61
and walking, 44, 46, 49, 60–4, 66–7, 74
and zoning, 53, 60–1, 72
Starnes, Debi, 91–2
Stone, Clarence, 103–4
StudioPlex, 84, 90, 97, 123–4

Tactical Urbanism, 9
transit and transportation. *See* Atlanta transit and transportation
Trees Atlanta, 123, 176
Trust for Public Land (TPL), 101, 111, 116–17, 123, 129, 176

urban planning, 14, 59, 170, 181, 185, 196, 221. *See also* Atlanta Beltline; city planners; infrastructure; zoning

vanMeter, Paul, 146–7, 164–6
Village of Euclid v. Ambler Realty Company, 60, 182

Washington, Booker T., 29
Weisz, Claire, 154–5
Westerman, W. W., 86
Western & Atlantic Railroad, 26
Whiddon, Alycen, 114
Woolard, Cathy, 93–8, 100–101, 106–7, 110–11, 114, 130, 198

Young, Andrew, 103
Youngblood, Mtamanika, 124

zoning
  and Atlanta Beltline, 56, 80, 90–1, 97, 111, 198
  flood zones, 168
  industrial zones, 20, 31, 34, 35
  mandatory inclusionary, 119
  and neighborhood conservation, 111
  and sprawl, 53, 60–1, 72
  and urban grids, 69
  and West Chelsea (New York City), 190